EDUARDO HALFON AND THE ITINERARY OF MEMORY

EDUARDO HALFON
and the
ITINERARY
OF MEMORY

Marilyn G. Miller

VANDERBILT UNIVERSITY PRESS
Nashville, Tennessee

Copyright 2024 Vanderbilt University Press
All rights reserved
First printing 2024

Library of Congress Cataloging-in-Publication Data

Names: Miller, Marilyn Grace, author.
Title: Eduardo Halfon and the itinerary of memory / Marilyn Grace Miller.
Description: Nashville, Tennessee : Vanderbilt University Press, [2024] |
    Includes bibliographical references and index.
Identifiers: LCCN 2024011667 (print) | LCCN 2024011668 (ebook) | ISBN
    9780826507051 (hardcover) | ISBN 9780826507044 (paperback) | ISBN
    9780826507068 (epub) | ISBN 9780826507075 (pdf)
Subjects: LCSH: Halfon, Eduardo, 1971---Criticism and interpretation. |
    Guatemalan literature--History and criticism.
Classification: LCC PQ7499.3.H35 Z77 2024 (print) | LCC PQ7499.3.H35
    (ebook) | DDC 863/.7--dc23/eng/20240709
LC record available at https://lccn.loc.gov/2024011667
LC ebook record available at https://lccn.loc.gov/2024011668

Front cover illustration © Alex Camlin

And when you open the Book of Memories
it speaks for itself—
for every human hand leaves its mark
an imprint like no other.

CONTENTS

Acknowledgments ix

INTRODUCTION. Reading Eduardo Halfon at the Crossroads 1

1 Numbers and Other Mnemonic Devices 15
2 Music and Memory, On and Off the Charts 41
3 The Threshold of Fiction 59
4 Untold Traumas 70
5 Acts and Arts of Survival 93
6 Memory Duels 107
7 Echoes and Refrains 129

Notes 151
Bibliography 189
Index 207

ACKNOWLEDGMENTS

I am extraordinarily grateful to the bookseller who handed me *Signor Hoffman* in Barcelona's La Central del Raval in the summer of 2018, as that's where my own itinerary of reading and engaging with the works of Eduardo Halfon began. Since then, I've given talks on his works in Havana, Jerusalem, New York, Seattle, Guatemala City, and virtually, and have benefitted enormously from the questions and feedback provided by fellow panelists and audience members. I'm especially grateful to University of Connecticut colleagues Jacqueline Loss, professor of Literatures, Cultures and Languages, and Avinoam Patt, previously the chair of Judaic Studies, who invited me to speak at UConn's annual Eyzaguirre Lecture. Undeterred by pandemic-related setbacks, they and other UConn colleagues convoked a two-day virtual symposium that included a deep dive into Halfon's works and an interview with the author himself on October 6–7, 2021—an event that served as a precursor to this book. Many other colleagues across an international diaspora of Halfon afficionados have accompanied me in this venture as well, including Gabriela Alemán, Esther Allen, Yuri Herrera, Anne McLean, Stephanie Pridgeon, and Estelle Tarica.

At Tulane University, I very much value the support of my colleagues in the departments of Spanish and Portuguese and Jewish Studies. To the many students who read Halfon's works together with me in graduate and undergraduate courses, thank you for sharing your insights and my obsession. To my colleagues Hortensia Calvo, Rachel Stein, Christine Hernández and Verónica Sánchez at Howard-Tilton Library at Tulane, *mil gracias* for graciously providing expert assistance and resources both to me and my students. I acknowledge as well the Office of the Provost, the School of Liberal Arts, the Stone Center for Latin American Studies, the Center for Engaged Learning and Teaching, and the Sizeler Professorship in Judaic

Studies for their support of my travel and research and of Eduardo Halfon's virtual visits to my classrooms.

Gianna Mosser, Patrick Samuel, Joell Smith-Borne, and the entire editorial team at Vanderbilt University Press skillfully shepherded this book to completion with patience and savvy. Thank you to Zack Gresham, the acquisitions editor who brought me aboard and provided witty encouragement for this volume and possible future projects as well. I also appreciate the efforts of the anonymous readers who reviewed the manuscript and offered helpful criticism on how to improve it.

Eduardo Alvelo (my "other" Eduardo), Joanna Bukszpan, Elizabeth Claman, Kristi Drake, and Judy Zachs each dispensed indispensable care and cheer along the way. Naomi Yavneh, unparalleled colleague, friend, and accountabilibuddy, walked this road with me, whether at Audubon Park or Oxford, always responding to my queries and quandaries with sagacious advice and unswerving affirmation. Eduardo Halfon, whose works inspired this adventure, was generous off the written page as well, engaging my questions and interacting personally with each lucky student who met him in his virtual visits to our classrooms.

INTRODUCTION
Reading Eduardo Halfon at the Crossroads

> *Creo que estoy haciendo una especie de rayuela.*
>
> —**EDUARDO HALFON**, in conversation with Franco Chiaravalloti

WHO'S/WHOSE EDUARDO HALFON?

This book offers an in-depth study of the primary works published thus far in English by the Guatemalan author Eduardo Halfon, including the volumes *The Polish Boxer* (2012), *Monastery* (2014), *Mourning* (2018), and *Canción* (2022). This single-author focus seems a straightforward enough enterprise, but in fact involves viewing these works from the crossroads where English and the Spanish original meet, and in relation to such diverse contexts as Latin American literary studies, Jewish studies, Latino studies, and the thematic fields of Holocaust and memory studies. The following pages propose a reading (several readings?) of these works from various angles, as well as a flexible approach to the author and his eponymous protagonist as complex and sometimes chameleonic characters in their own right. If a thorough study of Eduardo Halfon's literary production in English begins with the question of *who* the author is, it must also take into account his varied communities of readership, the question of *whose* author he is.

The opening pages of *Canción*, published in English in 2022, offer a strong case in point. When the organizers of a gathering of Lebanese authors asked Eduardo Halfon to participate in their event, he paused. *Was* he a Lebanese writer? The narrator admits he read and reread the invitation to make sure it was not a mistake or a joke. But the narrator—and, it seems, Halfon himself—would ultimately decide that having a grandfather who was born in Beirut was a good enough reason to accept the invitation, and besides, the conference would take place in Japan, an interesting destination. Halfon explains, "I accepted. I said, why not? I can play the part. I can take that costume out from the closet and pretend to be Lebanese for a few days, if that means going to Japan."[1]

So who's Eduardo Halfon? It's complicated, especially given the presence of a protagonist named Eduardo Halfon who narrates the works examined in this study. Author and character, person and *personaje*, both boast multiple origins, migrations, and transplantings to new environments and soils. Indeed, "diaspora" seems an insufficient descriptor for a family tree that includes Jewish grandparents born in Beirut, Aleppo, Alexandria, and Łódź, together with great-grandparents before them who hailed from Ukraine, Egypt, Palestine, and Spain. This foursome, bound by the accident or destiny that brought them as Jews to Guatemala, a historically Catholic country, engage in a complex choreography of what to hold on to and what to release or discard, what to remember from earlier lives and what to try and forget. The Lebanese grandfather, who shares the author's name, makes sure the cooks in his kitchen learn to prepare *kibbe* and *mujadarra*. The Polish grandfather, on the other hand, excises the Polish language from his life in Central America: "What do you want to go to Poland for? He used to say. You shouldn't go to Poland. The Polish betrayed us." So strong is this legacy of betrayal that when the protagonist of *Monastery* returns to Poland to search for the remnants of his grandfather's pre-war life, he is unable to shake off his grandfather's admonition. Sitting between two old men, he observes, "I thought they both looked a lot like my grandfather. I tried not to see them as traitors, not to judge them, not to condemn all old Poles. I made a futile attempt to forget my grandfather's words."[2]

As with the request of his Polish grandfather, the protagonist Eduardo Halfon will often go against his family members' directives to declare allegiances, to define his position, to take sides, and to take *their* side. There is the father who wants him to marry a Jew or relinquish his inheritance, the sister who wants to impose her ultraorthodox definition of Judaism, the maternal grandmother who wants him to confess which parent he likes best. But Halfon as character (quite possibly echoing the author himself) rejects these gambits outright for at least two reasons. First, he's engaged in his own pursuit of the answer to who's Eduardo Halfon, and he prefers to leave the question open. The second related reason, or perhaps another side of the first one, is that landing or settling on a fixed answer would mean the end of the quest at the heart of his writing and perhaps of life itself.

A second-generation Guatemalan and a third-generation Holocaust survivor, the author Eduardo Halfon also chooses which aspects of his variegated history to explore and appropriate, and which to set aside. "I adapt easily, but it's a superficial adaption," he has confessed. "It's not deep. I'm not deeply anything.... You know how I've constructed my identity? By destroying it."[3] Avoiding categorization has not prevented Halfon from donning certain strategic selves, however. As his protagonist in *Canción* explains,

> I'd never been in Japan before. And I had never been asked to be a Lebanese writer. A Jewish writer, yes. A Guatemalan writer, obviously. A Latin American writer, of course. A Central American writer, less and less. A US writer, more and more. A Spanish writer, when traveling on that passport was desirable. A Polish writer, on one occasion, at a Barcelona bookstore that insisted—insists—on shelving my books in the Polish literature section. A French writer, since I lived for a time in Paris, and some people assume I'm still there. I keep each of these disguises on hand, nicely ironed and hanging in the closet.[4]

This readiness to regard identity as flexible and optional rather than stiff and essential opens up Halfon's characters to exploration, experimentation, and a stimulating journey in which the reader is invited to tag along. Or as Juan Camilo Rincón put it, the reader of Eduardo Halfon's stories "receives a clue, like on a map, to finding a great jewel which is the cosmogony of the author. Individually, each book by the Guatemalan writer, from a Jewish background, stands on its own and is at the same time an essential part of a great journey toward the literary treasure that he freely shares."[5]

The reader should beware, nevertheless, that a "false" or assumed identity might in fact be a disguise with which to escape a real danger or assuage a troublesome memory. The disguise may become so natural that it can even supplant a "true" identity, as happened with Peter, a Polish Jew who was in fact not "Peter" but Yosef, who spent the war years living among the Nazis under the assumed identity of a lumberjack named Peter Zsanowsky. And "masked, camouflaged, lying, he managed to save his life. In Guatemala, until the day he died, even on his tombstone, he always called himself Peter."[6] As Halfon told Julia Tolo in an interview, "we all eventually become the mask that we wear."[7]

The settings of Halfon's stories are ever more diverse, reflecting the many places he's lived and others that he's visited. The United States, Poland, Serbia, Italy, France, Portugal, Japan, Germany, Israel, and the regional geographies of Guatemala itself all serve as backdrops. Connections with these places are sometimes strong, sometimes fleeting, but none are "home." Alexandra Ortiz Wallner describes this as a "mobile cognitive cartography," constructed around living and being "entre-mundos" or between worlds.[8] When

Gabriela Stoppelman called attention to the nomadism that characterizes his texts, Halfon replied, "Yes, that has a lot to do with my own wandering. I come from a nomadic family."[9] When another interviewer suggested that his characters live in permanent conflict with their origins, unrooted, in a kind of territorial nowhere, Halfon clarified, "I'm the one who feels uprooted. That's how I'm put together. I left Guatemala when I was little, and that meant not only that I was left without a country but also without a language, since English replaced Spanish. For me, uprootedness is a normal state, I don't feel uncomfortable in it."[10] But lest the cliché of the wandering Jew prove too easy a solution to this puzzle of who is Eduardo Halfon, his works show us that not all experiences of Jewishness and not all wanderers are equal.[11]

The fact that "Halfon" is a somewhat unusual and foreign-sounding last name in Spanish is another clue to the imprecise placement of the primary character. The surname is repeatedly misheard, mispronounced, and mangled in the author's works, most humorously in his 2015 volume *Signor Hoffman* and the story of the same name in *Mourning*. Indeed, according to the paternal grandfather for whom the author is named, the surname Halfon came from an old Hebrew word, or perhaps an old Persian word that meant "he who changes his life."[12] Author and protagonist live up to this definition, constantly changing geographical coordinates, linguistic settings, affiliations, and audiences, and adopting an ever more replete wardrobe of disguises.

What do we do, then, with a writer whose characters, as the following chapters will demonstrate, seem to eschew linguistic fixity, elide allegiances, slide in and out of religious or ethnic affiliations, and alternately claim both insider and outsider status? How do we study such a writer? Is Eduardo Halfon a Guatemalan writer? A Latin American writer? An American writer? A Latino writer? A Spanish writer (he holds a Spanish passport)? A Jewish writer? A Lebanese writer? Perhaps all of the above?

THE LATINO PARADOX

Front and center in this conundrum of categorization, at least for readers in English, is the particularly thorny question of Halfon's Latino identity. Those who awarded Halfon the 2019 International Latino Book Award for *Mourning*, the English version of his 2017 novel *Duelo*, clearly embraced the term and his embodiment of it. And at first glance, Halfon possesses the expected, even predictable profile of the Latino/x/a author in the United States. The journey from Central America with his family in 1981 when he was ten, their new life in Florida, the US schools he attended from elementary to university level, the negotiation of linguistic and cultural alienation and then absorption in the new host country; all these would seem to squarely situate him in the Latino experience, meaning, in his case, Guatemalan by birth, but North American by virtue of where he spent his formative years.

Halfon has addressed this paradox in different ways, usually to propose that the paradox cannot be resolved. In "Dicho hacia el sur" (Spoken Toward the South), he speaks of leaving behind his Spanish mother tongue and claiming English as her "stepmother" replacement:

> And so, just like that, before really understanding what was going on, already immersed in a new language which wasn't entirely foreign to me but which I didn't entirely possess, I found myself seated at a desk in a perfect classroom, solemn and artificially cooled. From that day forward I would belong simultaneously to two worlds, two countries, two cultures, but above all, two languages. My mother tongue would gradually give way to this barbaric intruder language, this new stepmother language. I would learn, in the years ahead, to love and hate them both.[13]

The autobiographical narrator in the tale "Mourning" represents this linguistic face-off quite differently, exchanging the metaphor of the sparring mothers for that of the diving helmet.

> I don't know at what point English replaced Spanish. I don't know if it truly replaced it, or if instead I started to wear English like some sort of gear that allowed me to enter and move freely in my new world. I was just ten years old, but I may have already understood that a language is also a diving helmet.[14]

This unexpected image evokes an antique, obsolete form of protection, a rigid enclosure that seals the diver's head from the surrounding water and provides him with oxygen, but also is heavy, clunky, and claustrophobic. It's notable, in any case, that "Dicho hacia el sur," perhaps the text in which Halfon most directly references his US immigrant experience, his assimilation into English, and his ostensible "Latino" bona fides, was published in *Sam no es mi tío*, a volume in Spanish that rejects in its very title a filial or familial relationship with Uncle Sam and what he has to offer. We find the speaker of "Spoken Toward the South" in Plantation, a northern suburb of Miami, where his family frequently spent vacations until increased violence in Guatemala drove them to Florida to live "temporarily." The author's choice of Spanish for this text makes a case for still speaking *from* the South as well.

Whereas the label "Latino literature" is usually attached to works in English by authors ensconced in enclaves where "life on the hyphen" is punctuated by code-switching and easy elision from one language to another, Halfon's characters rarely belong comfortably in any extended English-speaking "Latino community." After twelve years living in the US without becoming a citizen, the author returned to Guatemala and re-entered the family business there, reacquainting himself with his "lost" Spanish. Unhappy working in his father's business, he looked for answers in the study of philosophy, only to discover that in Latin American universities, philosophy and literature form a single course of study. Having never been a reader, much less a writer, Halfon was abruptly thrust into the world of fiction, a brave new world or perhaps addiction in which he was "at one point reading a book every one or two days, like some sort of literature junkie."[15] A stint as a literature professor at the Universidad Francisco Marroquín followed and it was from this long series of "accidents" that Halfon found his way as a writer of literature. Nevertheless, Guatemala was never fully "home" again, and the author subsequently took up residence in points as distant and disparate as Nebraska and New York City, before moving on to Paris, the south of France, and Berlin.

Halfon's decision to "relearn" Spanish after his return to Guatemala and then choose it as the primary vehicle of his creative work, despite his complete fluency in English, reveals something crucial to us about who he is, at least as a writer. But it's still impossible to place the author in a single linguistic or cultural camp. He claims booksellers can't even agree on where to shelve his works. A "Latino" or Latinx label can't fully capture his protagonists' propensity for navigating transnational and multilingual terrains. Nor does it account for his proclivity for moving in and out of Latin American, Jewish, and other spaces, finding the very notion of discreet domains motivation for fleeing toward creative freedom.

GOOD FOR THE JEWS?

Can readers and critics agree on Halfon's status as a *Jewish* writer, despite the persistent indeterminacy around issues of language and belonging that characterizes his works? Dan Reiter answers in the affirmative, describing him in a 2019 review as "born, brissed, bar-mitzvahed, a descendant of Holocaust survivors" and "inescapably, a Jewish author."[16] When Halfon won the 2018 Edward Lewis Wallant Award honoring a Jewish writer whose published fiction has made a significant contribution to American Jewry (explored further in Chapter 6), the announcement notably identified him as a "Latino Jewish" author.[17] Nonetheless, his negotiation of Jewishness, together with that of his fictional namesake, has not always endeared him to other members of the tribe. A Jerusalem taxi driver asks the protagonist of

"Tel Aviv was an inferno" (*Monastery*) if he is Jewish, to which he reluctantly replies "sometimes."[18] In his native Guatemala, Eduardo had explained to an Israeli girl, "I'm not Jewish anymore . . . I retired."[19] Halfon acknowledges that Jews are amongst his most frequent and vocal critics, taking offense at the attitudes and actions of his characters as well as with the comments he himself has made publicly.[20] And yet, what could be more Jewish than pondering the question of Jewishness, he wonders. "I think only a Jew questions his sense of Jewishness. A Catholic doesn't question why he's a Catholic. A Muslim doesn't question why he's a Muslim. They either are or aren't. But us Jews, inherently, neurotically, question our identity as Jews, we struggle to figure out what it means to be a Jew."[21]

Halfon's status as a Jewish writer has to do with more than bloodlines, religious practices, and his characters' individual negotiations of them. *The Polish Boxer*, arguably the anchoring text of his entire body of work, recounts his grandfather's Holocaust survival story, and the grandson's role as the heir of that survival and its memories. Whether or not his work can or should be described as "Holocaust fiction," the theme of Jewish survival is prevalent throughout, so much so that Erika Dreifus suggests that "even in stories that ostensibly focus elsewhere, the grandfather and his Holocaust history hover."[22] In her 2019 article "Why is Holocaust Fiction Still So Popular?" which mentions Halfon, Emily Burack provides four key reasons for the continuing popularity of the Holocaust trope: "a mix of *who* is telling the story (the third and fourth generations), the types of stories (not straightforward, but morally ambiguous), the historical truth at the heart of all these novels, and our current political moment."[23] All these characteristics describe Halfon's writings, even if not a single volume of his fiction is devoted entirely to Jewish topics.

As with all the labels considered here, however, we need an expansive notion of "Holocaust fiction" if we are to include Halfon's work in that particular category. When Eduard Aguilar asked him in 2018 if his work could be classified as "literature of the *lager*," the author responded, "The first thing that comes to mind when I read *lager* literature is literature that takes place in a concentration camp, within the lager, and in my case, it's not like that. In my work the lager never arrives. Although it's always there, circling, like some kind of ghost. I'm writing about the Nazi concentration camps because of my Polish grandfather. That's my heritage, my obligation."[24] Thus, while Halfon and his literary doppelgangers adamantly reject identity or thematic pigeonholing, Jewish memory stands out as a central theme and inspiration of his writing. In *Monastery*, the protagonist speaks of the scrap of paper his grandfather hands him with the address of his Polish apartment inscribed on it as "a mandate. An order. A dictate."²⁵ Thus, while the writer takes substantial liberties with the question of who's Eduardo Halfon, and to what community or communities he belongs, he remains bound to the task of telling Jewish stories, notwithstanding his doubts and skepticism. "I don't know if I believe in myself," he admits; "I believe more in the books I've written."²⁶

AGAINST MAGICAL REALISM

The upside of having so little authorial investment in any single identity, language, or history—even of Holocaust history—is that it opens the field to diverse readings and expands the range of correct answers to "Who's Eduardo Halfon?" And, as the author reportedly told Eric Gras at the end of their 2015 interview, "If you're missing anything or you need to elaborate whatever, you have my permission to invent it all."²⁷ The corollary question of *whose* Halfon, of which communities or publics or audiences can claim him as their own, also seems to have ever more possible answers. While the return to Guatemala and to Spanish after completing much of his schooling in the United States may have taken Halfon in a different direction from that of the "typical" Latinx author, it offered him the opportunity to consider his role in and commitments to a Latin American literary life. This insertion was also complex and incomplete, indicating once again Halfon's unique position(s) and voice(s). In a roundtable with the authors Daniel Alarcón and Santiago Vaquera-Vasquez, the author wondered out loud what it means to operate as he does, from a linguistic crossroads:

> But what happens with someone who appears to be writing in two languages at once, as we are, or as I am? What happens when writing is itself a translation in process? And here, of course, I can only answer from my own experience. With all its treacheries, with all its hardships and apparent contradictions (my mind immediately flashes back to my two sparring mothers), writing in two languages, or writing *from* two languages, is also like having two distinct treasure chests from where to grab gold and silver and diamonds. If at mid-sentence, for example, I reach for one chest and can't find in there anything I like, or anything that fits, I simply reach for the other one. And for some reason, the constant searching and the relentless tugging of these two languages seem to produce, through that same grammatical and syntactical tugging, a new language, a sort of hybrid or blended language. A self-language, really.²⁸

Given his own varied experiences, idiosyncrasies, and literary preferences,

Halfon has bristled at the stereotypes, clichés, and hackneyed expectations Latin American authors often confront, particularly from readers in the United States:

> I think most Americans still expect the same folklore from Latin American fiction, whether that folklore is magic realism, or political dictatorships, or the oppression of the indigenous peoples, or extreme poverty, or drug and border violence. Not Jewish protagonists. Jews belong in Eastern European literature, not in Latin American. Personally, though, I'm not interested in any pre-established folklore. I'm only interested in peeking where I'm not supposed to, in sticking my finger in the deepest wound, in throwing myself off the highest cliff.[29]

He also recognized that such stereotypes are not limited to the United States. As he discussed in an interview with Des Barry in 2013,

> there is still this idea that Latin American literature is defined by Gabriel García Marquez and the magical realist boom. They are looking for the new Gabriel Garcia Marquez, but magical realism exists only among a few writers. Throughout Latin America right now, the writing is far harder edged, far grittier, and much harder to classify or unify. There is a history we share, and a language. But as for literature, there isn't a lot of similarity between one country and another.[30]

Ironically, Halfon addresses some of these very themes in his work, most notably in regard to "Tomorrow We Never Did Talk About It" and *Canción*, in which the Guatemalan civil war and its impacts on the country's indigenous communities provide key themes. But even when he approaches such topics, he is emphatic about choosing what to write and how to write it, resisting external pressures and expectations. Determining to compose original works and publish them in a form of Spanish influenced by English, continuing to opt for the short form with its compunction that readers also practice a form of errancy, and situating his tales in an increasingly expansive global context all underline the heterogeneity of not just his own experience, but of Latin American literature writ large. Simultaneously, Halfon's first editions, released by editorial houses in Spain and Latin America such as Alfaguara, Anagrama, Pre-Textos, Sophos, and Libros del Asteroide, guarantee that his initial, if not primary, audiences, will continue to be Spanish speaking, whereas readers in English must approach him through a secondary platform of translation. While this decision would seem to limit Halfon's reach and the range of his audiences, renderings of his works into more than a dozen languages have constituted literary events in their own right, attesting to the multilingual nature of his transnational success. His varied list of awards, bestowed in several countries, prove that Halfon's fictions resonate with an ever more international and multilingual audience. A notable example is the bilingual publication in 2019 of *The Polish Boxer* in Spanish-Kaqchikel, opening the work to an audience of speakers of one of Guatemala's key Maya languages. As translator Raxche' Rodriguez explained, "Eduardo's people and my people, Jews and Mayas, have been historically persecuted.... So, it wasn't that hard to get all the nuances of his story."[31]

Is Halfon a different person, or at least a different writer, in his varied texts in Spanish, English, and other languages? Perhaps not, but the differences between editions remain important, as they reflect how readerships create cohorts of affinity and communities of belonging.[32] This volume focuses primarily on works published in English from the first two decades of Halfon's literary production, and their reception. While this is a limited sample, it nevertheless showcases Halfon's primary themes and forms, and the ways in which they interact with understandings of Latin American and Jewish memory in the English-speaking world. A more comprehensive study of Halfon's oeuvre would take into account a large body of material still unavailable to readers in English that includes *Esto no es una pipa, Saturno* (2003); *De cabo roto* (2003); *El ángel literario* (2004), *Clases de hebreo* (2008), *Clases de dibujo* (2009), *Mañana Nunca lo Hablamos* (2011), *Elocuencias de un tartamudo* (2012), *Signor Hoffman* (2015), *Clases de chapín* (2017), *Biblioteca Bizarra* (2018), *Oh gueto mi amor* (2018), and *Un hijo cualquiera* (2022), as well as subsequent editions of several of these works.[33] For these and other works published in Spanish, Halfon has won such awards as the Café Bretón & Bodegas Olarra prize for *Clases de dibujo*, the José María de Pereda prize in Spain for *La pirueta*, the Roger Caillois Prize in France, The National Prize for Literature in Guatemala, and The Cálamo Prize, also in Spain, for *Canción*.

THRESHOLDS

To what or whom does Halfon belong, then? It seems he belongs to fiction, even as he straddles its threshold with reality. Circling around and back again to events and encounters drawn from his own experiences or those of his family members, the "real" offers the author a point of departure, but not the destination. When Des Barry asked him why, if his stories are fictional, his protagonist almost always is named Eduardo Halfon, he explained:

> Perhaps because I want readers to have a visceral experience. I want them to believe what is going on in the story, that all this really happened. So if the author Eduardo Halfon has the same name as the narrator in the story then the reader is lulled into thinking that the events in the story are probably real. In writing them, they all start off as real in some way, and then they go somewhere else, somewhere less real, but just as true. Or perhaps even more so.[34]

As we have already seen, Halfon works from a linguistic threshold as well, in which he "belongs" to Spanish, even as he negotiates it from an overlay of English, from other languages temporarily inhabited in his sojourns, from the "self-language" that has emerged from all these experiences, and from the varied terrains of translation.

Offering a liminal territory in which fiction and nonfiction can overlap, the short-form *relato* provides Halfon with a genre that itself occupies a threshold. As Halfon asserted in one of his earliest works in Spanish, he hoped to write "on the very threshold that divides history and fiction."[35] Though there is no perfect English translation of the term, the relato typically falls between the *cuento* (short story) and the novel in terms of length and can refer to a tale that is conveyed orally or in writing. Additionally, the *relato* leaves room for the inclusion of non-fictional or historical facts.[36] Its Latin etymology "marks the prefix re-, to indicate a reiteration, in this case typical of narrating something that has already happened, likewise the component lāt- is appreciated, which is interpreted as transferring, understanding that in this framework, one takes the story to someone, being associated with the verb fero, knowing that it is presented as a statement that has variations."[37] In other words, a *relato* transfers or takes to someone (in this case the reader) a narration of something that has already happened, with an understanding that other variations are implicit in the narration as re-iteration.

Halfon's predilection for these episodic forms provides the ideal conditions for memory to act on the present and vice versa in his stories. Just as memories, always partial, may occur suddenly or abruptly, the "snapshots" or vignettes that together form Halfon's relatos sometimes appear to "lose the thread and never go anywhere," as one critic complains at the end of *Canción*.[38] The privileging of the intrusions of memory over narrative linearity has contributed to debates about whether Halfon's writing should be considered autobiography or autofiction, debates we consider further in the chapters that follow. Rejecting both labels, Halfon is adamant that all his work, in its entirety, is fiction: "I believe the key there is that they are not memoirs, I don't write memoirs, it's not autobiography, it's fiction. Everything I write is fiction."³⁹

This assertion prompts us to read his work through and with an eye to its fictional devices, whether our concern is the relationship of the text to historical fact or its relation to memory. Built in part on episodes from lived history and the memories of them, Halfon's works are full of such devices. As regards narrative time, analepses, prolepses, flashbacks and detours guarantee that neither the protagonist nor the accompanying reader will stay in one space or time for very long. His narratives oscillate, sometimes with discomfiting frequency, between past and future moments, interpolating remembered and new experiences. As regards narrative voice, the presence across several volumes of a narrator named Eduardo Halfon who "is and is not" the author, emphasizes the duplication or recreation of the self, however aware readers might be that an autobiographical narrator is always a fictional creation. Memory and recall enter as primordial vessels in Halfon's work, even if they are fallible containers for history and the construction of the self.⁴⁰ The narrative is so consistently interrupted by remembering that we can find the protagonist thinking of his grandfather, and of Auschwitz, and of his grandfather's green tattoo, as he pisses in a bar bathroom, as occurs in "White Smoke," a *relato* that appears in different forms in both *The Polish Boxer* and *Monastery*.⁴¹ Halfon's same-named protagonist moves through his own and others' memories to such an extent that memory itself becomes a character of sorts, a voice that might be ignored or suppressed, but cannot be silenced.

THE HALFON SHUFFLE

This book focuses on Halfon's first four novels to appear in English, as well as "Tomorrow We Never Did Talk About It," the title story from a larger collection that has yet to appear in translation.⁴² All of these works bear a relationship to the original Spanish editions, but rarely contain the same exact content. "All of my books in translation work this way," Halfon explains. "I add and subtract stories as needed or as we—each editor and myself—see fit. That is, every one of my books in translation is absolutely original."⁴³ This shuffle or reshuffle function in the assemblage of Halfon's works has become more complex over time, making it necessary for the author himself to chart the development of the principal works, the episodes in each, and their overlap with other publications. Using the metaphor of *matryoshka* or Russian nesting dolls, Halfon has organized his literary production in

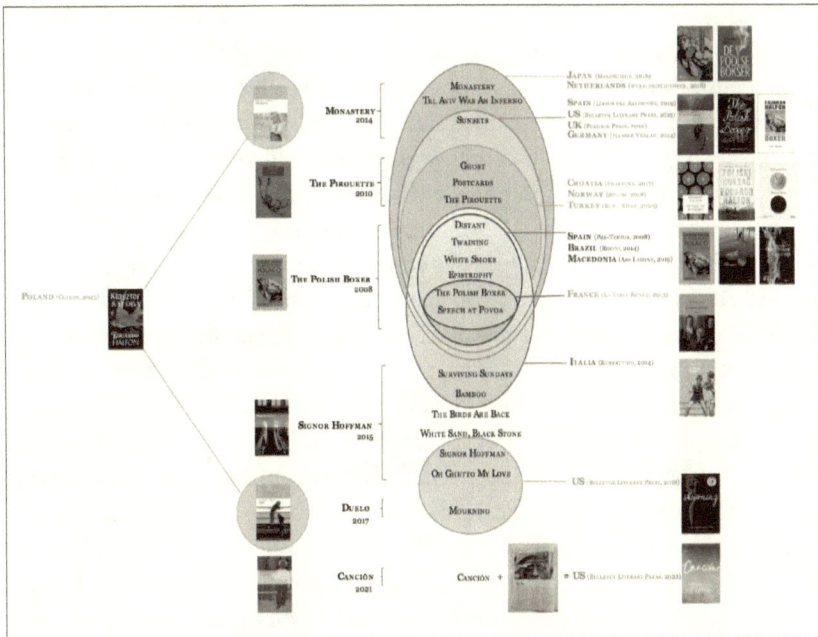

FIGURE 1. Matryoshka diagram created by author Eduardo Halfon explaining the relationships among his works published in English. Illustration courtesy Eduardo Halfon.

English in a chart that hints at his training as an engineer (see Figure 1). As this graphic suggests, its crucial to think of Halfon's stories as moving parts that are incorporated in different ways. We can compare it with the corresponding chart of his works in Spanish, an alternate document that Erica Durante and Maude Havenne have studied.[44]

These impressive graphic representations do not tell the whole story of Halfon's literary production, of course. They don't indicate that some editions of his work are divided into chapters with titles, while others have no titles at all or are ordered numerically. Missing from them is a whole host of stories that don't appear in Halfon's own volumes but can be found in a wide range of magazines, newspapers, and other story collections. Finally, trying to track which pieces appear (or reappear) in which volumes and treating the separate volumes as discreet projects may ultimately detract us from understanding Halfon's work as a unified project. For despite his declared preference for the short form—*The Polish Boxer* even begins with a professor discussing with his university students Ricardo Piglia's ideas on the functions of the short story—the author and his critics have also described his entire oeuvre, his work as a whole, as a *novela en marcha*, an ongoing novel.[45] In this larger frame, seemingly disparate parts converge in a large-scale project for which, at present, there's no end in sight.

Considering the sum total of Halfon's published works in English from *The Polish Boxer* forward as an ongoing novel has led me to organize this book according to a different logic from the usual one-chapter-per-book model. Chapter 1 deals with the ways in which *The Polish Boxer* marks a before-and-after inflection point in Halfon's work: his first major work to be published in English, the volume that first portrays his grandfather's story of surviving the Holocaust, and the Ur-text or starting point of the *novela en marcha*. Chapter 2 considers "Epistrophy," also included in *The Polish Boxer*, in which the protagonist's acquaintance with a gypsy musician sparks a conversation on jazz, other musical styles, and improvisation that carries through to other works by Halfon. *The Polish Boxer*'s penultimate chapter "A Speech at Póvoa" inspired Chapter 3, an examination of how fact and fiction combine in Halfon's (or his protagonist's) search for "ecstatic" truth. Chapter 4 considers "Tomorrow We Never Did Talk About It," the title story from the 2011 collection *Mañana Nunca Lo Hablamos*. That story's portrayal of the violence that characterized Guatemala at the beginning of the 1980s, when Halfon's family left his birth country for the United States, has produced some of the most important critical response to Halfon's work in Spanish and English. Chapters 5, 6, and 7 treat the subsequent works *Monastery*, *Mourning*, and *Canción*, respectively, though always with an eye to understanding each work's relationship to Halfon's larger writing project. The ongoing nature of Halfon's *novela en marcha* means that this study is incomplete as well.[46] The peripatetic itineraries of Halfon's characters will no doubt continue to spread out in fresh meanderings, new meetings, unexpected explorations, and memorable discoveries. "Clearly, this itinerant life is continuing," he explained to two fellow writers. "It's a nomadic existence, a Jewish type of life."[47]

CHAPTER 1

NUMBERS AND OTHER MNEMONIC DEVICES

> *If despair is contagious, so is memory: memory of our past, of our values, and even, as Hasidic teaching has it, of the future for which we yearn. And because listening to a witness makes you a witness, in reading these words, you the reader, have become a witness too.*

DISTANCE AND PROXIMITY

Eduardo Halfon's penchant for masterfully mixing history, story, and memory is perhaps nowhere more evident than in *The Polish Boxer*, his best-known work. It was first published in Spanish in 2008, and released in English in 2012, thanks to the efforts of an unusual team of five translators who workshopped the text, circulating drafts among themselves and the author over a few short, intense weeks, prior to its publication by Bellevue Literary Press.[1] There are several reasons *The Polish Boxer* is a key to fully understanding Halfon's entire writing project and its international resonance, some lodged in the work itself, some having to do with the book's relationship to subsequent works by the author, and some related to the role the volume played in expanding Halfon's international renown and readership.

Though not his first published work, *The Polish Boxer* is the first in which a first-person singular narrator also named Eduardo Halfon makes his debut, connecting a series of experiences—real or imagined—from different places, moments, and encounters. Halfon has spoken of the original text in Spanish as a gestational or foundational volume:

So, without me planning it, and without knowing what was going to happen, that first edition of *El boxeador polaco* has proceeded to function as a foundational book, or as a mother book, or as a sun, if you like, for all the subsequent books that orbit around it and form part of a project or perhaps of a single book, written in installments. I never know how it will continue. Nor how it will end. Maybe only that other Eduardo Halfon knows that.[2]

Besides serving as the narrative cornerstone for Halfon's larger writing project, *El boxeador polaco* thus marks the emergence of *two* important new voices: that of the author, and that of "that other Eduardo Halfon." While the narrator of *Boxer* (whether autobiographical, autofictional, or something else—a debate to which we will return) will reappear in subsequent works such as *Monastery, Mourning,* and *Canción,* suggesting an ever more familiar and reliable personal history and through-line, Halfon contends this development was spontaneous and unplanned.[3]

Although *El boxeador polaco* was favorably reviewed in the Spanish-language press and would be reedited in an expanded edition in 2019, its translation into English attracted attention from many new corners of the readerverse, soon garnering a surprisingly varied list of honors and mentions. It was an International Latino Book Award Finalist, a *New York Times* Editors' Choice, a *Los Angeles Times* "Holiday Gift" selection, a *San Francisco Chronicle* "Top Shelf" selection, and a *Shelf Unbound* "Top 10 Book of the Year" selection.[4] The author confirms it was the English version that made it possible for many people to read his work who wouldn't have found it otherwise, subsequently awakening interest in other countries and languages. There's a "before" and "after" of *The Polish Boxer,* Halfon ascertains; the appearance of the work in English was crucial to his recognition as an author with both a local and global appeal.[5]

Indeed, the different lives of this work in English and Spanish establish a precedent for how Halfon works and how to understand his authorial universe, one in which translations and even subsequent editions of any given work should be understood not as parallel texts, but as reconfigurations or even, in some cases, reinventions. As Erica Durante and Maude Havenne have pointed out: "In fact, despite the fact that the titles might superficially maintain the illusion of equivalence between editions in Spanish and versions in other languages, the contract of fidelity that usually defines the relationship between an original and its translation finds itself betrayed by this author, who like Borges makes fun of the notion of authorship, giving us a work that is unpredictable and concentric."[6] For example, while *El boxeador polaco* contains six separate stories or segments, *The Polish Boxer,* published some four years later, contains ten. The 2019 edition of *El boxeador polaco* contains three new tales not included in the Spanish original, but which did appear in the first English edition. The reconfigured *Boxeador* also sports fresh metatextual elements, such as a short preface and a newly designed cover featuring a photo of the author's grandfather, a photo newly alluded to in a reworked version of the book's final story.

The resounding resonance of *The Polish Boxer* within Halfon's own oeuvre, as well as across generations, languages, territories and publics, is evident in the strikingly diverse list of awards it has received, and its growing list of translations, including both British and American English versions, as well as versions in German, Italian, Portuguese, French, Japanese, Croatian, Dutch, Macedonian, Norwegian, Turkish and Kaqchikel, one of the Maya languages of Halfon's native Guatemala. The formats of these translations are notably varied as they add to or dispense with texts included in the original Spanish version (as mentioned, even the 2008 Pre-Textos and 2019 Libros del Asteroide editions in Spanish are not identical). Despite facing pressures to produce lengthier volumes, especially for US publishers, Halfon continues to prefer the short form, both in terms of choosing the *relato* as his primary genre and considering possible configurations of short texts together. His favorite version of *The Polish Boxer*, he admits, is the shortest one, containing only "The Polish Boxer" and one other story: "In my opinion, it's the most beautiful of all of them: a short, intimate book about a grandson and a grandfather."[7]

The Polish Boxer (or perhaps more precisely, its Spanish-language precursor) thus initiates a series of compositional rituals to keep in mind while moving through this and later works. The remaking of a text in a translation, the reorganizing of texts in shorter or longer volumes in different languages, the alteration and repurposing of texts in subsequent projects, together urge us to read any of his texts not as fixed and finished, but as part of a larger work in progress. Paradoxically, it is this focus not just on a multilingual experience, but also on this openness to reconfiguration that allows the parts to cohere, whether in a single volume such as *The Polish Boxer*, or in the sum total of his writing.

A final point to highlight in this relationship between *The Polish Boxer* and later works is their underlying logic of intertextual memory. That is, not only do each of the episodes draw in large part on a memory bank of experiences, whether those of the narrator or those of a family member as recounted to the narrator, but so too will other, later works draw on the "memory" of *The Polish Boxer*. Halfon himself has acknowledged as much in his graphic illustrations of his works as interrelated and overlapping narratives or *matryoshka* (see Figure 1 in the Introduction). Before taking a closer look at the title story itself, then, it's a good idea to see how some of the other parts of his books establish this context for an intertextual itinerary of memory.

The first story in *The Polish Boxer*, "Distant," stages the culture clash between the distinct worlds and worldviews that inhabit the finite geography of Guatemala itself.[8] No doubt reflecting something of the author's own experience teaching literature at a private university in Guatemala City, a professor reflects on an in-class discussion of a celebrated essay by Ricardo Piglia on short story form. In it, the Argentine writer proposes that "a story always tells two stories," and "the visible narrative always hides a secret tale."[9] Besides providing us with clues as to Halfon's own preference for short fiction, "Distant" illustrates Piglia's theory by presenting two tales. The first is about an instructor confronting the boredom and indifference of his students as if he were "speaking some Bantu language" and asking himself "if this shit was really worth it."[10] But adjacent to the faces marked by ennui and acne assembled before him appears that of a student with an entirely different semblance and story, another language even: thin, dark-skinned Juan Kalel, a seventeen year-old native of Tecpán: "Everything about Juan Kalel was out of sync with the other students in my class, and of course, the whole university. His sensitivity and eloquence. His interest. His appearance and social status." Kalel appears like a rare "shooting star" who, thanks to his devotion to all types of learning, "exposes the falsehood and hypocrisy not just of the other students, but sometimes of the professor and his stultifying ivory tower."[11]

The second or "secret" tale that "Distant" reveals, then, is that of another register of knowledge, another kind of creativity, an out-of-classroom experience of eloquence. Away from the halls of the university and its patina of superiority, Kalel explains to his professor, also named Halfon, that the word for poetry in his Kaqchikel-speaking community is Pach'un tzij, a neologism that means "braid of words."[12] Besides implicitly asserting the superiority of poetry to the short story genre his professor has promoted, "Distant" allows us and other readers to glimpse this alternate field of comprehension and understanding, suggesting that in certain literary matters, Juan Kalel's skills supersede those of his classmates and even his professor. As Halfon explained in an interview,

> The Guatemalan of a certain social class and from the capital is one kind, the kind from which I come. But there is also the Indigenous Guatemalan, which is 80 percent of the country, which I sometimes interact with. Like Juan Kalel,

in *The Polish Boxer*. I like that story so much because of the inversion that occurs between student and teacher. Kalel becomes the one who guides the one who was his professor toward another Guatemala, the Indigenous and rural Guatemala where my narrator Eduardo Halfon goes to look for him. That's why the title is "Distance," for the distance that exists between the two Guatemalas and the need for Juan Kalel to guide his professor in a world that's unknown to him and where he feels insecure. In the same way that Juan Kalel feels in university life in the capital. They're two worlds in which each one is a foreigner in the territory of the other.[13]

Different ways of seeing are on display again in "Twaining," the second story in the English version of *The Polish Boxer*.[14] Here, the narrator travels to a Mark Twain conference at Duke University in the United States, where he confronts his own boredom, before seizing the opportunity to espouse his ideas on the similarities of Twain to Cervantes, especially in *Huckleberry Finn*. Later, he takes a walk with a seasoned Twain critic named Joe Krupp, who tells him the surname was originally Krupowsky. Joe's Polish surname triggers the narrator's memories of his Polish grandfather and of "the bottle of whiskey we'd drunk together while he told me about Sachsenhausen and Auschwitz and the Polish boxer."[15]

In contrast to the Twain-Cervantes comparison, which Krupp gently advises has already been explored by a host of critics (including at least one writing in Spanish), the grandfather's account of life in the camps is the protagonist's personal inheritance of memory, serving here, perhaps, as the secondary tale which Piglia considered the key to the short story form and all its variants. As in several other stories in *The Polish Boxer*, then, we find cameo appearances of the crucial character of the narrator's Polish grandfather, who like Halfon's own maternal grandfather, survived by following the advice of a fellow Polish-speaking prisoner at Auschwitz who was still alive to dispense that advice because the Nazis liked to watch him box.

HOLOCAUST TESTIMONY AND *THE POLISH BOXER*

In a 2008 interview with Luis Figueroa at the university where the author was then teaching, Halfon explained the process by which he began to create *The Polish Boxer* as a unified project, as a "novel" of sorts.[16] As he wrote "Distant," "Twaining," and other *relatos* as discreet, self-contained short stories, he sensed there was a thread connecting them, which he finally recognized was a conversation he had with his grandfather in 2001, who after nearly sixty years of silence, had agreed to speak of his wartime experiences in a succession of Nazi labor and death camps. Halfon filmed that conversation, describing it as "very chaotic, very disordered. He himself unraveled the story; he didn't himself know what had happened first, what had happened later." Despite these memory lapses, the conversation proved to be a revelation, not just to the author, but to other members of the family as well: "He spoke of things which my mother, my aunts and uncles, my grandmother didn't know."[17] The grandfather's belated consent to speak after maintaining silence throughout most of his adult life suggests a recognition that "the Holocaust stands behind any contemporary sense of Jewish identity, whether it is addressed obsessively, ambivalently, or not at all."[18]

Within this nonlinear conversation, the anecdote of the Polish boxer, recounted in just a couple of minutes, leapt out to Halfon as "tremendously literary" from the moment he heard it. "I grabbed that anecdote, I put it in my bag, and I carried it around with me everywhere," he explains. Nonetheless, as Halfon told his interviewer, despite recognizing the literary value of the Polish boxer episode within his grandfather's account, he resisted the topic of the Holocaust for many years, so horrific and at the same time so cliché. Yet another grandson. Yet another grandfather. Yet another survivor. Hadn't enough people already written about this? "I was trapped between fear and respect," he admits.

While scholars and family members tend to focus entirely on the role of the *provider* of survivor testimony, the *hearer* also faces a complex task, as Dori Laub has noted: "The listener to the narrative of extreme human pain, of massive psychic trauma faces a unique situation. In spite of the presence of ample documents, of searing artifacts and of fragmentary memoirs of anguish, he comes to look for something that is in fact nonexistent: a record that has yet to be made."[19] The key to the book's integrity, Halfon says, was to find a starting point that seemed to be literary, but that quickly led beyond the literary to the terrains of history and memory.

If a film version of *The Polish Boxer* is made, it will undoubtedly include a close-up of the figure of the Polish grandfather and his Auschwitz tattoo, a short (or long?) story unto itself: "This, he said, rubbing his forearm gently. It was in Auschwitz, he said."[20] In an interview with Dwyer Murphy for *Guernica*, Halfon acknowledged the importance of just such a number and conversation to the gestation of *The Polish Boxer* and his global project:

> EDUARDO HALFON: *A number on my grandfather's forearm was the beginning of The Polish Boxer: this one image in my head of growing up as a kid in Guatemala, and looking at my grandfather's forearm, and him telling me it was his phone number.*

GUERNICA: *And how did you go from image to story?*

EDUARDO HALFON: *I guess that that image—of a Holocaust tattoo as his phone number—later became a conversation. One rainy afternoon, I was drinking whiskey with my grandfather when he told me the true story behind that number, behind those five green digits. A very brief story that had to do with Auschwitz, and a twenty-dollar gold coin, and a boxer, and the saving power of words. He spoke for hours that afternoon, about many things that had happened to him. But that story about a boxer instantly crept under my skin.*[21]

The story of the Polish boxer who appears in the grandfather's excavation of his own troubled memory, carefully guarded until that moment, creeps under the skin of the author to be fleshed out in a fictional text that serves as a kind of intergenerational memorial. The author's under-the-skin reaction suggests an embodiment or imprint paralleling his forbear's Auschwitz tattoo, as well as a measure of empathy combined with his curiosity. The grandfather's tale is compelling enough to propel the writer forward on a search that is both personal and literary, leading to a "mosaic of episodes" that extends beyond *The Polish Boxer* itself.[22] Indeed, we might argue that Halfon's authorial voice in large part emerges from this specific conversation marked by a decades-long prelude of silence. As Janet Jacob notes, "the research on the intergenerational transmission of trauma focuses primarily on two modes of survivor communication: storytelling . . . and deep emotional silences." The backstory to "The Polish Boxer" is the "untold story" of "feelings and emotions that permeated the emotional climate of the survivor household."[23]

NUMBERS

"The Polish Boxer" emphatically begins not with a word but with a number, the very number that was tattooed on the arm of the author's grandfather. The story begins *in media res*, or mid-conversation, as it were: "69752. That it was his phone number. That he had it tattooed there, on his left forearm, so he wouldn't forget it. That's what my grandfather told me. And that's what I grew up believing."[24] The advantages of this first "word" of the story being a number are many, if not immediately obvious. First, "the skin acts as a document or archive. . . . The serial number tattoo is a certificate of authenticity."[25] The number carries across alphabetic languages as an indexical sign, a mark of translingual or even universal comprehensibility. The tattoo "is an 'artifact' even though it is part of the living, mobile body," and "a physical manifestation of a specific time and place, an icon of atrocity" that "remains 'objective' despite the passage of time and the shifting landscape of the grandfather's post-war life."[26] It provides evidence not only of the existence of the concentration camps the grandfather names in his account, but also of the existence of survivors like him. As such, it is a potent kind of shorthand for a larger experience shared by thousands but experienced in each case uniquely.

In fact, the number features as the principal protagonist in a curious element of ephemera, the "book trailer" or publicity video associated with the release of *The Polish Boxer* in its US and UK editions, accessible on YouTube.[27] Less than two minutes long, the video features twenty-eight individuals holding a poster-sized piece of white cardboard bearing only the number 69752 in black ink. Most of the subjects look directly at the camera. The first of these number-bearers is filmed against a wall where two framed versions of the 1981 Richard Avedon portrait "Nastassja Kinski and the Serpent" hang. In the second frame, one smiling woman holds the sign while another heats tortillas on a wood-burning stove next to her; both wear typical indigenous dress. Others who bear the 69752 poster include a barber cutting someone's hair; a woman in front of a military helicopter; a boy and his father holding a rooster; a vendor in a fabric store; a man in a boat; people in a horse-drawn transport; a fireman or other first responder; a woman standing behind a fountain in the shape of a mermaid, from whose breasts water flows in two streams; a man squatting with his pigs in a pigsty; a conductor or orchestra teacher, surrounded by his students and their instruments; a woman selling piñatas; a fisherman framed by his nets; a fruit vendor; an older man killing time with three of his cronies in a park; a man harvesting coconuts; a woman and her child in a rural setting; several kids in school uniforms; and two smiling boys in matching hats, sitting on a stone wall.

What is the point of these individual cameos with the numbered posterboard and the montage they create together? At minute 1:10 of the video, five cyclists who have dismounted at a mountain viewpoint hold other white signs with one word each that together form the sentence "It was my grandfather's number." In the next frame, five men hold up signs that make the phrase "It was in Auschwitz." And then, six men at the beach create the sentence "It was with the Polish Boxer." Finally, the author himself appears, sitting at the edge of a boxing ring, holding a sign reading "The Polish Boxer" and then another (or the flip side) reading "(Me)," followed by two posters that declare the names of the English version's five translators. The logos of the US and British publishers appear, as well as an image of the cover of *The Polish Boxer*, before the video closes with two preschool-aged children holding up the 69752 sign between them, one of them waving goodbye to the camera. The soundtrack for the video is an unattributed version of the Russian Jewish folksong "Tumbalalaika," seemingly unrelated to–or even contrasting with—the region and contemporary era captured on the video.[28]

By being filmed holding the posters with the Auschwitz tattoo number of the author's grandfather, these Guatemalan compatriots of different ethnic backgrounds and settings in turn become memory bearers, however briefly, for the grandfather's Holocaust story and its place in the national narrative. The number that features at the beginning, end, and symbolic center of "The Polish Boxer" here forms a kind of logic of a local and transnational community linked by memory. By extension, *The Polish Boxer*—particularly in its English-language format—can resonate in a broader global context, while still referencing the Central American origins of its author. However much of this history the participants in the video understand, the book trailer generalizes the experience of the European concentration camps the tattoo number references, suggesting that the number is broadly legible both within and beyond national boundaries. The video also portends a shared legacy of traumas, whether external or internal to Guatemala, that Halfon will address elsewhere in his work.

For the children and grandchildren of Holocaust survivors, the number tattoo arguably has much more intimate meanings than this book trailer suggests, however. It can represent a riddle, reflecting unanswered or prohibited questions, or the key or code to solving mysteries surrounding this crucial episode of a family member's experience. For the child version of the grandson who narrates "The Polish Boxer," the number was *hypnotic*, a sign inscribed on the surface of the body that reached far beyond the physical: "That's how I played with his number. Clandestinely. Hypnotized by those five mysterious green digits that, much more than on his forearm, seemed to me to be tattooed on some part of his soul."[29] Indeed, the Auschwitz tattoo number is so important to "The Polish Boxer," the narrator invokes it explicitly at both the beginning and end of the text. In the last paragraph, he considers again his grandfather's number:

> Once more, I sat looking at my grandfather's number, 69752, tattooed one winter morning in '42, by a young Jew in Auschwitz. I tried to imagine the face of the Polish boxer ... but all I could imagine was an endless line of individuals, all naked, all pale, all thin, all weeping or saying Kaddish in absolute silence, all devout believers in a religion whose faith is based on numbers, as they waited in line to be numbered themselves.[30]

This striking image of camp prisoners "all weeping or saying Kaddish... all devout believers" may be more imaginative than factual, as the group of approximately 400,000 people who received tattoos on their bodies at Auschwitz and its sub-camps was constituted of Jews and non-Jews alike.[31] Additionally, only "*69 percent of the survivors surveyed claimed to have believed in God before the Holocaust*," and only about 55 percent of this group can be regarded as religiously observant, according to one study.[32] Even the narrator's own grandfather does not know how to recite Kaddish: "What else have you got left when you know the next day you're going to be shot, eh?" he says. "Nothing. You either lie down or cry or you lie down and say Kaddish. I didn't know the Kaddish. But that night, for the first time in my life, I also said Kaddish."[33] The imagined scene emphasizes not the rote recital of a familiar prayer known by all, but the extremity of a moment in which men and women of all levels of faith (or none at all) understood the precariousness of their lives and sought to mitigate their terror with prayer.

Indeed, though the number tattoos, together with murder in the gas chambers, are among the best-known symbols of the Holocaust, most Jews were not tattooed, and most did not die at Auschwitz or by gas; the principal causes of death during the genocide of European Jews were starvation and illness in the ghettos, or immediate death from a gunshot in the German conquest of the east.[34] Nonetheless, by returning full circle to the number with which he started, Halfon alerts us to the continuing imprint of the camp experience on the diverse individuals imprisoned there, and of the continuing search for a way to negotiate the unspeakable nature of such experiences in language. The number, as well as the silence or lies accompanying it, is the indelible mark of the unspeakable, and the unspeakable or the inability to speak is itself the invitation to generations that follow to speak.[35] In his memoir *Survival in Auschwitz*, Primo Levi uses a surprising term to describe the ritual of being tattooed together with other prisoners: "My number is 174517; we have been baptized, we will carry the tattoo on our left arm until we die." The use of "baptism" in this context suggests a desecration or betrayal rather than a sacrament, or perhaps the unavailability of a suitable term in the Jewish lexicon. Despite his many efforts to convey in writing what he underwent, Levi ultimately concludes that "language lacks words to express this offence, the demolition of a man."[36]

NUMBERED

The Auschwitz number is legible across space, language, and time as "anyone fluent in the language of Holocaust memory" can identify or read it. As

Nina Fischer notes in *Memory Work*, "the tattoo links to a number of temporal levels in the network of memory: the tattooing process, the ensuing horrors of Auschwitz, and also life after survival that is indelibly marked."[37] The number even provides us with a geospatial record of survivor dispersion to places such as Central America, where the narrator's Polish grandfather arrived in 1946.[38] But what do we do with it in the present? The 2012 Israeli documentary *Numbered* suggests that the meanings and significance of the Auschwitz tattoo could not be more disparate or contradictory for its varied interpreters.[39] Fifty Holocaust survivors living in Israel who had been forcibly tattooed each tell their stories, some alongside their younger relatives who have chosen to reinscribe those numbers on their own bodies as well. *Numbered* thus "provides several perspectives of the relationship each person has to their number and how that number functions daily in their lives as a trace of memory."[40] The creators argue "the film's protagonist is the number itself, as it evolves and becomes both a personal and collective symbol from 1940 to today. These scars, paradoxically unanimous and anonymous, reveal themselves to be diverse, enlightening, and full of life."[41]

Despite this affirmation, *Numbered*'s subjects respond to the Auschwitz tattoo with little unanimity as to its purposes and effects. Some have chosen, like the character of the grandfather in Halfon's story, to hide it or invent another reason for its presence on the body. Some speak of taking steps to remove the tattoo, due to the post-war stigma that only the cruelest prisoners survived.[42] Indeed, the word *stigma* "derives from the Greek and refers to a kind of tattoo mark that was cut or burned into the skin of criminals, slaves, or traitors to visibly identify them as blemished or morally polluted."[43] For some, the experience of being tattooed signified a different level of degradation within elaborate systems of persecution and deprivation. Imogen Tyler writes that the "Czech holocaust survivor Ruth Elias recalls how she survived near-starvation in the Jewish ghetto of Theresienstadt near Prague, but it was only when she lined up to be tattooed at Auschwitz that she understood that she was no longer considered a human being: 'The numbers on our forearms marked our depersonalization.'"[44] The grandfather in "The Polish Boxer" alludes to this stigma by creating an alternate, neutral explanation for the "telephone" number on his body.

Numbered in fact highlights a wide range of sentiments ranging from horror to beauty, from stigma to medal of honor.[45] The film begins with an emblematic citation by Levi: "With time, my tattoo has become a part of my body . . . I show it unwillingly to those who ask out of pure curiosity; readily and with anger to those who say they are incredulous. Often young people ask me why I don't have it erased and this surprises me: Why should I?

There are not many of us in the world to bear this witness."[46] Levi traverses a range of responses here: reluctance to expose his number, anger at those who would question its veracity, and surprise at those who think he should remove it, given his sense of obligation to "bear this witness."

From the moment of its inscription through to the present, the Auschwitz tattoo simultaneously marks both trauma and survival. "Although a marker of dehumanization, the number meant in fact a certain degree of security, as only those deemed fit for physical labour or were in other ways of interest to the Nazis received them," notes Tanja Schult.[47] The character Vladek in Art Spiegelman's graphic account *Maus II* "understands the Auschwitz tattoo as a positive marking," aided in this interpretation by a Polish priest who does a kabbalistic reading of the digits in his number and finds that their sum is the number 18, a number that corresponds to the letters in the Hebrew word *chai* or life.[48] Commenting on the multiple perspectives of those who appear in *Numbered*, Lisa Costello believes the most important element "is the way in which this film focuses on the tattooed number in positive relationship with others. Instead of being depicted as an object of judgment or pity, a thing that separates that person from the rest of 'us' who are physically 'unmarked' with trauma, the film shows the tattooed number as a connector."[49] In Halfon's tale, the tattoo accomplishes both these tasks: it serves as the marker of silence and creative mistruths on the one hand and as a connector between generations and overdue conversations on the other.

Numbers ascribed on prisoners' bodies at Auschwitz take on more meanings as some in the second and third generations elect to tattoo them on their own skin, identifying this action as a memorial to their loved one who survived the Holocaust, as the literal imprint of the responsibility to "never forget." Nonetheless, these "progenic" tattoos have been controversial as they enact "a mode of postmemory through a resignification of the original sign that makes visible the intergenerational trauma of the Holocaust."[50] In her influential development of the term postmemory, Marianne Hirsch explains it is "meant to convey its temporal and qualitative difference from survivor memory, its secondary or second-generation memory quality, its basis in displacement, its vicariousness and belatedness." This work "defines the familial inheritance and transmission of cultural trauma" but is essentially different from the experiences of victims, survivors, witnesses, or perpetrators: "Postmemory is a powerful form of memory precisely because its connection to its object or source is mediated not through recollection but through representation, projection, and creation—often based on silence rather than speech, on the inviable rather than the visible."[51]

As in "The Polish Boxer," in which both first and second-generation members of the family (including the marked member himself) choose not to discuss the grandfather's tattoo, such actions inevitably raise questions about whether a progenic tattoo in fact only repeats a trauma, reifying its power of abjection. Daniel Brouwer and Linda Dian Horwitz point to at least three contexts in which the use of a tattoo as a medium to practice public memory of the Holocaust remains problematic: the explicit prohibition against tattoos in the Torah, the belief that a tattooed body cannot be buried in a Jewish cemetery, and the overdetermined meaning of "Jewish tattoos vis-à-vis the Nazi experience."[52] Analyzing this gesture within semiotic, affective, and pedagogical rhetorical frames, Brouwer and Horwitz nonetheless acknowledge the number's plasticity and potential for resignification:

> For Auschwitz survivors, the tattoo indexes a direct experience of Nazi atrocities. For progeny of survivors, wearing the tattoo retains a poignant but altered indexical function while newly activating other functions and effects of signification. When progeny retain the content, style, medium, and familiar placement (on the left forearm) of the sign, yet drastically change its meaning through the sign's historical circumstance, they suggest how resignification can be a powerful rhetorical strategy.[53]

The progenic tattoo thus becomes a "memory text" that is read differently by different people. While some Holocaust scholars are wary that such gestures "keep the wounds open," Brouer and Horwitz argue that the progenic tattoo "practices the imperative to 'Never Forget' while inducing others to engage in active memory of the Holocaust."[54] Ultimately, the Auschwitz-inscribed number, like the one on the grandfather's arm in "The Polish Boxer," is an especially charged and contested mnemonic device, then. In his evocation of the symbol, Halfon travels the same contested terrain, though the fictional or semifictional nature of his story arguably diffuses the tattoo's trauma. It is one of the touchpoints of memory that extend through his entire line of literary creation. As the author himself noted, "Every time I write, it's my grandfather's number, it's the relationship with my brother, it's leaving Guatemala, it's my father, it's my mother, it's my sister, it's all based there."[55]

Even if systematically "erased" through a bearer's denial of its true significance or through the ravages of time that cause the tattoo to fade, the tattoo continues to exert a profound influence on later generations. Not surprisingly, then, the shadow of the grandfather's tattoo, its forbidden signification, appears elsewhere in Halfon's writing. In the version of "White Smoke" that precedes "The Polish Boxer" in this volume, the protagonist, slightly drunk and sporting a slight erection after meeting two Israeli women in a bar, thinks even then and there about his grandfather, "about Auschwitz, about the five green digits tattooed on his forearm," which for all his childhood he had believed were a phone number.[56] In a reworked version of "White Smoke" for *Monastery* (2014), the protagonist notices the graffiti on the wall, and his tendency to search for "anything crossed out, anything forbidden," as in the canvasses of Jean-Michel Basquiat, who believed you'd see words more if they were crossed out: "the very fact that they were obscured, he said, made you want to read them." These are the messages that make him think of his grandfather, of Auschwitz, of the "five green numbers tattooed on his forearm that throughout my entire childhood I'd believed were there, as he himself had told me, so that he wouldn't forget his phone number— his way of crossing them out, I suppose, of forbidding them."[57]

USING WORDS SPAR(R)INGLY

We might say that in "The Polish Boxer," the tattoo stands in a contrapuntal relationship to the words of the pugilist himself, a fellow prisoner in the dark hole of the camp who shares with the protagonist's grandfather what to say at his Auschwitz hearing the next day to avoid the gas chambers and remain alive. The grandfather explains:

> He told me in Polish that he had been there for a long time, in Block Eleven, and that the Germans kept him alive because they liked to watch him box. He told me in Polish that the next day they'd put me on trial and he told me in Polish what I should say during that trial and what I shouldn't say during that trial. And that's how it went. The next day, two Germans dragged me out of the cell, took me to a young Jewish man, who tattooed this number on my arm, and then they left me in an office, where I was put on trial by a young woman, and I saved myself by telling this young woman everything the Polish boxer had told me to say and not telling the young woman everything the Polish boxer had told me not to say. You see? I used his words and his words saved my life and I never knew the Polish boxer's name, never saw his face. He was probably shot.[58]

In *Last Traces: The Lost Art of Auschwitz*, Joseph Czarnecki includes a reproduction of an 8.5-inch pencil sketch titled "The Boxer," photographed in Cell 18 of Block 11 of the main camp of Auschwitz. Part of a larger group of "strange scratchings, paintings, inscriptions, decorations" that Czarnecki located, photographed, and assembled from the walls of Auschwitz in the 1980s, "The Boxer" was uncovered in the camp's most famous cell, that of a Franciscan priest named Father Maximilian Kolbe who offered to exchange his own life for another man condemned to die by starvation.[59] When Pope John Paul II visited the cell in 1979 and paid homage to Kolbe, it had already become a shrine of sorts, covered with tallow and soot that made recovery of the boxer drawing difficult.

Czarnecki was also perplexed by the subject: "I simply could not imagine what a boxer might have to do with Auschwitz," he admitted. Later, though, he read about a boxing match in the autobiography of a former camp prisoner and linked the information to Tadeusz Pietrzykowski, who arrived in Auschwitz in June of 1940, and in the 1980s was living less than an hour's drive from the camp. Czarnecki meet "Teddy" and heard firsthand his account of how boxing saved his life at Auschwitz, following a fight in which he outwitted Walter Duning, a German light-middleweight champion and kapo, though Pietrzykowski's weight had by then dropped to 93 pounds, about half as much as his well-built opponent. "Teddy had thirty-seven fights at Auschwitz and won all of them except two matches with a Jewish boxer, Lew Sanders, the Dutch light-middleweight champion," Czarnecki notes. In fact, it appears that Pietrzykowski unknowingly defended Father Kolbe himself from a vicious beating by a kapo, allowing him to push to the front of a *kommando* and offer to die by starvation in place of another prisoner, the action that resulted in Kolbe's later beatification.[60]

Whether or not Teddy Pietrzykowski is the historical figure the grandfather references in the account dramatized in "The Polish Boxer," *Last Traces* suggests at least three ways to "survive" at Auschwitz: first, that of Father Kolbe, who became the "martyr" and "saint" of Auschwitz, offering his own body in place of another's; that of Pietrzykowski and other boxers who could parlay their skills in the ring into better treatment, better work assignments, and better rations that aided their survival; and finally that of the scribes and "artists" who left their mark, literally, on the walls of latrines, attics, basements, and other spaces of confinement at Auschwitz and elsewhere. As Chaim Potok notes in the introduction to *Last Traces*, "there exists an inventory on cards of almost all that can be seen on the walls of that silenced inferno," an inventory which together with Czarnecki's photos, presents to us an art "encased in a membrane of experience so unique that it forces a reevaluation of all notions of good and bad art."[61]

Halfon's story documents a possible fourth route toward survival: that of endowing one's fellow prisoners with the power of what to *say* to stay alive. As Ángel Díaz Miranda points out, the boxer becomes the "trainer" of the prisoner who will one day be the narrator's grandfather.⁶² His words are like a charm or secret incantation that bestows upon the hearer a way to fight for his life, while also providing the possibility for the life of the grandson who now listens to the story and in turns re-presents it. But are they real? Did the grandfather indeed speak like this, repeating "he told me in Polish" in this invocatory way? Or is this anaphoric construction a device that emphasizes the shared bond of the grandfather and his listening grandson, the privileged recipient of a long untold trauma, now expressed (in the original, at least) in Spanish? Isn't there an inherent contradiction between the boxer's lifesaving words in Polish and the grandfather's refusal to speak Polish in his post-war life, considering it the language of his betrayers?

The boxer's advice to the narrator's grandfather is conspicuous not only because of its power to grant life that extends to subsequent generations, but also in contrast to the damaging nature of language in contexts such as the Nazi camps. Steffi Hobuß notes that "we are able to actually hurt others by using language," and "conversely, we are vulnerable to others because we speak . . . we are willingly or not susceptible to them . . . and this vulnerability cannot be overcome."⁶³ In *The Drowned and the Saved*, Primo Levi reflects on the German translator's lack of awareness of this dimension of language, even as he rendered *Survival in Auschwitz* into the language of Levi's former oppressors or indifferent spectators, now converted in readers: "*per force* he did not know the degraded, often satanically ironic jargon of the concentration camps . . . I wanted that in the book, particularly in its German guise, nothing should be lost of its harshness and the violence inflicted on the language."⁶⁴

Against this backdrop of language as a weapon of hurt and proof of the prisoner's vulnerability, the Polish boxer's words endow the speaker with the possibility of life and continued humanity. But these words never actually appear in the story; we know where he said them and in what language he said them, and when he said them relative to the life-or-death moment at the crux of the story, but we don't know what the words themselves were, even in translation. The number, on the other hand, remains inscribed on the very body of the hearer/bearer of those words more than a half-century later, however faded. Far away from the country of his birth, the grandfather can choose to not speak Polish, (though he cannot avoid its influence in his speech), but the tattoo continues to testify to his experience and his outliving of that experience. "I liked his Polish accent," says the grandson. "But most of all I liked that number. His number."⁶⁵ As he comes of age, though, he realizes there is a "historical origin" behind the "telephone joke," and he makes up possible scenarios to fill that history, as neither his grandfather or anyone else chooses to talk of the true source. Its presence is only ghostly, symbolized by faded green ink and digits blurring together.

How alike, then, is Halfon's reinscription of a number on his text to other second-and third-generation survivors' reinscription of their loved ones' Auschwitz tattoos on their own bodies? As Schult suggests, "taking over the number once enforced on a beloved relative can be seen as a refusal to accept that this person's memory dies with its bearer. . . . The tattooed number acts as a memory repository and a reminder."[66] Jacobs acknowledges, "the reinscription of a grandparent's tattoo may have many meanings, including an act of remembrance and the strengthening of affective ties across generations."[67] Halfon's enlistment of the Auschwitz tattoo also accomplishes many of these tasks; paradoxically, its inclusion in the storytelling process "fleshes out" the character, granting him the personhood symbolically erased by the assignation of a number.

MEMORY TRIGGERS

As we see throughout Halfon's works, names—including his own and the many deformations of it—are a central theme.[68] But in "The Polish Boxer," names, like the boxer's life-giving words, are noticeably missing. Of course, being rendered nameless, reduced only to a number, was a central strategy of the *lager*. The character of the grandfather recalls a moment soon after his arrival at Sachsenhausen, when the camp commander found him hiding, hoping to avoid that day's work detail:

> I don't know how, but the lagerleiter found me hidden under the cot and dragged me outside and started beating me here, at the base of my spine, with a wooden or maybe an iron rod. I don't know how many times. Until I passed out. I was in bed for ten or twelve days, unable to walk . . . I don't remember his name, or his face . . . he had very elegant hands.[69]

The grandfather explains that he "never knew the Polish boxer's name, never saw his face."[70] In fact, there are no real names in this story, other than "Oitze," a nickname and term of endearment that grandfather and grandson use with each other: "I called him Oitze because he called me Oitze, which means something soppy in Yiddish."[71] This mirror name conveys a special connection, a bridge across intergenerational distance, even if the protagonist has only a vague idea of the word's Yiddish meaning, "treasure." Halfon enhances the mirror effect by not using quotation marks or clear attribution in the dialogue, creating a kind of overlap of the two voices that mutually address each other as "Oitze."

The mirror name also brings to mind the citation from Henry Miller's *Tropic of Cancer* that Halfon uses as the epigraph to *The Polish Boxer*: "I have moved the typewriter into the next room where I can see myself in the mirror as I write." That is, the grandfather acts as a mirror in which the protagonist sees himself as a reflection of his forbears, but uniquely engaged in the act of writing at the threshold of history and fiction, as discussed in the Introduction to this volume.[72] Though Halfon has rejected the categorization of his work as autobiography, the inclusion of autobiographical elements provides an apparatus with which to alternate or oscillate between a focus on the act of creative writing itself, and a series of lived or historical events that endow him with the vocation to do that creative work.

As we have seen, the grandfather's memories of his experiences in the camps are "disorderly" rather than lineal in the conversation he has with his grandson in "The Polish Boxer." He starts his testimony, at least in its narrative recreation, by referring to his tattoo, rather than to the period he spent at Sachsenhausen and other camps before arriving at Auschwitz, the only camp (with its subcamps) where prisoners were tattooed. As Halfon has repeatedly sustained, the point is not to create autobiography or biography, but precisely to use the act of writing as a point of origin for his own identity. The strategic absence of key pieces of information, such as what the Polish boxer said or the names of key characters, signal the author's navigation of wartime and family memory not as an empirical project, but as a creative or restorative one. Confusing and confounding the distinctions between author, narrator, and principal protagonist is a tool Halfon uses, like a high-wire artist uses a crossbar, to steady his balance on the threshold of fact and fiction. While rejecting the pretense of memory as entirely recoverable, he nonetheless portrays the grandfather's memories of his Holocaust experience as viable and credible, perhaps because of its lacunae, anachronisms, and even contradictions. When his grandfather falls silent in the process of finally revealing the true story of his tattoo and the experiences of the camps themselves, the narrator is not sure why, but knows to wait, observing, "Maybe because memory is always pendular. Maybe because pain can only be tolerated in measured doses."[73] Memory "swings back and forth, between past and present, alternating between opposites."[74]

Together with these apparent lapses or memory swings, there are other ways "The Polish Boxer" powerfully calls Holocaust memory into place. The grandfather's account is peppered with "foreign" terms; for example, the story mentions two culinary elements typical of Eastern European Jewish cuisine, *gefiltefish* and *chrain*, the latter a beet-colored condiment. These foodstuffs have been transported to his postwar environment and integrated to the Guatemalan table, where they are known to the grandson by their Yiddish names.[75] Nina Fischer considers food's powerful connections to memory and its ability to produce *mémoire involuntaire*. She explains that food has a particular power as a node connecting several generations to pre-Holocaust memory because "it can be recreated rather than only contemplated and discussed."[76] Halfon develops the opening tableau of this tale around foods that the grandfather has clearly not banished from his gastronomic repertoire, despite rejecting his Polish mother tongue.[77]

Food is a powerful memory trigger in another sense as well. With his grandson, Oitze describes the valuable objects of the incoming Jewish prisoners that could be traded for food at Sachsenhausen, alluding to the camps' unique economies of survival. Nonetheless, the most extravagant example in "The Polish Boxer" of the hoarding Fischer explores among survivor populations doesn't have to actually do with *food*, per se:

> I remembered one time when, as a kid, I heard him tell my grandmother that she needed to buy more Red Label, the only whiskey he drank, even though I had recently discovered more than thirty bottles stored away in the cellar. Brand new. And I told him so. And my grandfather answered with a smile full of mystery, with wisdom full of some kind of pain I would never understand: In case there's a war, Oitze.[78]

The whiskey is an interesting symbol of insecurity, as it could not assuage the actual hunger or thirst suffered in the camps or the ghettos, where so many died of starvation, or the continuing trauma associated with that hunger. Nor does the grandfather associate his unquenchable need for whiskey explicitly with the Holocaust, but only with "the war," suggesting a residual need for its anesthetic or escapist qualities, perhaps even its ability to help him forget, if only temporarily.

We might consider "The Polish Boxer" to be a story about stashing away certain words as well. To describe his concentration camp experiences, the grandfather uses several German words that he has apparently silenced and hidden for many decades: he speaks of how the *lagerleiter* or camp commander named him *stubendienst*, the "one in charge"; he recalls that he greeted Jewish prisoners as they arrived to the shouts of *Juden eintreffen*. He remembers the terror of the *Gnadenschuss*, the shot to the back of the neck that prisoners received at Auschwitz's Black Wall.[79] And he speaks of *Kaddish*, the Hebrew prayer for the dead. These terms from other languages generally are not marked off as such by the use of italic but appear as an organic part of the grandfather's recollections, suggesting both the untranslatability of these phenomena as well as the impermeability of certain memories.

With gestures such as these, "The Polish Boxer" shows us how the literary frame can "document" the tragedy of the Holocaust or other traumas in ways that historical narrative cannot. It demonstrates how creative improvisation was necessary both to survival *in* the Shoah and survival *of* the Shoah as a living memory. This "fiction" in which we can't necessarily discern what parts are truth and what parts invention, resurrects "real" people and "real" experiences hidden or altered by camouflage or silence, and offers them as a spur for understanding and expressing the intergenerational effects of violence in new ways.

The grandfather of "The Polish Boxer" is by all accounts a faithful representation of the author's own predecessor. But as we shall see elsewhere in this volume, the grandfather is not immune to bending or reinventing history in the same way he has explained away his Auschwitz tattoo as a telephone number. Or perhaps the author is the one who puts these words in his mouth. In any case, these varied, imperfect, and unfinished representations contribute to a portrayal of history that recognizes its lodging in the unverifiable, its susceptibility to revision according to the needs of a given moment. Or, as Nina Sankovitch puts it, "even fiction portrays truth: good fiction *is* truth."[80] A story about a specific moment in a family member's life, remembered much later, points us back to the now-distant event while also hinting at how such an experience transits time and transmits something authentic to subsequent generations. Using a number as a point of departure and register of "what really happened," provides a way for the author to honor his duty to keep his grandfather's memory alive. At the same time though, the author's concurrent insistence on the "fictional" nature of his tale releases him from the burden of proving the veracity of his, his grandfather's, or others' memories, thus providing a more protected space from which to explore the enduring effects of extreme violence and its residual traumas.[81]

CHECKING THE DATA

We can't help but wonder: was 69752 the number inscribed on the body of Halfon's Polish grandfather? "Mourning," as we see further in Chapter 6, "verifies" key elements of "The Polish Boxer," including the number with which Halfon starts and finishes it. In fact, it adds this number to others, discovered only as the autobiographical protagonist makes a reluctant visit to Sachsenhausen. There, after several fruitless hours perusing dust-covered files with the camp museum's archivist, the protagonist is tempted to abandon his search for documentation proving his grandfather's time in that camp or others. Finally, it occurs to him to search using a first name that his grandmother alone used for her husband, a name that indeed produces a bewildering assortment of numbers:

> My grandfather, Leib Tenenbaum, not León Tenenbaum, first prisoner number 9860, then prisoner number 13664, had been in Sachsenhausen until his transfer, on November 19, 1939, to the concentration camp at Neuengamme, near Hamburg, where he became prisoner number 131333. A little more than five years later, on February 13, 1945, now as prisoner number 69752 (the number he received and was tattooed with in Auschwitz), he'd returned once more to Sachsenhausen... I didn't understand the jumble of numbers. Why so many numbers? Why keep changing the numbers? As though in war a prisoner were, in fact, many prisoners, and a man many men.[82]

This eponymous tale from the volume *Mourning*, published about a decade after *El boxeador polaco* first appeared in Spanish, not only confirms the digits of the Auschwitz tattoo featured in the earlier book, but provides a date on which the grandfather had returned to Sachsenhausen with this last number indelibly inscribed on his body. With the correct name, history comes into focus in the dusty documents of an accounting system designed to strip individuals of their personal identity and personhood itself. The later text serves as a source text for the first; Halfon's decision to use "The Polish Boxer" and "Mourning" as the titles of each respective volume also acts as a kind of secondary guarantee of the reliability of the information, telling us that each tale is so significant or momentous, it merits serving as the title of the volume itself.

3G REMEMBERING

While the number of the grandfather's Auschwitz tattoo is a potent symbol with many possible meanings in "The Polish Boxer," the story ultimately showcases its power as a prod, as a mysterious if unspeaking cipher that propels author, narrator, and reader toward a deeper search for clarity and context. The text exemplifies the contention that shifting conditions of discourse across time alter decorum concerning the representation of the Holocaust. That is, "the passage of time alters the conditions for a new understanding of what type of response counts as timely."[83] Halfon and other "3G" survivors—those who have inherited a family history that was tragically affected by the Holocaust two generations earlier—participate in and invite others to participate in "never forgetting," while simultaneously signaling the imminent loss of the generation of firsthand witnesses. As the grandson of a survivor, Halfon together with other "third generation authors are necessarily self-referential at the same time that they write about a past that is in many ways deeply disconnected from them."[84] Jessica Lang suggests that without direct access to the events themselves, *readability* is an essential condition for representation. Maybe "readability" is what Halfon has in mind when he speaks of his texts as being fictional. In Lang's analysis, readability alters the slant of the text from reflecting backward to leaning forward, providing authors and their readers an opportunity not only to participate as witnesses of traumatic events, but also to benefit from the restorative powers of literature:

> The nature of this restoration is twofold. On the one hand, authors work to restore survivor memory and history with the belief that through doing so some element of the healing power of literature will exert itself, that is, the act of restoration mends a rift in time and place between the survivor's history and the contemporary reader or writer's understanding of it. On the other hand, however, this pull toward readability does not come easily. Unreadability stands as a form of memorialization, a recognition of the trauma that efforts toward readability hope to excise. An element of remembrance is deeply embedded in recognizing the unreadable.[85]

Perhaps unsurprisingly, the manner in which 3G survivors manage their roles as inheritors of this testimony "confounds assumptions of a second generation that scarcely could imagine the practice as a legitimate form of memory work. In this sense, the third generation's practice disturbs fundamental expectations about what can be said by whom and in what way."[86] The third generation's engagement with this legacy often vacillates between, on the one hand, a sense of remove or disconnection from the firsthand survivor's experience and on the other, a sense of ownership and responsibility in relation to that experience.[87] Jules Bukiet allows that others might bring wisdom and compassion to their evocations of the Holocaust, "but for us, it's genetic. To be shabbily proprietary, we own it."[88] When Halfon explains to his interviewer the unease he felt as he confronted the task of writing his own family's Holocaust story, of being caught between respect and fear, including fear of that story being cliché, disconnection and ownership are both present. Is such a possession a treasure or a trap? An honor or an obligation? A sacred trust or a temptation? As Ana Mendoza suggests,

> It's difficult to resist the temptation to convert your family past into literature, if, as happens with the Guatemalan Eduardo Halfon, you have a Polish grandfather who saved himself from dying in Auschwitz thanks to a boxer who taught him the exact words to say in order to survive. And it's even harder if that grandfather wears tattooed on his forearm the number 69752, and, every time his grandson asked him about it, he would only respond by saying that it was his phone number, tattooed there so he wouldn't forget it.[89]

Halfon's decision to imprint his grandfather's number on his text provides a highly legible point of reference for readers across several generations, enhancing its readability. Not just an aid to a faulty memory–as the telephone story suggests—the number prevents both the bearer and the contemporary reader/viewer from forgetting. With his lie about the tattoo's origin, the grandfather no doubt hoped to shield his young grandson from the trauma it referenced.[90] But he later agrees to carry forward the record of that experience in an alternate format, though conscious of the ultimate unreadability of his account by those who did not share the experience, including his own grandson. The fictional armature Halfon builds around his grandfather's account provides a fuller if still incomplete history while also acknowledging the reasons individuals resist sharing such memories.

Ultimately, Halfon's fiction in general, and this story in particular, argue, paradoxically, that such experiences can only be retold "reliably" by acknowledging their susceptibility to silencing, suppression, and alteration across time. Of the two categories of imaginative and testimonial literature about the Holocaust that Sidra Ezrahi identifies, the first "static" or absolutist, locating "a non-negotiable self in an unyielding place whose sign is Auschwitz" and the second "dynamic" or relativist, approaching the representation of memory of that place as a site for "ongoing renegotiation of that historical reality," Halfon clearly chooses the second option.[91]

By employing fiction, Halfon remixes the mandate to "never forget" for twenty-first century readers. "The Polish Boxer" exemplifies Jessica Lang's contention that "perhaps the most notable quality of third-generation texts is the effort exhibited within them to render visible the unreadable narrative."[92] As a text written in Spanish by an author who speaks from Guatemala—where he was born and spent his early childhood and to which he returned as an adult—as well as from other sites in the United States, Poland, Serbia, Italy, France, Japan, and Germany, "The Polish Boxer" offers a crucial contribution to the creative representation of Holocaust memory. Just as the progenic tattoo practice "enacts a mode of postmemory through a resignification," so too does Halfon's fictional gesture. As a "memory text," "The Polish Boxer" offers us a point of entry to the events and experiences of the Shoah "distinct from traditional Holocaust memory practices like visiting museums and memorials," and distinct, perhaps from the category of individual "counter memorials" as well.[93]

Identifying herself as one of the forebears of the 3G writers, Erika Dreifus notes that Halfon's work stands as an influential precursor to later efforts of this cohort, despite its original publication in Spanish. *The Polish Boxer* is crucial to the international and "universal" appeal of his fiction, despite (or because of) the particular focus of the title story and its treatment of the post-Holocaust, post-testimony (Lang), postmemory (Hirsch) and 3G experience (Aarons, et al.) considered here. Dreifus cites a 2012 pre-publication review of the English translation in *Publisher's Weekly* that already recognized *The Polish Boxer*'s positioning "in the murky half-light where fiction meets memoir meets memory and the impossibility thereof" that exemplifies 21st century engagement with postwar memory and genre blurring more generally.[94] She notes how other stories in the English-language version of *The Polish Boxer* also allude to a "special kind of kinship" among 3G writers. These include the reference to the grandfather's account of Auschwitz and Sachsenhausen in "Twaining;" the narrator toying with the idea that he might be related to an Israeli woman he meets in a Guatemala bar who shares his Polish grandfather's surname, Tenenbaum, in "White Smoke;" and his understanding of the role of fiction through the lens of his grandfather's Holocaust testimony in "A Speech at Póvoa," to which we will return in a later chapter.[95]

There is one more curious component of *The Polish Boxer*, not available in either edition in Spanish, to keep in mind in relation to the discussion of the volume's title story. In "Sunsets," the final piece in the English volume, the narrator visits his grandparents' home soon after his Polish grandfather has died. It is a moment in which he is expected to pay his respects by participating in the specifically Jewish rituals that accompany death. The story emphasizes how small the Jewish minority is in Guatemala, where there are only "a hundred families, they usually say," and where "the rabbis are always imported" from Miami or Panama or Mexico or Argentina.[96]

The occasion of his grandfather's death provides a coda to the volume as a whole and adds another layer of questions to those explored elsewhere in the book. If the standalone story of "The Polish Boxer" considers the responsibility of subsequent generations, and especially the third generation, to preserve the memories of their family members who experienced the Holocaust firsthand, then "Sunsets" asks what it means when that family member dies. How can or should one keep remembering the now absent witness? The protagonist resists having the meaning of this moment imposed on him through rituals and traditions; he chafes at being asked by an unkempt rabbi to show his respect by donning a kipa or yarmulke (explaining to the reader in the process that these are the Hebrew and Yiddish words for *skullcap*). Respect for whom, he wonders? He remembers Carlos, a jazz-loving rabbi from Argentina who "arrived just in the years when I began to distance myself from Judaism and from my family (you can't do one without the other)." Having recently left home, which also meant "leaving behind my father's religion and everything about his glass-house world," he appreciated chatting with Carlos about Louis Armstrong and John Coltrane and Charlie Parker and Thelonious Monk (a fascination with jazz indulged in the story "Epistrophy," also included in this volume). But finding a common musical ground with the young rabbi ultimately did not help him resolve the question of his own Jewish identity. In their last encounter on the street, Carlos quoted a well-known passage from Genesis: "Get thee out of thy country, and from thy kindred, and from thy father's house, unto a land that I will show thee. Lech l'cha, he said in Hebrew with a wink, and that was all."[97] "Sunsets" does not make it clear how the protagonist interpreted this advice. Was Carlos giving him his blessing to leave the country, the family, or the faith? Or perhaps all three? Or was he suggesting that Eduardo was now free or perhaps obligated to interpret the injunction to "go forth" as he wished?

As "Sunsets" resurrects the grandfather figure central to "The Polish Boxer," resurrecting as well the thematic focus on the Holocaust and how difficult and foreign it is to be Jewish in Guatemala, it also offers a view of Jewish identity as inescapable and central to the narrator's character, despite his efforts to distance himself from it. "Sunsets" tells us, for example, that there in his grandfather's room "still hung the only photo my grandfather had managed to keep of his family," all of whom died in the ghettos or concentration camps. He includes the names of these relatives in both Spanish and Polish, and the professions of his great-grandparents. The protagonist remembers the moment he told his grandfather that he wanted to visit Poland, and his grandfather's violent reaction. "You mustn't go to Poland," he warns, though he later will provide a small piece of yellow paper with an address jotted on it, and precise details how to arrive there.[98]

Clearly, the grandfather has not forgotten the number of his last apartment before being detained, and his grandson, at the scene of his death, remembers as well the number tattooed on his arm, and the telephone story that went with it. But in "Sunsets," Halfon also expands on the way the Auschwitz tattoos and the camp experiences themselves mean different things to different survivors:

> And I thought about Rena Kornreich, another Polish survivor of Auschwitz, who years later, as she herself told it, had her number surgically removed, 1716, but instead of throwing it away, she had kept that small piece of skin, that small piece of herself, in a bottle of formaldehyde. And I thought about Primo Levi, about the number tattooed on Primo Levi's forearm, 174517, and how, whereas my grandfather avoided his number, hid it, made a joke out of it so as not to acknowledge it, and whereas Mrs. Kornreich tore hers off, Primo Levi left instructions for his to be engraved on his tomb. And so there, on a tombstone in the Jewish cemetery in Turin, both his name and his number are engraved: his family name and that other, more sinister name. Both, I suppose, like it or not, intrinsic elements of his identity.[99]

One thing Halfon purposely left out of the scene of his grandfather's lifeless shape on the bed, and the family sitting shiva, is the copy of *El boxeador polaco* on his grandfather's nightstand, deeming it "a little too corny to put in the story."[100] As he told Dwyer Murphy in an interview,

> I published *El Boxeador Polaco* in Spanish in 2008, and my grandfather died in 2009. My mother had read it out loud to him, she told me, as he cried. He became very sick at the end of his life. He was delirious. He couldn't sleep. He thought there were German officers in his room, waiting for him. On the morning he finally died, I went into his room and saw him lying on his deathbed. And there, on his nightstand, was my book, his book, his story.
>
> I think he was very proud of the book, or proud that his story would stay behind. By him not wanting to talk about it for so long, his legacy was going to be lost. So perhaps he felt a sense of pride, not only in his grandson the writer, but in leaving behind his story, his testimonial.[101]

It's easy to see why Halfon avoided including the book in his narrative, judging it to be too self-referential, too tidy a prop for tying up loose ends at the end of this volume, which also offers us a manifesto of sorts. But it certainly would have been Cervantine, or Borgesian, or both, to have the last story of *The Polish Boxer* refer to an earlier version of that same book.

CHAPTER 2

MUSIC AND MEMORY, ON AND OFF THE CHARTS

I'd like to think that the windows to my work aren't so much in other books, but in the films of <u>Bergman</u> or <u>Kiarostami</u>, in the music of <u>Monk</u> or <u>Dylan</u>

IN LOVE, WITH MONK

Borrowing its title from a famous 1941 composition by jazz innovators Thelonious Monk and Kenny Clark, the tale in *The Polish Boxer* titled "Epistrophy" invites readers to consider the perpetual quest to understand one's role as a creator in the juicy interstices of repetition, improvisation, and memory. A Serbian piano prodigy named Milan Rakić appears on the scene of a cultural festival in Antigua, Guatemala, and despite a long list of characteristics he does *not* share with the protagonist (country of origin, mother tongue, profession, taste in women), the wandering musician's search for himself in different styles of music and in performing them immediately resonates with the narrator. Together with "Postcards" and "The Pirouette," also included in the English version of *The Polish Boxer*, "Epistrophy" shows how displays of musical creativity often inspire Halfon's fictional terrains.

A close cousin to the literary term "epistrophe," the obscure term that serves as this story's title will likely be familiar only to a select *cofradía* or membership of jazz aficionados. Halfon uses it in ways that supersede a song title or literary figure as he draws us into the musical histories and worlds of classical, jazz, and Gypsy music.[1] Signifying the repetition of the same word or words at the end of successive sentences, phrases, or clauses, "epistrophe is the trope of obsession," explains Mark Forsyth in *The Elements of Eloquence*. "It's the trope of emphasizing one point again and again," so common in music that we tend to take it completely for granted, as in Leonard Cohen's "Hallelujah." But outside the musical frame, it appears in more subtle ways.[2] Halfon's allusion to the term seems to cover more ground and more sounds, as his "Epistrophy" includes references to Che Guevara's motorcycle journey through the Americas, a woman's orgasms, and the possible meanings of *epistrophy* itself.

Even before the memorable concert in which they hear him play for the first time, the story's narrator and his girlfriend Lía decide to get acquainted with the rakish Rakić at an upscale Antigua bar called the Panza verde, where the trio chats as a marimba, Guatemala's national instrument, plays somewhere in the background.[3] The members of an Austrian quartet (who Lía reports had played Mozart earlier that day), a Venezuelan baritone, and "some Guatemalan poets, drunk already," have bellied up to the bar at the Panza verde, too.[4] In this first conversation over tequilas, Rakić and the protagonist soon discover their shared musical tastes and propensity for both venerating and challenging the traditions of a specific period or genre. Rakić mentions Stravinsky as one of the composers he might play the next day in his scheduled concert, which in turn leads to a conversation about the jazz saxophonist Charlie Parker, who revered Stravinsky as the consummate example of classical composition.

> Ah Charlie Parker's favorite, I said just to say something. Milan smiled. You like jazz? I told him that in my last or second-to-last incarnation, before making the small leap over into a Judeo-Latin American cosmology, I must have been a third-rate black jazz musician playing in some brothel in Kansas City or Storyville (a name so lovely, it seems made up), although I could just as easily have been a black hooker from Kansas City or Storyville who spent all night fucking to the rhythm played by some third-rate jazz musician. Which is to say, I said with all the seriousness of a poor forgotten harlequin, I've got jazz deep in my gonads.[5]

The obsession with jazz that Eduardo confesses to Rakić is such that he speculates he has been either a Black jazz musician or a prostitute in the creative hotbeds of Kansas City or New Orleans in an earlier life. He identifies with the form as imagined in these early settings where music and sex comingled, in the process establishing the brothel as an important setting in his works for intense experiences of sensation and connection. With jazz, or immersed in jazz, the protagonist can imagine many possible shape shifts of era, birthplace, race, gender, language, and the secrets to musical genius and survival itself.

From this confession, it's an easy slide into a disquisition on jazz itself, with the narrator dropping the names of his favorites: Bird, Miles, Coltrane, Tatum, Powell, Mingus, and of course, Monk: "And then, as if we were invoking the names of Aztec warriors or of strange Nordic runes, we took turns reciting the titles of everything written by Melodious Thunk, as his wife called him."[6] Though Rakić's Spanish is "impeccable," thanks to his Argentine girlfriend, and the narrator himself manages to work in a few phrases in Serbian, thanks to having watched a lot of Kusturica films, it is in the shared language of jazz and musical performance that Eduardo and Rakić find their common ground and groove. Both profess deep respect for the creative masters but also value improvisation and reinterpretation.

With Lía's help, they ponder the possible meanings of *epistrophy* itself, whether a botanical term (Eduardo), a rhetorical or musical term that involves repetition (Lía), or a term from Greek mythology, a definition mentioned by Rakić but immediately dismissed as "crap" or "nonsense"—"Some things signify nothing and are beautiful all the same. Epistrophy, he said, and the word fell like a dead dragonfly in a bowl of warm lentil soup."[7] While there might be some truth in all of these definitions, Lía's answer gets closer to the full resonance of epistrophy in relation to Monk's use of the term, as well as in Halfon's redeployment for his tale. "Epistrophy" was Monk's first copyrighted composition, a piece he had initially titled "Fly Rite" and then "Iambic Pentameter," both suggesting grounding in rituals or repetitive forms renovated in the flight path of each specific performance.[8] Monk played "Epistrophy" hundreds of times, and included it as the final theme for most of his live shows and on many of his recordings.[9] Other prominent jazz innovators also covered the piece; trumpeter Cootie Williams used it as the closing *and* opening tune of his performances.[10] In the late-discovered landmark recording of the Thelonious Monk Quartet with John Coltrane at Carnegie Hall, for example, "Epistrophy" appears twice, midway in the recording with a four and a half-minute version played to close out the early set, and again in a second version lasting less than two and half minutes that closed out the show. The two cuts demonstrate Monk's fascination with the idea of a recurring refrain with a recognizable melody that also offers endless opportunities to engage in fresh renderings.[11]

In a biography subtitled "Epistrophy Blues," David Dicaire explains that whomever and whatever his influences, "almost from the beginning, Monk was not interested in the music that surrounded him but more in creating his own universe with its logic, rules, and fun."[12] Dicaire is not the first to consider epistrophy in relation to creative acts beyond music. In a section of *Afro-Blue* titled "Epistrophy: The Performance of (Re)Memory," Tony Bolden posits that as used by Monk, epistrophy "suggests a unique African American style of cultural production that is both vernacular and sophisticated."[13] It is perhaps no accident then that the protagonist in this story imagines an earlier life in which he inhabited an African American body in a place like Storyville, where sex and vernacular music cross-pollinated each other.

In an analysis of blues sonnets from the Harlem Renaissance, often considered precursors to the jazz forms that emerged in the 1930s, Timo Müller pinpoints a style of formal repetition or epistrophy that is both subversive and affirmative: it is subversive in that it demonstrates the iterability of supposedly authentic or essential conventions, and affirmative because in the very act of simulating such conventions, the writer or musician revitalizes cultural (re)memory.[14] In *Epistrophies: Jazz and the Literary Imagination*, Brent Hayes Edwards offers us the complementary notion of "transmedial consonance," of the interface that can occur between sound and writing. He also shows how jazz players employ a "poetics of the reprise," another redolent aesthetic frame with which to consider Halfon's fascination with musical form, literary form, and the ways to imbue each with fresh interpretation.[15]

Whereas other works by Halfon, including those studied here, often focus on the conscious or unconscious suppression of memory in relation to trauma, "Epistrophy" calls us to reflect on memory as a renewable resource, one that can be perpetually enhanced with ever different moods and riffs, just as jazz players reinvent a piece, each time they play it. By continually "turning about" tales and episodes, as the Greek etymology of the word suggests, Halfon treats his own compositions in a way we might also describe as epistrophic, reprising stories and themes and remixing and reshuffling them for different translations and editions of his works. As with Monk and his own famous piece, the familiar or the remembered paradoxically offers the author an invitation to rework existing compositions, defamiliarizing them for the reader/hearer.

Despite his impressive knowledge of jazz, it is with classical music that Halfon's new friend Milan Rakić will serve as a poster boy of mnemonic techniques in "Epistrophy." Foregoing the sheet music, he draws on his (re)memory of the canonical scores of art music, while also recreating and renewing the compositions so that he and other listeners hear them afresh. He explains to Eduardo that he learned this from his teacher Lazar Berman, a Russian Jew and Listz expert with whom Rakić had studied in Italy as a child. He remembers how he had once played Liszt's "Sonata in B minor" for Berman, "a very complex piece;" his teacher had not said a word until he returned the next day and began to play it again, prompting Berman to shout at him in Russian that he was playing the piece the same way he had yesterday; had he not noticed that today it was raining?[16]

FLOW CHARTS

After their conversation with Rakić, Eduardito and Lía return to their hotel room where they engage in "a naked thing that trembled with a thousand legs and a thousand hands and a thousand guava-flavored tongues that could never be enough to make love with." Lía emerges not just as Eduardo's lithe love interest, but in fact, someone with her own memory projects. A cultural polyglot who studies medicine, knows her quantum physics, and is also versed in classical and jazz forms, she has recently returned from studying capoeira, Brazilian Portuguese, and sunbathing in Salvador de Bahia, where she also acquired a new nickname for her boyfriend, "Dudú." In the morning, Eduardo finds Lía glowing amber and sitting up in bed with an almond-color notebook on her lap. In it she is recording her own sensations and creative flows, not based on musical scores but composed of sketches that track her physical pleasure and release. Since their first time together, the narrator explains, Lía liked to draw her orgasms, "to make graphs of them for me, like a scientist would."[17] Although Eduardo thinks the drawings of mountains, plateaus, fluvial jets, clouds, and spirals are designed to be shared with him, some elements, like Lía's drawing of zigzagging lines that look like lightning bolts, are off-limits: "that was her one secret, she used to say, and it was of the upmost importance." The grapevines, clouds, maps, and ellipses in the orgasm sketchbook elicit envy from Eduardo, but also fascination; her "studied scribbles," fleshed out with the dedication of a Flemish painter, reveal to him the details, signs, and keys for interpreting her most unfathomable mysteries.[18]

Lía's graphic pleasure journal demonstrates how repeated sexual encounters, even with the same partner and the same "script," serve as another example of repetition as re-creation. Her sketchbook, some of which she shares with Eduardo, some of which she retains for her own private remembering, charts and preserves sensory stimulation that is to some extent off the charts, both in the vernacular and empirical senses. This visual inventory of pleasure complements Lía's ability to recount her dreams, which the narrator tells us she always remembered in great detail.[19] After showing Eduardo her most recent drawing, this one "a raging sea viewed from a small boat," the couple goes back to sleep. And in a state somewhere between dreams and waking, Eduardo remembers that Liszt had been the lover of a princess related to Ludwig Wittgenstein, a philosopher-poet whose theories on language have influenced later debates concerning the ethics and aesthetics of memory.[20] Still savoring the sex, the dream-state after, and the tantric or tantalizing illustrations in Lía's journal, the couple sets off to hear Rakić play the Liszt he had promised them the night before. The Serbian prodigy has had his own intimate encounter before the concert, his with the dark-skinned girl who had been dispensing tequilas the night before at the Panza verde. If for the narrator, her hands had seemed too small, like "muddy starfish" or "sad, puffed-up tarantulas," Rakić had quickly discovered her name, initiated a flirtation, and left the bar with her after whispering to Eduardo, "What a beauty." Surprised, perhaps jostled from reigning local stereotypes in which indigeneity too rarely is equated with "beauty," Eduardo (and, implicitly, the reader along with him) is compelled to see the Mayan woman in a different light, from Rakić's appreciative perspective.[21]

The concert takes place in the ruins of San José el Viejo, a Catholic church built in Antigua in 1762. The event is just one offering in a wide-ranging cultural festival that on this occasion includes a talk on neo-Baroque architecture, an Irish children's choir, a Far Eastern dance troupe, Salvadoran melodramas, and other events which barely pique the narrator's interest. Rakić's performance, however, will prove to be utterly unique. As he sits down at the piano, his silent concentration is such that the narrator doesn't know what to make of it:

> I thought at first he was waiting or people to be quiet, but then, after the quiet had come, I thought maybe he was reviewing in his mind all the pieces he was going to play (there weren't any scores), but after that, when more than a minute had passed and people, somewhat perplexed, began looking around, I thought maybe he'd just awakened and had a filthy hangover and couldn't remember a thing, neither how to play the piano nor what the hell he was doing in a ruin in Guatemala.[22]

Milan's approach to the piano, despite all his international training, is more than merely technical, more than merely a matter of memorization; he must commune with the instrument and the moment before playing Liszt or any other master. When the keys of the piano begin to sound, "like water in a slow cascade," the couple strains to figure out the piece he is playing. Lía is the first to realize it is Beethoven, though his name might not have appeared on the program. "For some reason," Eduardo says, "Beethoven's sonatas always make me feel like changing the world, or at least changing out of my own world."[23]

In the pause before the second piece, Eduardo advises Lía that any printed program is a ruse, that Rakić is channeling "Bazar Lerman," a play on the name of Rakić's teacher that echoes "Melodious Thunk," the nickname Nellie Smith used for her musician husband. Unperturbed by the cries of hungry baby pigeons screeching for their dinner from a nest high up in in the church's rafters, and a child's delighted shout upon discovering the birds, Rakić serendipitously folds unforeseen and unforeheard elements into his well-trained memory of the masters, launching into his performance as if the bird noises "had been set down in the score by Rachmaninoff himself." With this avian accompaniment, Milan renews the Russian master's composition as if it were "the unstoppable zephyr of a hurricane or of Lía's raging sea." Rakić's Rachmaninoff takes on "Amazonian" tones, "screeching with a precise logic" that seems to Eduardo chaotic, bold, fortuitous, and moving.[24]

After another long silence, the musician launches into a third theme, this one forceful, energetic, a "din of opposing emotions" and ups and downs and peace and anxiety.[25] In the middle of this tangle, Eduardito thinks he hears several of Monk's iconic melodies: "Straight. No Chaser," "Tinkle, Tinkle," "Blue Monk," and maybe even a small segment of "Epistrophy." But over lunch following the concert, Milan identifies the piece as one by Liszt, a composition with which even the Liszt experts are often unfamiliar. "It's an arrangement by Liszt for organ and later by Busoni for piano, from an opera by the German, Meyerbeer. But a strong arrangement, dark, beautiful, and one that for some reason no one knows about," he explains.[26] As he had with the dark-skinned Mayan barmaid, Rakić defamiliarizes Liszt for his listeners, even the experts, endowing the piece with a many-layered origin story not unlike his own. When Eduardo asks him why he has such an affinity with Liszt, he finally answers that perhaps it is because Liszt offers an open structure and allows for improvisation, so that playing his works is "like being able to play and stretch and fly inside a framework made of air" (inevitably calling to mind Monk's "Fly Rite"). As he chews his tortillas, Rakić eschews the boundaries laid down within a piece, or between styles of interpretation, or even between fixed forms and genres. "Why create boundaries between genres?" he asks. "Why differentiate between one type of music and another?" Eduardo engages him further on this point, questioning why Rakić wants so much to challenge boundaries, to rebel against them, to act in such a revolutionary or seditious way. "I'm fascinated by internal rather than external revolutions," Rakić admits. He finds Che Guevara's motorcycle journey, in which his ideas were formed and "where something magical incubated inside him for the first time" much more interesting than the revolutions he later fomented. Revolutions of the spirit, he believes, whether artistic or social or whatever, are "far more honest" than the spectacles that follow, whether in the form of a painting, a novel, a piano recital, or in the "pure spectacle" of the Cuban Revolution itself.[27]

It is only later, after this series of confidences, that Milan admits to Eduardo that he is the son of a Gypsy accordionist, and the music he has deep in *his* gonads is Gypsy music; he can embark on his nomadic journeys without Liszt or Chopin or Rachmaninoff, but not without his Boban Marković, Oláh Vince, or Šaban Bajramović. Throughout their conversation, Rakić always uses the word *Gypsy* (*gitano* in the Spanish original) for his community and its music, rather than Roma or other terms deemed less offensive in contemporary parlance.[28] Milan, despite his twenty-five years at the piano, studying with the best classical masters, dreams only of "being among Gypsies, playing and dancing and feeling the pain of their music." This confession prompts Eduardo to wonder how it is that some people flee their ancestors, while others yearn to enter their fathers' worlds. Eduardo can't "get far enough away from Judaism," while Milan can't even let his father know of his longing to leave the classics behind in order to completely immerse himself in Gypsy music. That revelation must be for Eduardo's ears only.[29]

SOUND TRACKS

"Epistrophy" stages an important through-line in Halfon's work, that of the interaction between music, memory, and the creative quest. Musical references elsewhere in his works enhance this thematic thread. In "Tomorrow We Never Did Talk About It," the final story in his 2011 volume *Mañana nunca lo hablamos*, an autobiographical narrator remembers the last piano lesson he had on the eve of his family's departure from Guatemala, just as he was about to celebrate his tenth birthday. Once again, migration has become necessary in the wake of war and violence, this time spilling over onto the street in front of the narrator's elementary school. In a room full of echoes from the removal of everything but the Steinway, his indigenous teacher Otto indulges the boy's ruse of following the score, when he is really only playing by ear. As in "Epistrophy," where two kinds of racial difference are associated with musical mastery as marked by reinterpretation and innovation, the racially othered Otto seems to secretly agree with his pupil that it is much more important to play and feel the music than it is to read it, to follow the chart.[30]

Other memories involving music also suggest a distrust with traditions, and in at least one case, a full-blown betrayal. In "Tel Aviv was an Inferno," the first episode of *Monastery*, we find an adult narrator at the Kotel or Western Wall in Jerusalem, trying to remember the history of the second temple, so central to Jewish history and experience. He is put off by the heavy-handed proselytizing at the site, however, and instead recalls "the song by the Cure," a reference to the English rock band's moody and piercing "Wailing Wall," which incorporates Middle Eastern melodies and the sharp cries of a wooden flute. Described by historian Chris Gerard as a "sound painting," "Wailing Wall" is a foray into "exotic sonic hypnosis" that "explores the intense devotion of those who hold religious devotion to their core."[31]

Further on in the same tale, watching two very young Israeli soldiers walk by holding machine guns and wearing black berets, the protagonist remembers when he was fifteen or sixteen and was invited to play with a heavy metal band that called itself—much to his parents' horror—Crucifix. When he shows up for the gig looking too buttoned down for the band's brand, his fellow musicians disguise him as a punk rocker, finishing off the look with black makeup, black boots, and a black beret. It wasn't until he arrives home, still euphoric from the performance, that he saw that

> on the black beret, smack-dab in the middle of my forehead, was an enormous swastika. A Nazi swastika. I snatched the cap off my head to inspect it from up close, without the distortion of the mirror. The swastika was embroidered in black thread. Factory stitching, expert stitching. I remembered that as they were dressing me, someone had hurriedly stuck the beret on my head. I never saw it, never saw myself with the beret on, never knew that I'd played two hours to a full audience dressed as a Nazi punk rocker. Did that make me a Nazi, at least for those two hours, at least in the eyes of those teenagers? I felt something in my stomach. Nausea, maybe.[32]

The protagonist's longing to be a musician and enjoy the public's adulation as a musician lead him to unknowingly betray himself, his Jewish community, and perhaps Jewish history itself. The "Crucifix" memory is one of the few places in Halfon's work where a disguise, rather than saving its wearer, implicates him.

In "White Smoke," which follows "Epistrophy" in the English edition of *The Polish Boxer* and reappears in *Monastery*, the voices of Bob Marley and Bob Dylan provide the soundtrack for the narrator's discussion of his doubts about God and renunciation of Jewishness with two Israeli women he meets in a different bar in Antigua. "White Smoke" is followed in *Monastery* by "Surviving Sundays," in which the protagonist heads up to Harlem to hear the jazz jam at Marjorie's apartment at 555 Edgecombe Avenue. In the process he recalls jazz clubs of earlier eras as well as the renowned musicians of those eras: Count Basie, Duke Ellington, Coleman Hawkins, and the pianist Marjorie Eliot, known for hosting jazz jams on Sunday afternoons in the parlor at the famous address.[33] Musical subthemes also appear in the title story from *Monastery*, where Prokoviev, Strauss, and Ravel have cameos in another allusion to Wittgenstein, who, Eduardo recalls, not only learned to play piano with one hand after losing his right arm in World War I, but tasked these composers with writing works for him based entirely on the left hand. Even Thelonious Monk/Melodius Thunk comes to mind as Eduardo remembers a gem from Monk's notebooks: "a genius is the one most like himself."[34]

In all these allusions and interludes, we should be reading the music as more than just a theme in Halfon's oeuvre. It's arguably a repeat, reappearing refuge from the rational in his writing method. The author himself acknowledges:

> It's all over the place. It's sometimes subtle, just a reference. That happens a lot in *The Polish Boxer*. Sometimes it's direct, straight up about a pianist or about a piano teacher, but more important than that, and I insist on this all the time, is me seeing language as music . . . there's this rhythm to my prose that I'm really conscious about, so I'll read it out loud, I want to hear it. So, my approach to language is musical. It's a frustrated pianist writing . . . I'm always turning to music to understand other things.[35]

It was the Argentine Julio Cortázar—another writer for whom music was an essential formal and thematic element—who Halfon says showed him "how to be less of an engineer. Less myself. He taught me not be afraid of that darker, bleaker, more sinister, more musical, irrational side."[36] This explains why the author portrays music as a safe space in which to draw on both the brain's hemispheres, as it were:

> There is this duality in me between the irrational and the rational, between the emotional and the structured. Maybe that is the reason why I felt so safe when I played music, as a child and teenager, because in music you can be both, you have to be both. And in my type of writing, I have to be both, as well . . . I want to create an emotional response, similar to what a musician would do through music . . . I'm always going back to music. Music is the only art that needs no rational mediation—it either goes straight in or it doesn't.

There's a strong lyrical component to what I write—in beats, repetitions, the words themselves—and that's very tricky to achieve, and almost impossible to fix when it's not there.[37]

Even the choice to write the original versions of his works in Spanish seems tied to music, as Halfon himself has surmised, "maybe I write in Spanish because it was my first language, my baptism into words and their music."[38]

POSTCARD *PATRIN*

Despite being "all over" in Halfon's body of work, the best place to pick up the musical thread that begins in "Epistrophy" is in the previously mentioned episodes of *The Polish Boxer* which occur after Rakić's Antigua concert in narrative time. In "Postcards," Eduardo and Lía receive a one-way stream of communication that Milan dispatches from a string of stops on the journey that follows his departure from Guatemala. "He liked sending postcards, not receiving them," the narrator explains. Regarding his refusal to supply a return address, Rakić has replied, "I don't have one, he said jokingly, or on second thought, perhaps seriously. I live on the lungo drom, which in Romany means the long road, with no set destination and no turning back. He said: I travel in a caravan of one."[39] Nonetheless, each postcard contributes to a kind of conversation with Eduardo's confession in Antigua that he wants to know more about Gypsies and their music, understand them better.

The first of Milan's cryptic messages, this one sporting a photo of acrobatic dolphins at a waterpark in Florida, is titled "The naked isle." "Gypsy singer Šaban Bajramović was born in the Yugoslav city of Niš in 1936," the message begins. After deserting from Tito's army for a woman, Bajramović was sent to Goli Otok, the "Naked Isle" a harsh prison on the coast of Croatia that served as an Adriatic gulag between 1949 and 1989. The postcard (and the book in our hands) cites lyrics from one of Bajramović's songs without marking them off with quotation marks or italics. The first verses, "I am writing a letter and crying/ I am dying in prison here / The years pass, flying / And they are not freeing me," are from "Pelno Me Sam," (I am imprisoned), the song that launched the flesh and blood Bajramović's career.[40] Rakić's first postcard also includes lyrics in which Bajramović's plaintive speaker laments losing all his money and friends and spending his days "roving around, all alone, who knows where. No ties or responsibilities or boundaries of any kind. No boundaries." Perhaps Rakić doesn't know how the Nazi invasion of his birth city affected Bajramović, but it is not coincidental that Bajramoić's history was also marked by the trauma of World War II. As Garth Cartwright writes,

> Šaban's childhood was interrupted by the Nazi invasion—a concentration camp was built outside Niš and the area's Roma ruthlessly murdered. A Gypsy song from the war goes:
>
> > Give me, God
> > two big wings
> > that I may fly
> > to kill a German.
> > To take from him the great keys
> > and to open the Niš camp.[41]

Eduardo pins this first postcard on the wall, next to Lía's only orgasm sketch not included in her almond-colored notebook.[42]

A series of postcards follows, more evidence of Rakić's nomadic life and his immersion in Gypsy music, despite its forbidden quality. One postcard arrives from Mexico City, recounting the story of Papusza, a Gypsy woman convicted of being *mahrine* or contaminated for associating in mixed company with non-Gypsies; in another, with a scene of the Arizona desert, Rakić provides an origin story for the millions of Gypsies scattered across the earth. "The Gypsies' origins, Eduardito, are eminently musical," Rakić explains on the dorsal of a giant postcard picturing Philadelphia but sent from Hawaii. He offers several possible stories of how the Gypsies discovered music, stating before each version, "This is how it happened" and then concluding each origin story except the last with the epistrophic caveat, "No. That's not how it happened, Eduardito."[43]

A communiqué postmarked in New York conflates jazz and Gypsy music, offering on the front side a photo of four jazz masters in front of Milton's Playhouse, "Melodius Thunk" among them, and on the other a biography of a legendary, perhaps even mythical figure named "Yusef":

> The old people say listening to Yusef's accordion was like listening to a siren's sweet song. The old people say listening to Yusef's accordion was like listening to the cries of Christ on the cross. The old people say Yusef managed to survive four years in Chelmno Nazi extermination camp, on the shores of the river Ner, playing at German officers' party every night. The old people say Yusef, night after night, played one piece for every Gypsy killed that day

in the gas chamber.... The old people say when he was freed after the war, Yusef unstrapped his accordion and left it on the green grass of Chelmno."[44]

The story connects Milan's history to Eduardo's by way of the Holocaust and its primary referents of racial hatred, gas chambers, extermination, the arts of survival, and the silences that followed in the wake of extreme trauma.

As elsewhere in Halfon's oeuvre, the history of a people, their unique forms of expression, and the ways in which they remember and preserve their origins, are never set in stone, despite the stone tablets of his own Jewish tradition. Here's how history happened, Rakić tells us ... or perhaps not. Competing versions are equally worthy not because they lead to or confirm a single truth, but because they showcase the arts of memory and survival as an ongoing, open-ended narrative. Whether or not the story of Yusef is a true one—a subsequent postcard admits that Milan's own father claimed he never existed—, it can tell us something truthful of a persecuted people's use of memory and improvisation to survive and even thrive. A bit later, Eduardo receives a postcard-sized biography of Django Reinhardt, a Manouche Gypsy considered the greatest jazz guitarist in the world, despite losing the use of his third and fourth fingers in a caravan fire. When the Spanish guitar master Andrés Segovia heard Reinhardt play, Rakić's card recounts, he was so impressed that he asked to see the score, "but Django just laughed and told him that there wasn't one, that it was a simple improvisation."[45]

Liszt himself reappears in another of Milan's condensed lessons on Gypsy culture. Rakić cautions that however he had responded to Eduardo's question in Antigua about his attraction to the Hungarian composer, "there's always more than one truth to everything." He recalls a movie about Liszt that tells one of these other "truths," one more specious and troubling.[46] At the center of the story is a boy violinist named Josy, who Liszt reportedly hears play at a Gypsy carnival in Pest, Hungary "with such virtuosity that he immediately reminds him of Paganini." Later, trying unsuccessfully to recall one of Josy's dazzling melodies at the piano, Liszt tracks down the boy in a Gypsy camp and tries to convince his family that such talent must not be wasted. Liszt "wants to save him from savagery. He wants to Europeanize him." He finally brings Josy into his home, hoping to train him for the annual music competition. But Josy, besides eating with his hands, running wild, and scribbling on a bust of Beethoven, "is wary of musical scores, believes in improvisation, refuses to learn music theory, and keeps playing by ear."[47] Rakić's postcard describes a key scene in the movie: Josy has just heard his teacher play a recital and is enthralled. But at a dinner following the recital, where Josy himself is set to play, a woman screams that someone has stolen her gold bracelet, implying, of course, that it must be the Gypsy boy. Liszt returns home to find Josy in the bathtub sobbing, trying to scrub away his "Gypsy color." The scene, Milan says, always makes him want to vomit.[48]

Later, a postcard featuring the London Underground will appear, recounting the tale of a Gypsy trumpeter named Gyorgy Krompasky who Rakić had met. Another arrives from New York City, recommending Eduardo add the multi-genre multi-instrumentalist Félix Lajkó to his expanding playlist. Milan describes Lajkó as "the most famous Gypsy violinist" from the Serbian city of Novi Sad; a Rough Guide describes him as a "Hungarian virtuoso violinist and zither player from the Vojvodina region of Serbia, whose eccentric fusion of folk, Gypsy and jazz inspires a devout following."[49] Rakić confesses he had heard Lajkó play at Madison Square Garden, and was even part of the dinner party fellow Serbs hosted for the musician after the concert, but had been so starstruck, he was unable to reveal his own part in this musical lineage:

> I didn't say a word the whole night. I spent two hours sitting next to one of my idols, in the most absolute silence, petrified. When the coffee was finally served, Lajkó turned to me and said that he knew an accordionist whose last name was Rakić who was also from Belgrade, and maybe he was family. Without looking up from my espresso, I whispered that no relative of mine was an accordionist in Belgrade.[50]

Milan's refusal to acknowledge his Gypsy family and musical legacy at the table with one of the greatest masters of that community seems to spring from some internalized and involuntary response of shame even he can't explain, despite his defense of the much-maligned movie character Josy. While Rakić's response is very different from Eduardo's provocative and unfiltered renunciation of his Jewishness in "White Smoke" and elsewhere, both figures wrestle with the foregone conclusions of personhood that have accompanied them on their journeys, looking for ways to question such definitions and instead decide for themselves who and how to be in the world.

In the course of this parade of postcards, Eduardo has taken Rakić's recommendations to heart and acquired a respectable collection of Gypsy music, which he packs up for the weeklong vacation escape that he and Lía will spend at a Guatemalan biosphere reserve, a "frozen, secluded cabin in a village called Albores, in the Sierra de las Minas, almost three thousand meters above sea level." There, they will make love listening to Lajkó's violin and magic sitar as well as a host of other Gypsy musicians "and a lot of flamenco . . . Lía, like a doctor, or perhaps more like a scientist, or perhaps more like a zealous disciple of quantum physics, ended up associating various types of Gypsy music with different positions."[51] Whether from the music, or the altitude, or the cold, or their joint solitude, Lía's orgasms and the sketches representing them are "transformed," creating a seven-page parenthesis in her almond-colored notebook unlike any other pages, seemingly created by another hand.

When the couple returns to the city, there is one last postcard from Rakić awaiting them, this one telling the story of a half-Serbian, half-Gypsy boy who wants to be a Gypsy musician and travel in a Gypsy caravan, though something has held him back. In the forests of Belgrade, the boy meets a large man with purple eyes, little horns on his head and a hoof for one foot who says he can turn him into a great Gypsy musician, on one condition. "There's always a condition, right, Eduardito? Always a sacrifice." So the boy, both happy and sad, bids his mother and father farewell, and weeping in the forests of Belgrade which were now to become his home, performs a single pirouette.[52]

This last word, with its end-point whirl in the woods, will lead the reader forward in *The Polish Boxer* to "The Pirouette," in which Eduardo embarks on a long and difficult search for Milan Rakić in the cold streets and Gypsy encampments of Belgrade. First published in Spanish as a standalone short novel in 2010, *La pirueta* contains portions of the stories "Ghosts," "Epistrophy," and "Postcards," though they appear in a different order than in *The Polish Boxer*.[53] In "The Pirouette," Eduardo will go looking for Milan after the trail of postcard *patrin* (a Romany word for signs placed along the way) suddenly dries up.[54]

Halfon's Spanish publisher described *La pirueta* as "the fathomless and prohibited story of a Serbian pianist, told by someone named Eduardo Halfon. But it is also the story of a Balkan odyssey, of the obsession of a jazz player, of a mysterious and erotic chase, of how this tale first escapes the boundaries of any friendship to later overflow the limits of any short story and finally find its way toward these pages."[55] Halfon was asked, "Do you find the Jewish experience of harassment and exile to be similar to what the Gypsies of Eastern Europe have dealt with, and are dealing with?" Not only is there is a strong connection between the two communities in *La pirueta*, he responded, but this is especially evident in the friendship that develops between Eduardo and Milan, a friendship based on common roots, on a common struggle with their identity, with their family history, with their people.[56] *La pirueta* was also praised for introducing readers to a protagonist who knows what it means to live "in a country far away from where the decisions are made," one who meets a Serbian pianist whose personality and way of interpreting the music of Thelonious Monk fascinate and drive him.[57] But did Milan ever play Monk for Eduardo? Eduardo *thinks* he hears Rakić weave in whispers of Monk tunes in the last Liszt piece he plays in Guatemala, but Monk's presence in the Liszt is mostly ghostly, just as Rakić's will become following the last of his postcards punctuated with the pirouette.

Amid snowfall, dark rooms, dense clouds of cigarette smoke, and secret enclaves, Eduardo will doggedly search for his Serbian friend and his Monk-influenced piano playing in Belgrade and its environs, in the process amassing an immersion experience in Romany culture and its contentious relationship with the Balkan environment in which it is perpetually othered. In one frustrated, whisky-soaked moment, the protagonist remembers the half-Gypsy boy of Milan's postcard and concludes, "Epistrophy doesn't actually mean a fucking thing."[58] In another, he rereads the correspondence from Rakić for buried clues to his whereabouts, resigning himself to the failure of not finding his friend. In that "sea of postcards," a white card appears with a drawing of Lía's orgasms, from the last time they were together before his trip to Belgrade:

> I looked at the drawing carefully, trying to decipher it, but instead I thought about all the lines of Lía's orgasms, about the lines of her body, about the lines on my palm, about the lines that join the stars to form constellations, about the five lines of the musical stave that held Milan back so much, about the lines that unite and divide and reunite the Balkan countries only to divide them again, about the ideological and religious lines that fracture the world and are making it more wretched all the time, and about the tangled web of events and people that, like the tiny dots of a single flourishing sketch, had led me to the banks of some river in Belgrade.[59]

Despite the frustrations, Eduardo will continue looking for Rakić and for the meaning of the pirouette in Roma culture, sifting the clues he is offered, such as "Gypsies sometimes do a pirouette before they die." His linguistic skills in English, Spanish, Hebrew and other languages are of little help here, and every piece of information that his sources reluctantly share with him must go from one mouth to another and then another, from Romany to Serbian and then to English, which "finally, like the last little deformed doll of a matryoshka, I translated for myself into Spanish."[60] In an "apocalyptic" snowstorm that keeps him inside and off Rakić's trail for a day, Eduardo reads and listens "to a few pieces by Melodius."[61] In another unsuccessful foray, he begins to wonder if he is the one who's lost. At one juncture, Eduardo gets close enough to a group of men on the street to see that one has a swastika tattooed on his neck, a discovery that sickens him, paralleling Rakić's desire to vomit every time he sees the child prodigy Josy try to wash off his Gypsyness in the movie about Liszt. In a bar he orders a vinjak, the local cheap whiskey with which "slowly, the sickness or fear or whatever it had been started to fade."[62]

Finally, a serpentine, secretive path leads Eduardo to a subterranean Serbian brothel, but by this time, he is incapable of speech itself: "I had gone beyond language. Beyond any rational concept. Beyond myself. Beyond any understanding of what was happening. Beyond any god or doctrine or gospel or borderline between one thing and another. Just beyond."[63] In this unmoored or undone state, he faintly hears what he thinks are the sounds of a piano, and he ascends a steep staircase (though it seems a descent at the same time) where he hears an "invisible tune," an "ethereal note," that "had to be Milan."[64] The door that he opens, rather than revealing his friend, frames the figure of a young woman, a "spectral Gypsy" clad in turquoise, who places her bare feet on top of his, who slides her hands down his neck and torso, who presses her groin against his. In this sensory overload, he thinks he sees Milan's face, and then perhaps both their fathers' faces together: "I thought I saw Milan's father's face, which at the same time was my own father's face, calling me in Romany or maybe in Hebrew and holding out one of his hands so that I'd take it and he could help me." In this dense superimposition of father figures, Hebrew and Romany, Gypsy and Jewish history and experiences, the protagonist thinks he hears far off, perhaps subliminally, "as though threaded through the rest of that music and all the music of the universe, one of the syncopated melodies of Melodius Thunk. Impossible to know which one. Better that way."[65]

This is how "The Piroutte" ends, with a return to Monk's music that advocates for maintaining its quality of mystery, and implicitly, maintaining the mystery of Rakić himself, who will prove to be "untrackable, unreachable, almost missing, peregrinating, with no roots or ties."[66] The end of "The Pirouette" returns the reader to the smoky and intense interiors of the brothel setting summoned forth in "Epistrophy's" reference to Storyville, though we are in a different country, a different climate, a different language and a different musical genre. The protagonist's sensation of finding himself beyond rationality, beyond language, beyond himself, beyond understanding any god or doctrine or gospel or even the borderline between one thing and another, and finally, "just beyond," becomes a kind of epistrophe. From here, the protagonist of *The Polish Boxer* will travel on to Portugal, to the book's last chapter, which also considers the dividing line between story and history, fiction and reality, a line ultimately beyond his and our grasp.

CHAPTER 3

THE THRESHOLD OF FICTION

*I am not enough. I need fiction
in order to say what I want to say.*

LITERATURE TEARING AT REALITY

When Eduardo Halfon states, in the prologue to his 2004 book *De cabo roto*, "Quería narrar en el lindero mismo que divide la historia y la ficción," how should we translate it?[1] In the Introduction and elsewhere in this volume, I have taken the phrase to mean, "I wanted to narrate on the very threshold that divides history and fiction." But there are other options to consider. We could understand *lindero* as the *border* of history and fiction or the *boundary* between the two or maybe, the *limit* point that divides them. *Historia* is also a persistent puzzle, signifying both *story* and *history* in Spanish, but here pointing more convincingly to the latter. What is crucial about this desire, expressed in the earliest stages of Halfon's life as a published author, is its emphasis of adjacency. For Halfon, history and fiction are not binary opposites or even discreet terrains, necessarily, but adjacent domains.[2] Multigenerational migrations, the Holocaust, the kidnapping of a family member, state violence, and assimilation to new environments all contribute to a series of family histories marked by trauma, silences, and conflicted memories. Against a backdrop undeniably built, at least in part, from autobiographical elements, a repeat-appearance narrator traverses near and distant terrains marked by diasporic origin stories, unclassifiable identities, and linguistic quandaries. The primary actions and emotional landscapes of his works translated into English involve experiences of estrangement and otherness both on the home front and beyond those familiar terrains.

In the encounters and disencounters of his protagonists, incomprehension and confusion produce results that are sometimes humorous, sometimes frightening, but that always contain important questions. Paradoxically, bewilderment, dissonance, and otherness best "define" the narrator's exploration into who he is and where he fits. Even in "A Speech at Póvoa," with its innocuous title suggesting nothing more than the repurposing of a talk the real-life Eduardo Halfon gave at a writers' festival in Portugal, this blurring between literature and reality prevails. The tale incorporates varying versions of historical events, unresolved linguistic mysteries, and a palimpsestic overlap of fictional, journalistic, and autobiographical elements impossible to disentangle from one other.[3]

The closing text in Halfon's celebrated *El boxeador polaco* and the penultimate story in the book's English translation, "Discurso de Póvoa"/"A Speech at Póvoa" references the author's 2008 appearance at the Correntes D'Escritas festival in Póvoa de Varzim, a coastal Portuguese city about thirty kilometers from Porto.[4] Its narrator describes the preparations that went into his participation in the event, including his interlinguistic wrangling with its baffling theme, "A Literatura Rasga a Realidade," a phrase his translation team for *The Polish Boxer* rendered as "Literature Tears through Reality." As with other conundrums associated with arranging historical episodes or stories to better impact readerly or live audiences, the narrator ultimately determines he can best address this riddle by recuperating the Holocaust survival story of his Polish grandfather.

The structure of the tale strongly suggests that "A Speech at Póvoa" *is* the talk Halfon gave at Póvoa de Varzim, as it begins, no doubt, as Halfon himself began, facing his audience, and proclaiming, "A few weeks ago, I got an email notifying me of the subject of this conference, 'A literatura rasga a realidade,' 'Literature Tears Through Reality,' a very beautiful phrase but one that ultimately left me no more enlightened than I'd been to begin with."[5] Whoever reads these pages at whatever moment finds a first-person account in the present tense that starts off "a few weeks ago." The narrator explains that he had written to Manuela Ribeiro, the real-life director of the festival, to seek clarification on the topic: Did it refer to the intersection of literature and reality? To the irruption of reality in literature? To the irruption of literature in reality? Or what? Ribeiro had quickly responded in Portuguese, *isso mismo*, that exactly. The narrator tells us he had then queried his Brazilian friend and co-presenter João Paolo Cuenca, who together with other real-life writers Ignacio del Valle from Spain, and Pedro Teixeira Neves and Valter Hugo Mãe from Portugal, would also be weighing in on the topic at the event. Cuenca had responded, "*eu tambem não faço idea*," (I don't have a clue either).⁶ Such was Halfon's perplexity, even when finally standing before his audience, that an actual website for the Póvoa de Varzim festival reported, "A really nice phrase, but one that leaves me confused; revealed Eduardo Halfon, referring to the topic."⁷

The speaker (both as a character at a literary conference and as the narrator) goes on to explain how he hoped to distract himself from the task of preparing a talk on this puzzling subject by watching an Ingmar Bergman film, finally realizing after a fitful night of insomnia that the film itself perhaps provided an answer to the riddle of literature tearing at or through reality. But just as at Póvoa, the protagonist leaves the reveal of *which* Bergman film and *what* answer it provided for the end of his disquisition (which I will do as well). "What is reality? I don't know," he admits to his audience. "How do I conceive of reality? No idea." The protagonist considers the accepted meanings of the verb *rasgar* in Spanish, hoping he can count on its parallel etymology in Portuguese. Could literature *tear* reality, as if reality were a piece of fabric or paper? Could it *shatter* reality like a car window, considering another use of the term *rasgar* in Spanish? What link did his own experience as a writer establish between literature and reality? "How has my literature torn through reality?" he asks his Póvoa audience and the readers of these pages.⁸

Those familiar with Halfon's works likely will not be surprised at the answer the speech giver supplies to these rhetorical questions. Solving the problem of what to say or what to write involves returning in historical and narrative time to the experiences at Auschwitz of his Polish grandfather, experiences that his forbearer for all intents and purposes silenced during nearly sixty years in Guatemala, after migrating there following the war. Finally, just a few years before the event in Portugal, the grandfather had consented to speak of his experience on camera, "A Speech at Póvoa" tells us, not just for the sake of posterity, but so that his descendant might tell that same story himself, might pass it on. The speaker recalls how his grandfather then revealed details of being picked up in his neighborhood in Lodz while playing dominoes with friends, of the last time he saw his family, of the almost six years he spent in a series of concentration camps, and most crucially, of a fellow Pole at Auschwitz who advised the grandfather what to say and what not to say to save himself from an early death.

The grandson is immediately attracted to the apparent "simplicity" of this story and the importance of well-chosen words to the survival of his grandfather, and by extension, his progeny. But he also likes it because he finds the account "powerfully literary."⁹ However faithful to history, however reliable the account his own grandfather or the grandfather in the story shared with him on videotape of his experience in the camps, his primary interest is in its fictional power:

> I work with fiction. Or I work in fiction, I work through fiction. . . . I am not interested in the facts of my grandfather's story. . . . The story is based on an anecdote that my grandfather told me, and he told it to me very quickly. To him it was nothing more than an anecdote. I think he told it to me in about a minute . . . 'I was sent to Auschwitz because of this, this happened, I survived.' And when he told me that story, I immediately saw the ripples. I saw the texture of that story. But I knew that I needed a vehicle for it.[10]

For several years, the speaker at Póvoa tells us, he carried the story around under his arm, unsuccessfully testing out different narrative techniques. Finally, though, he was able to get it down on paper in a slightly altered version: "I managed to write a piece in which a grandson interviews his grandfather about his experiences in Auschwitz while he's looking at the five green numbers on his arm and they're drinking a bottle of whiskey together."[11] This fictional twist, which the narrator displays for us by noting that *a* grandson interviews his grandfather, this time in the third person, is the key to the success of the character and narrator named Eduardo Halfon, and, it seems, a key to the success of the author Eduardo Halfon as well. An anecdote from lived experience is released from its testimonial (truth) limitations and re-placed in fiction to give it more emotional heft, or to create an "ecstatic truth," to use a term from Werner Herzog with which Halfon has declared an affinity and to which we will return.[12] "I had managed to carry reality over into literature. I had managed, through literature, to penetrate reality. All lovely and perfect and smelling of printer's ink," the speaker-narrator explains.[13] All was perfect, that is, until he had opened a Guatemalan newspaper to find a photo of his grandfather showing off his Auschwitz tattoo and providing the reporter with a substantially *different* explanation of his survival, this time crediting not the Polish boxer but his skills as a carpenter. What carpentry skills? the speaker wonders out loud. And what of the boxer, his grandfather's Scheherazade in disguise, who had given him the words to say to continue living?

The true story that the grandson had waited all his life to hear, the familial and intimate account of Holocaust survival—a sacrosanct subject to be sure—suddenly proves susceptible to alteration, variant plotlines and even reinvention, perhaps as much for the reader as for the protagonist. In a 2020 interview for a Colombian newspaper, Halfon was asked to clarify whether the grandfather character survived for being a good carpenter or thanks to the help of the aforementioned Polish boxer, to which he responded, "We'll never know. He had both versions. When I asked him why these two explanations exist, and why he told the reporter that it was because of being a carpenter, he answered, 'I give each person the version they deserve.' As if the reporter at that moment did not deserve the version of the boxer. But I don't know. And when he told me, he didn't grant it much importance."[14]

THE CONTRADICTORY PACT

The speaker's pre-festival wrangling with "A literatura rasga a realidade," his preparatory interactions with the festival's director and his fellow presenters, his tale of finally making sense of the festival topic by connecting it to his grandfather's recounting of his Holocaust experiences sixty years after the fact, and his explanation of how that revelation provided him with the *materia prima* of his own literary project, all lead us to read "A Speech at Póvoa" as *the* talk Halfon gave at the 2008 festival. Even the narrator's shock at later encountering an entirely different version of his grandfather's survivor story in a Guatemalan newspaper—an element conveniently left out of the tale "The Polish Boxer" itself—adds to the effect of replication. A reference in Portuguese to Halfon's speech on the Póvoa de Varzim website further compels us to conflate the author and narrator of "A Speech at Póvoa," to read this as the textual record—a duplicate of sorts—of Halfon's address in the 2008 festival.[15]

Ultimately, though, there are crucial differences between Halfon's speech at Póvoa and "A Speech at Póvoa." Whereas those in attendance at the festival could take his words at face and ear value, listening to him speak (in Spanish, one assumes) during his allotted fifteen minutes, our *reading* of "Discurso de Póvoa"/"A Speech at Póvoa," especially in relation to the other texts in *The Polish Boxer*, produces different results. The talk now belongs to a fertile intertextual and intermedial field. There is an intense interplay between the various levels, formats, and times of narration. There is the text of which Halfon is author, the narrator's *discurso* or speech forming that text, the grandfather's oral account that the narrator claims is at the heart of his speaking and writing project, the mentioned film recording of the grandfather's testimony, and the allusions to the intertext of "The Polish Boxer." There is also, reportedly, a *second* survivor account proffered to the Guatemalan press by the grandfather, which in turn calls into question the "truth" value of the first version of those lived events, the accurate remembering of them, or the faithful representation of those memories.

Given the complex, multileveled authorial function in "A Speech at Póvoa" and in *The Polish Boxer* more broadly, a consideration of these texts in relation to the term *autofiction* is perhaps de rigueur. Alexandra Ortiz Wallner has written that the "autofictional wink," the writings of the "I," and the subtextual intertwining of many stories "*like reflections in a distorted mirror*" all characterize the various stagings of the task of writing in Halfon's works.[16] Nicolás Campisi notes that beginning with *El boxeador polaco*, "Halfon's works have begun to blur the lines between fiction, non-fiction, and autobiography" and the text "asks to be read as a series of autofictional mosaics that offer a kaleidoscopic view into Halfon's literary project."[17] Stephanie Pridgeon warns that even being careful not to conflate author and narrator, "the two often seem interchangeable due to Halfon's use of autofiction."[18] Charlotte Gartenberg partners the characteristics of autofiction found in *The Polish Boxer* with the notion of haunting, with the author's attempt "to forge a settled sense of self in circumstances which expose the impossibility of such a thing."[19]

In an essay that pairs Halfon's works with *autofiction* in its very title, Matías Barchino cites a definition by Manuel Alberca that notably draws on the language of spatial relations to weigh in on the controversial term:

> Autofiction is a tale that presents itself as a novel, that is, as fiction, or without a fixed genre (never as autobiography or memoir), characterized by having an autobiographical appearance, confirmed by the shared name of author, narrator and character. It is precisely this intersection of genres that configures a space of contradictory narrative outlines, since it transgresses or at least contravenes the principle of distance between author and character that reigns over the fictional contract and the principle of veracity of the autobiographical contract.[20]

Barchino explains further that the autofictional narrator of *The Polish Boxer* represents a search for a "hypernarrative" structure, a term often employed to describe electronic or digital materials that allow for interactive participation on the part of the viewer or reader.[21] The sentence that Halfon borrows from Henry Miller's *Tropic of Cancer* for the epigraph to *El boxeador polaco/The Polish Boxer*—"I have moved the typewriter into the next room where I can see myself in the mirror as I write"—seems to further vouch for the book's "autofictional" nature.[22] In autofiction, in other words, both writing and reading are treated as constitutive acts, as *reflective* in both senses of the term.

Nevertheless, Halfon himself has rejected the term "autofiction" outright, while one of his interviewers has chided critics for using it as a "crutch" for understanding the writer's oeuvre, together with "metalanguage," another false support.[23] Notwithstanding definitions of the term as including "all the processes of the fictionalization of the Self," Halfon insists that "autofiction doesn't exist," that "all literature is fiction and all literature is autobiographical" and that "that other Eduardo Halfon is very different from me.... He carries my name and my biography but is not me."[24]

Further elaborating on the definitions of the (for Halfon unnecessary and onerous) term in her 2018 study *The Story of Me: Contemporary American Autofiction*, Marjorie Worthington shows how some critics place more weight on the "auto" half of the term, on the text's referential function, while others highlight its fictional characteristics. She cites its use by the French narratologist Gerard Genette, for whom "true autofictions ... are those which are more fictional than not, but which maintain the onomastic connection between author and protagonist."[25] For Genette, in fact, any text in which an author of fiction includes his own person or a character with the same name as the author should be considered an autofiction.[26] In *Fiction and Diction*, Genette speaks of the "intentional contradictory pact" of autofiction, in which the author proposes a protagonist who declares, "It is I and it is not I." Under this rubric, the French structuralist analyzes such illustrious works as Dante's *The Divine Comedy*, Cervantes's *Don Quijote*, and Jorge Luis Borges's "The Aleph."[27]

Accepting this seeming contradiction, Worthington asserts that American autofiction "combines the clearly fictional with the seemingly accurate biographical history of its authors."[28] But is *American* autofiction somehow distinct from these other traditions Genette identifies? And does Halfon belong to this "American" group? Despite affirmations of Halfon's increasing importance to "American" letters, his relationship with such a category remains a fraught one. Though fully bilingual, Halfon's first and chosen language for writing is Spanish, as the original text of "Discurso de Póvoa" in *El boxeador polaco* suggests. Nonetheless, the writer owes much of his international success to English language translations of *The Polish Boxer* and subsequent works, success which in turn led to his works being translated into more than a dozen languages, as well as an audiobook format.[29] As I suggest in the Introduction, as both author and protagonist, Halfon shifts in (and out of) delimiting categories such as "American," "Latino," "Latin American," and "Spanish-language author." Thus, while we might say that Halfon's place in literature of the Americas is increasingly well established, his works have also been discovered by an ever more vast and diverse cosmopolitan audience. Diaspora is now a condition not only of the author and his principal narrator, but also of his works.

The resulting overlap of authorial functions, genres, and linguistic systems both reflects and is generative of the conflicting and indeterminate subject positions and postures of Halfon's characters. Returning to Alberca's definition cited earlier, an autofictional text represents an "intersection of genres that configures a space of contradictory narrative outlines." Borrowing from the languages of geography, migration, and law, he argues that autofiction produces a terrain of displacement since it transgresses or at least *contravenes* the principle of distance between author and character that reigns over the fictional contract and the principle of veracity of the autobiographical contract.[30] Indeed, the primary narrator in *The Polish Boxer* and the works related to it so often expresses and simultaneously *rejects* labels and affiliations, including the author's core identities as "Guatemalan" and "Jew," we might speak of *contravention* (with its attendant meanings of breach, violation, infringement, trespass, disobedience, transgression, infraction, conflict, interference, contradiction, refutation, disputation, and counteraction) as a semantic key to interpreting both form and theme.

Despite Halfon's objection to the term, then, Alberca's focus on the language of space and place and on the trespass and transgression that characterize autofictional narratives brings us back to the central emotion of his work, that of dis-placement in the standard confines of nation, language, religion, or genre. As the author himself has said, "It's almost like living in a permanent diaspora, away from a homeland and away from a religion and away from language itself."[31] Or as he explained in his interview with Damián Huergo, "I don't have a homeland, a city, a country, a place that calls me ... I wish I did. Perhaps that's why I move through the world looking for it. I can make any city mine, or to say it better, I can make it seem like mine. But it never is."[32] The restless movement of Halfon's protagonists through ever-changing physical, temporal, and self-interpretive scenarios disturbs the notion of tidy chronology that characterizes memoir and autobiography, once again propelling the author toward fiction. As he told his interviewer in a translation workshop, "I am not enough. I need fiction in order to say what I want to say, which is to give the reader an emotional journey."[33]

FORGETTING AND ECSTATIC TRUTH

At the end of "A Speech at Póvoa," the narrator circles back to the Bergman film he had watched as a distraction from preparing his talk for the writers' festival, in the process stumbling on a solution to the problem of "literature tearing at reality." The heretofore unidentified film is Bergman's *Skammen* in Swedish, or *Shame* in English, *Vergüenza* in Spanish, *Vergonha* in

Portuguese. A dark and foreboding story of a musician couple in the Swedish civil war, the film is "much more than that," the speaker-narrator assures. In the final scene, Jen and Eva, having lost everything in the ravages of war, attempt to escape their island in a boat that circumnavigates a host of floating cadavers. In this horrific setting, the character Eva, played by Liv Ullman, recounts a dream in which a wall of roses is set afire by a plane above, in which an imagined infant daughter clings to her, the child's mouth next to her cheek. Throughout the dream, she knows there is something she must not forget, something someone told her that is crucial she remember, but which she nonetheless forgets. Literature is exactly like this, Halfon's narrator avers in Póvoa. As we write, we know we have something important to say about reality, something close at hand, within reach, on the tip of our tongues, something we must not forget, but which we invariably do forget. Remembering is both an urgent task, and one at which we are bound to fail, as Eva discovers in the dream she recounts at the end of *Skammen*. So it is that literature "needs to construct one reality by destroying another... and then reconstituting itself from its own debris," a survival tactic or creative mechanism the narrator believes his Polish grandfather would have understood intuitively.[34]

Is it mere coincidence that the film that supplies the solution to how literature tears at reality for the protagonist of "A Speech at Póvoa" is *Skammen (Shame)*? In "Bergman's Nazi past," Peter Ohlin argues that *Skammen* stages Bergman's attempts to come to terms with his and other family members' complicity in National Socialist politics and activities.[35] Bergman had reflected in an interview

> The original background to *Skammen* is a horror show. How would I have behaved during the Nazi era if Sweden had been occupied, if I myself, in one way or another, had held a position of responsibility or some institutional function or just been a threatened private person? How much courage to stand up for my beliefs would I have been able to bring forth against physical or psychological violence or against the war of nerves implied by the occupation of a foreign power?... the continuous, cold threat that wears you down—how would I have managed that?[36]

Perhaps, then, both author and filmmaker share a preoccupation with the events of World War II and their personal relationship to those events, though from very different positions and generations. Bergman might well have rejected the equivalence the Póvoa speechmaker establishes between Eva's account of forgetting in her dream and the impetus for writing literature, however, as the celebrated filmmaker believed the two creative forms to be fundamentally different from one another:

> Film is not the same thing as literature. As often as not the character and substance of the two art forms are in conflict. What this difference really depends on is hard to define but it probably has to do with the self-responsive process. The written word is read and assimilated by a conscious act and in connection with the intellect, and little by little it plays on the imagination or feelings. It is completely different with the motion picture. When we see a film in a cinema we are conscious that an illusion has been prepared for us, and we relax and accept it with our will and intellect. We prepare the way into our imagination.[37]

Is the Póvoa speaker's "solution" to literature tearing at reality invalid, then? Or can we salvage a connection between literature and the memory-forgetfulness tug-of-war in *Shame* by highlighting the symbol of the infant daughter Eva cradles in her dream? Though the couple at the center of Bergman's narrative has no flesh-and-blood child that will survive the apocalyptic aftermath of war, the daughter that clings to Eva in her dream represents a kind of progeny of imagination. By connecting the scene to the mandate or function of literature in relation to reality, the protagonist of "A Speech at Póvoa" (and/or Halfon himself) represents this surviving generation and its ability to recount a traumatic past, if only through fiction, or perhaps, most appropriately and effectively through fiction.

Another film, or at least its director's musings about it, might ultimately provide us with a fuller solution to the problem of literature tearing at reality in "A Speech at Póvoa." At the beginning of his 1992 film *Lessons of Darkness*, Werner Herzog "cites" this epigraph from Blaise Pascal: "The collapse of the stellar universe will occur—like creation—in grandiose splendor." But in a talk he gave in Milan after a film showing, Herzog admitted to putting those words in Pascal's mouth:

> The words attributed to Blaise Pascal which preface my film *Lessons of Darkness* are in fact by me. Pascal himself could not have said it better. This falsified and yet, as I will later demonstrate, not falsified quotation should serve as a first hint of what I am trying to deal with in this discourse. Anyway, to acknowledge a fake as fake contributes only to the triumph of accountants. Why am I doing this, you might ask? The reason is simple and comes not from theoretical, but rather from practical, considerations. With this quotation as a prefix I elevate [*erheben*] the spectator, before he has even seen the

first frame, to a high level, from which to enter the film. And I, the author of the film, do not let him descend from this height until it is over. Only in this state of sublimity [*Erhabenheit*] does something deeper become possible, a kind of truth that is the enemy of the merely factual. Ecstatic truth, I call it.[38]

Later in his address to the Milan audience, after sharing several fantastical anecdotes in which he was compelled to rethink the relationship between reality and fiction, and between *cinema verité* and other approaches to reality, Herzog added, "We must ask of reality: how important is it, really? And: how important, really, is the Factual? Of course, we can't disregard the factual; it has normative power. But it can never give us the kind of illumination, the ecstatic flash, from which Truth emerges."[39] Unlike Bergman, Herzog does not distinguish between the genres of literature and film as regards their relationships to truth, as for him, "in the fine arts, in music, literature, and cinema, it is possible to reach a deeper stratum of truth—a poetic, ecstatic truth, which is mysterious and can only be grasped with effort; one attains it through vision, style, and craft." And thus, Herzog sees the words he attributes to Pascal at the beginning of *Lessons on Darkness* "about the collapse of the stellar universe not as a fake ['counterfeit'; Fälschung], but as a means of making possible an ecstatic experience of inner, deeper truth."[40]

This, Halfon affirms, is what he is after, too: "What I want to give my readers is not my family's history. It's not the story of my grandfather in Auschwitz; it's the feeling or the sense of that story, or the emotional content of that story, something Werner Herzog calls the ecstatic truth. So not the factual truth, but the truth of ecstasy, of a sensation."[41] Whereas Barchino had associated Halfon's works with the term *hyperreality* to reference the reader's role, Herzog supplies us with a more elegant and more resonant explanation of this interaction between reader and text: "The soul of the listener or the spectator . . . actualizes truth through the experience of sublimity: that is, it completes an independent act of creation."[42] In the case of "A Speech at Póvoa," Halfon provides us with tools and tactics to remove obstacles on the paths to history and its truths, including the stumbling block of the contradictory nature of memory and forgetfulness, and of the contradictory nature of lived experiences and their literary evocation.

CHAPTER 4

UNTOLD TRAUMAS

The difficulty of the current conjuncture is to think memory and amnesia together, rather than simply to oppose them.

GLIMMERS OF A LOST PARADISE

As its title story translated into English as "Tomorrow We Never Did Talk About It" illustrates, Halfon's 2011 volume *Mañana nunca lo hablamos* captures in its anachronic syntax the uncertainty the narrator recalls feeling upon abruptly leaving the country of his birth with his family in 1981, laden down with the unanswered questions of a ten year-old.[1] The book contains ten textual snapshots that together create a collage of memories from his Guatemalan childhood: hand-in-hand with his father at the seashore; drawing with his brother in the dust caused by the 1976 earthquake; learning of the death of his baseball hero Thurman Munson; enjoying a family meal at El Rodeo, where his father identifies a woman across the restaurant as one of the guerrillas who kidnapped his grandfather in 1967; soldiers barging into a family gathering at his grandparents' house as his uncle reads the residue of his Turkish coffee. As David Pérez Vega has noticed, beginning with the sixth of these episodes, the theme of political violence progressively builds throughout the last section of the book, culminating with the title story itself.[2]

Jeffrey Browitt has described the stories in this volume, written after *The Polish Boxer* but never translated in its entirety, as "linked by an adult narrator remembering his younger self during key affective moments of his idyllic childhood, his *paradise lost*."[3] Words spoken by Halfon himself in a 2011 publicity video for the book, included on the back cover of some editions in Spanish, support this reading of his early experience in Central America as a lost paradise:

> Without setting out to, and almost without realizing it, I return time and again to the narratives of my childhood. The stories of my youth. As if, by writing them, I'd like to also recuperate something or remember something, or just return to that bright white space from which I was banished.... Sometimes I think that's why I write. To try and return to the illusory and fragile purity of my childhood, in the Guatemala of the turbulent '70s.... To retrace my steps as a child and walk through those doorways again and perhaps now, in a handful of pages, and through the nebulous prism of memory and fiction, recuperate glimmers of a lost paradise.[4]

Guatemala is "frequently idealized" in the book, according to Vanessa Perdu, with the characterization of the Guatemalan space as "white" a notable example of this idealization.[5] Such gestures, she argues, represent the country with the "consistency of a paradise lost."[6]

Nonetheless, it would be a mistake to read "Tomorrow We Never Did Talk About It" and its companion tales as wholly idyllic. Each invokes some kind of fear in relation to illness, death, near-death, or loss, whether the loss is of innocence or of the familiar or even the favor of one's parents. As Javier Goñi observes, "little by little, the landscape of childhood of this writer-child subtly becomes invaded, a corner, a horizon, a blurry area. Military boots, Machine guns. People missing. Guerillas. Terrorism. Guatemala in the 80s. And the family can and does: flee."[7] An ominous undercurrent, already present in literal form in the first text of the volume, "El baile de la marea," (The Sway of the Sea), builds to the crescendo of the final chapter with its curious, discordant title.[8] This last window into childhood remembrances captures the crucial moment when escalating armed conflict in Guatemala City propels the protagonist's alarmed parents to flee with their three children to the United States. Though the narrator's father promises he will explain "tomorrow" the turmoil that drives this decision, that conversation never occurs. The anachronism of the title suggests that fields of personal and national memory can contain silences that become chronic wounds or traumas. And by using "we" as the subject of that story and the subject of the volume title, Halfon invites and implicates us as his readers in that silence and its still-pending truth-telling.

"The Boy in the Bubble" is how Browitt characterizes the narrator protagonist of *Mañana nunca lo hablamos*, stating, "the class positioning of the young child against the backdrop of war creates a secondary emotional tension between the political stance of the adult narrator and his own family."[9] But is the child in fact fully protected from the violence around him? If the bubble were effective, would the protagonist be left eternally awaiting a crucial conversation? Would Halfon have presented us, his readers, with these "fond" recollections increasingly tinged with fear, flight, brutality, and death? Though the narrator remembers his childhood bewilderment regarding the events around him, his questions—perpetually deferred until a never-arriving "tomorrow"—reveal a transtemporal longing to sort out those events, to understand more fully who he is as a Guatemalan. Shuttling back and forth between the perspective of an uncomprehending child and an adult still waiting for answers to decades-old questions, this work implies that what's left unsaid or untold constitutes its own kind of open wound. As Browitt observes, "The scene of writing, then, is Halfon's attempt to stage the way fragmented memory, especially of traumatic moments, can haunt the present, especially through moments of affective intensity linked to unresolved contradictions on both the psychological and emotional level."[10]

Given these allusions to a paradise lost, we might assume that non-indigenous or *ladino* privilege, in both its ethnoracial and economic dimensions, differentiates and insulates the narrator and his family from the conflict surging around them—at least until their decision to flee north.[11] Browitt posits that both class and race help "quarantine" the family from the terror experienced by "the mass of poor Guatemalans."[12] Indigenous actors predominate on both sides of the conflict, leaving the child protagonist confused about how to distinguish between identities and affiliations. Jorge Ramón González Ponciano warns us, though, that when scholars view the dichotomy between "Indians" and "ladinos" through the troubled history of race relations in the United States, "ladinos effectively appear as whites . . . reducing Guatemalan racism to anti-indigenous sentiment and making ladino racism against Indians the sole axis on which Guatemala's deep historical and social contradictions—and thus its inability to achieve social harmony—turn." Such a position "requires ignoring both the geographies of imperial whiteness that situate Guatemala as a banana republic and the internal complexities of pigmentocratic hierarchies within Guatemala."[13] Instead, he finds post-genocide Guatemala to be characterized by a symbolic war between a cosmopolitanism from below, influenced by the immigrant Mayan and ladino diaspora throughout North America, and a cosmopolitanism from above that continues to sustain the oligarchic values attached to the plantation economy and export agriculture. A particular privilege of this latter group is that of "moving freely on a global scale," with the result that transnational ease of movement itself becomes "somewhat racialized."[14] When the family at the center of "Tomorrow We Never Did Talk About It" leaves suddenly for the Miami area, where the father already owns an apartment, they exercise this privilege, though the protagonist experiences the abrupt removal as a rupture, a "tearing in two."

The benefit of "whiteness" enjoyed by the narrator and his family will also be called into question in contexts such as the anglophone US setting to which they flee. Ultimately, it is never the family's only distinguishing characteristic. Rather, privileges associated with economic class, access to private education, ownership of personal and business property, etc., exist in tandem with marginalizing and estranging markers such as Jewishness and immigrant status, both in Guatemalan and US spaces. As Judith Kay warns, "racism is an inadequate and misleading way to frame anti-Jewish oppression," as "the sheer existence of Jews from many cultures and regions reveals the irrationality of the division that pits Jews against people of color."[15] A sense of belonging, whether of the extent to which the protagonists belong to the national family, or the extent to which Guatemala's history and events can belong to them, are both called into question. The memory fragments gathered here thus provide a portal through which the reader can glimpse, albeit "through a glass darkly," the personal and communal costs of Guatemala's long civil war (1960–1996) at the personal and familial level, even for its privileged members.[16]

Halfon's text followed in the wake of two major reports that sought to clarify the nature and human costs of that war, ostensibly providing facts and explanations never shared explicitly with the narrator at the center of his story. In 1998, the Recovery of Historical Memory Project (Recuperación de la Memoria Histórica or REMHI) issued *Guatemala Nunca Más!* (Guatemala Never Again!), a project supported by the Catholic Church and its "guiding light" Bishop Juan Gerardi, who on April 24, 1998 presented the findings to a large audience at the cathedral in Guatemala City. Two days later, Gerardi was bludgeoned to death in the garage of his residence, "underscoring the contemporary relevance of the horrors documented in the report."[17]

The members of the United Nations-sponsored Comisión para el Esclarecimiento Histórico (Commission for Historical Clarification or CEH) worked between 1997 and 1999 on a separate report, one that charged the Guatemalan military with genocide, a charge that had never been leveled against any other country in the hemisphere, despite similar patterns of targeted violence, torture, disappearances, and murder of "subversives" by state actors. The CEH concluded that more than six hundred massacres took place, and that two hundred thousand people were killed or disappeared, "93 percent at the hands of state forces and related paramilitary groups."[18] The Commission found that racism, expressed "as a doctrine of superiority," drove the "indiscriminate nature and particular brutality with which military operations were carried out against hundreds of Mayan communities."[19]

Besides revealing these harrowing findings, the Commission also exposed the active role played by the United States in the Central American conflict. While "the involvement of the Central Intelligence Agency in the campaign of terror against Mayan and leftist insurgents had long been an open secret," the CEH report "confirmed the C.I.A.'s participation" in the war and revealed that "American training of Guatemalan military officers in counterinsurgency played a significant role in the torture, kidnapping and execution of thousands of civilians." President Bill Clinton visited Guatemala in March of 1999 and apologized for this intervention, declaring, "I state clearly that support for military forces and intelligence units which engaged in violence and widespread repression was wrong, and the United States must not repeat that mistake."[20]

In labeling its report *Memory of Silence*, the CEH called attention to the still-taboo topic of the national conflict and its casualties, even in the context of the postwar project of reconciliation and the mobilization of memory. More than a decade later, Halfon similarly invokes the fraught relationship between memory and silence in *Mañana nunca lo hablamos*. Despite the CEH and REMHI reports and the historic apology of a US president, he presents the civil war as a perpetually untold story. His work brings to mind Judith Zur's declaration that "the entire history of *la violencia* can be read as a war against memory, an Orwellian falsification of memory, a falsification of reality. The military state attempted to deny people access to truth, thus contaminating their morality and their memory."[21] At the same time, Halfon's "fictional" text acts as a corrective against the reification of memory as infallible, trustworthy, or untainted by political expediency. Beatriz Manz recalls Holocaust survivor Primo Levi's warning that "human memory is a marvelous but fallacious instrument" and that memories not only "tend to become erased as the years go by, but often they change, or even grow, by incorporating extraneous features."[22]

UNTOLD TRAUMAS

The word *untold* can be understood in at least two senses in English, one associated with abundance or excess, as in "untold riches" and the other with lack, absence, or a missing piece, as in "the untold story." The ten short texts of *Mañana* implicitly ask readers to keep both these senses of the word in play, along with their apparent contradictions. One of those contradictions has to do with the family's place in the Guatemalan social landscape. The family members' inclusion in the nation, facilitated by their prominence in the economic life of the country, is tempered by their exclusion or unbelonging as non-Catholics and immigrants or descendants of immigrants. Both factors influence the posture the adult members of the family will assume toward the conflict itself, including their refusal to remain in the country or to discuss their reasons for abandoning it. We might read "Tomorrow We Never Did Talk About It," then, as a multi-voiced *silence*, a shared *un*telling, a familial and by extension communal lacuna.

In the year prior to publishing *Mañana*, Halfon responded in part to the question "What would you like to include in your work that you haven't yet?" by explaining his discomfort with Guatemala as a subject, or even in relation to concepts such as homeland or citizenship: "Guatemala, for me is a big issue. I have a big problem with Guatemala. I left so young that I don't identify at all with the country, with the people. I see Guatemala as most people from the outside see it, as an outsider, so the subject matter of Guatemala, socially, politically, the civil war, that, you know, went on for forty years, the poverty, the violence of it, that is also one of those subjects that I'm tentative about."[23] *Mañana nunca lo hablamos* responds to this hesitancy. In a 2021 interview coinciding with the release of *Canción*, which explores more fully the 1967 kidnapping of his grandfather, Halfon admitted that the more recent volume also engages with a topic he had been avoiding, that of "dealing with a war that I did not consider my own. This was due to my distancing, my fear perhaps, of writing about an internal conflict which I did not consider mine."[24] These admissions suggest a recognition of conscious or unconscious complicity in the silencing or "untelling" of the civil war experiences and casualties to which *Mañana nunca lo hablamos* alludes. At the same time, by evoking these silences and the tendency during and after the Guatemalan civil war to mute testimonies of trauma and defer indefinitely the processes of reckoning, Halfon asks us to reflect on how this stubborn silence operated at the most intimate level of the family. Interweaving memory and fiction, the author exposes the difficult task of full discussion and disclosure, even into subsequent generations.

THE SILENCE TREATMENT

Truth commission investigators, activists and scholars alike have addressed the systematic silencing of accounts of atrocities suffered or witnessed during the Guatemalan civil war as a hallmark case of state impunity. When the documents from the National Police Historical Archive (Archivo Histórico de la Policía Nacional, AHPN) were discovered in 2005—documents that would lead to a report that echoed and expanded on the CEH document—a state official reportedly commented, "Why waste time on this mountain of old paper." Indeed, to those who discovered them, the documents themselves appeared to be "victims" that begged for a chance to finally speak and seek healing:

> This is how [the documents] were actually found, piled on the floor, victims of time, humidity, laziness and pests, but above all, of secrecy and deception. From the first moment, the commitment on the part of those of us who worked in the Archivo Histórico de la Policía Nacional was that we would not be limited to rescuing those "old papers" from dust but, above all, to liberate them from oblivion and secrecy in order to uncover their content. Guatemalan society has a right to recover the truth, to provide dignity to their victims, and to want to know about the past, in order to begin healing. People who don't know their own history cannot understand the present, and don't know who they are.[25]

As Carlos Aguirre explains in the preface to the 2013 English version *From Silence to Memory: Revelations of the AHPN*, "For quite a long time, the efforts by victims, relatives, human rights attorneys, NGOs, and other social agents to find out 'what happened' and to bring to justice the perpetrators of atrocious acts of violence *crashed against a wall of silence and impunity.*" We find a notable reordering of the wording of the CEH report *Memory of Silence* in the later effort to produce the AHPN's *From Silence to Memory*. Its publication in the second decade of the twenty-first century thus became an "emblematic case of the worldwide effort to preserve what are known as 'archives of repression' but also a model of what can be called archival activism: records ought to be considered not inert pieces of evidence but actual carriers of powerful symbolism and weapons in the multifaceted effort to create a more just society, empower hitherto marginalized and silenced individuals and social agents, and promote a culture of transparency and human rights."[26]

Halfon's fictional account demonstrates how effective this silencing was at the level of the individual and the nuclear family, across temporal and spatial divides, even for those who were not direct physical victims of the war. Whether or not *Mañana nunca lo hablamos* itself contributes to this effort of archival activism is one of the questions we can consider in our analysis. Particularly in its eponymous final text, the volume bears witness to concrete dates, actual events, and documents, but also to the context of sustained efforts to silence, obfuscate, and repress the dirty and deadly details of the civil war. It offers a series of origin stories, a return to and recuperation of the roots of its Guatemalan author, as well as a prequel to the displacement, estrangement, and opportunities of its protagonist's new life in another country. At the same time, it seems to exemplify the assertion by Steffi Hobuß that "every claim that understands silence and speech as simple opposites can be seen as wrong," and that "remembering can itself consist of practices of remaining silent."[27]

To some extent, we can read Halfon's 2011 "Tomorrow We Never Did Talk About It" or its parent volume as a next-generation response to Victor Perera's 1996 *Rites: A Guatemalan Boyhood*, which also combines poignant, often trenchant personal recollections of the country left behind, recuperated from the perspective of a Jewish child who feels himself to be an outsider, one who can only watch from the sidelines as his friends participate in the mainstream religious and social milieu.[28] Perera's return to Guatemala as an adult in 1981, the same year the family in *Mañana* and Halfon's own family flee the country, provides a much starker and straightforward assessment of the extreme level of violence that characterized the period; Perera speaks of a violence "which turned neighbor against neighbor, friend against friend, and provoked respectable heads of family to hire contract killers to rid themselves of an offending relative over a petty argument or political disagreement. In the highlands, the army's war of counterinsurgency against three guerrilla organizations had cost the lives of more than 40,000 Guatemalans, the great majority Indians of Mayan descent."[29] The epigraph of Halfon's *Mañana*, "That great cathedral space which was childhood," contains no explicit allusion to this violence, however.[30] Lifted from Virginia Woolf's "A Sketch of the Past," the metaphor of the cathedral suggests the "complex and solemn architecture" of the childhood experience and the sacred nature of its recuperation, though in Halfon's hand, it might also be read ironically, given the author's Jewish background and the backdrop of the Guatemalan civil war.[31]

Translated into English by Anne McLean, "Tomorrow We Never Did Talk About It" seems to place weight on the definition of *untold* that highlights an absence, here the conversation that never occurred. The ungrammatical future ≠ past disagreement in the title amplifies or exacerbates this sense of the perpetually postponed (re)telling, its *mañana* clashing with the possible senses of the verb. The effect is strongest in the Spanish original, in which the first-person plural *hablamos* can be read as either present or past tense, meaning either "tomorrow came and we never *talked* about it" in a finite past tense, or "tomorrow comes, and we never *talk* about it," in a continuing present tense. The same verb might even refer to the future, as when the father promises his son, *lo hablamos mañana*, "we'll talk about it tomorrow," without using the future-tense form of the verb.[32] Undoubtedly, this ambiguity, the very asynchronicity of the title, also draws in the reader, hinting that the thing not talked about might here be revealed. So too does the first-person plural subject of *hablamos*: who is this "we"? At a basic level, it refers to the child-narrator at the center of the story, and the father who promises to answer his question "tomorrow" but never does. But can we also understand the pronoun as a national "we," as the failure of Guatemalans more generally to come to terms with what is not discussed? Might it implicate non-Guatemalan readers, or readers across the globe as well?

If "Tomorrow We Never Did Talk About It" marks the persistent gap or absence of an untold story, it also leaves room for the *untold* as excess, as a quantity to which a specific figure cannot be attached. The moment when the narrator's parents spirit the family away to the United States falls within the period historians consider the "most intense period of the military onslaught, from 1981 to 1983" when "as many as 1.5 million people, out of Guatemala's 8 million, were displaced internally or had to flee the country."[33] It was also in this period that the Guatemalan military began to collectively identify Mayan groups as allies of the insurgent forces, intentionally exaggerating their support, "based on traditional racist prejudices."

> The consequence of this manipulation, extensively documented by the CEH, was massive and indiscriminate aggression directed against communities independent of their actual involvement in the guerrilla movement and with a clear indifference to their status as a non-combatant civilian population. The massacres, scorched earth operations, forced disappearances and executions of Mayan authorities, leaders and spiritual guides, were not only an attempt to destroy the social base of the guerrillas, but above all, to destroy the cultural values that ensured cohesion and collective action in Mayan communities.[34]

This was especially true, according to the CEH, "between 1981 and 1983, when the scorched earth operations and more than half of the massacres occurred."[35]

The mention of an armored tank situated across the street from a school in the second line of the story alerts the reader to a new intensity, a more exacerbated level of armed conflict during the protagonist's ninth and final year in the country of his birth. The narrative begins at the end of a long day of sustained violence in an upscale neighborhood with a bucolic name, Vista Hermosa (beautiful view). That neighborhood was home to the Colegio Americano, one of the most exclusive schools in the country, close to a private, elite university. The memories the narrator brings to mind align with real events that took place in July of 1981, when a guerrilla safehouse was bombed in the area, reportedly killing ten men and four women. This moment of conflict is important not only in the context of the civil war as a whole, but also because it obligated Guatemalans in "safe" urban neighborhoods such as Vista Hermosa to come face to face with a conflict that for many years they had attempted to ignore.[36] After many hours sheltering in place with the rest of their classmates, the narrator and his friend Oscar are finally able to leave aboard a fleet of yellow buses flanked by a police escort. The driver's steering gives them a better view of a tank, as well as a chaotic assortment of soldiers, journalists, paramedics, firemen, and family members of those affected by the violence.

The temporal focus then shifts back to 10 in the morning, when the first shots had sounded.[37] The narrator tells us he hadn't heard those shots, but by the seriousness in the faces of Oscar and his other schoolmates, he can tell something important had happened. Later, they all hear a volley of gunfire. This was the summer of 1981, and these were days characterized by gunfire. But these shots were too close for comfort. Their North American teacher has the kids sing songs and clap along, hoping to drown out the disturbing soundtrack of the nearby streets.[38] Then an enormous explosion shakes the entire school and paralyzes everyone "in silent fright."[39] Even after they are herded into the refuge of a large gym-like room, the wooden floor echoes with the sounds of the shelling, sirens, and helicopters close by. The students are isolated there for almost seven hours, "shut away" from the mêlée. When the protagonist's teenage cousins find him at school to assure him that everything will be fine, he thinks, "But of course everything was going to be fine. Everything was always fine. What could be wrong?"[40]

The school grounds provide a refuge from the violence, as do the police-escorted school buses, as does the boy's home, defended by a guard who sits up all night with a rifle across his lap, and as does the boy's father, though he himself now needs the extra protection of an all-hours bodyguard. This level of protection is both a testament to the growing unrest in the capitol and a shield from it available only to a privileged few with the resources to pay for it. But ultimately it is not enough, either as guarantee of physical safety, or as a barrier to the reality of the war's growing casualties. As their bus advances through the embattled streets, Oscar points out a dirty bundle surrounded by other people, and whispers, "look . . . a dead woman."[41]

Where does weeping fall on the spectrum between sound and silence? All though dinner, the boy's mother cries, though she says nothing. The young women who work in the house, Pía and Márgara, deflect phone calls, asking those on the line to call later. These deferred conversations foreshadow the promised conversation that the boy will never have with his father. Later, the parents appear in the doorway of the bedroom of the boy and his brother, and the father begins to speak in a different tone, "perhaps more nervous or hurried," stammering "chaotically" about the day's fighting, the workers at his textile factory, the Americans, the "Indians," the guerrillas, the Communists, of the kidnapping of the boy's grandfather fifteen years earlier, of the bars they had to install on the windows of the house, of the new bodyguard with a pistol in his waistband, of the new night watchman.[42] Snooping around, the protagonist has even discovered that his dad now sleeps with a gun under his pillow. But the family also has other resources, other options, most notably an apartment on a golf course north of Miami, where they've previously spent family vacations. When his father speaks of their decision to leave the country, there are a few seconds of strange or estranged silence, and then another stubborn silence from both parents when the protagonist asks what to tell his friends when they ask how long he'll be gone. The house has been sold. Their departure is imminent. The child now "understands" why his mother has been crying the entire evening, calling into question once more the "boy in the bubble" characterization.

Irene Levin reminds us of Foucault's emphasis on the power both speech and silence possess: "Foucault refuses to look upon the two as dichotomies. He views silence not as the end of speech nor as the other side of a definite border; rather, silence is in a close relation to speech, in complex social interaction."[43] The loud silence that punctuates "Tomorrow We Never Did Talk About It" suggests the "telling" power of absent speech. As Stephanie Pridgeon notes, "As a way of exploring the identifications between people and the breakdown in transmission of memory . . . silences play a central role throughout the novel."[44] Ilan Stavans, in his afterword to the English version of the story, describes it as the kind of tale in which "what is said, what the narrator understands, and what the reader knows, is as important as what is kept out of sight, what falls into that nothingness we call silence."[45]

The protagonist awakes the day after the armed conflict arrived on the doorstep of his elementary school and is disappointed to find that little has changed. Despite his mother's crying, his father's declaration of their imminent departure, and even what he and his classmates witnessed from the convoy of yellow buses, things seem to be in place around him, with the happy exception that classes have been cancelled. After pleading with his mother, he gets permission to go to Oscar's house, although for the first time, Rolando, a member of the family's staff, has to accompany him, holding his hand the whole way. The boy finds Oscar in the treehouse where he spends time "playing, reading comics, planning pranks, storing forbidden things."[46] On this day, the important forbidden thing is a newspaper Oscar has rescued from the trash, despite his parents' prohibition. Together, the boys look at "two whole pages that told the story of the previous day's battle" and read the headline proclaiming the destruction of a guerrilla headquarters in the Vista Hermosa neighborhood. They look at a photo of something that might be dead bodies and read that "After artillery shelling from a small tank, fourteen guerrillas were crushed to death, eleven men and three women." A curious detail is that in a shelled living room of a house in Vista Hermosa, the lifeless body of one of the guerrillas was found "alongside a charred guitar." An accompanying headshot shows a dark-complexioned indigenous man. The boys read that "'According to the authorities, this guerrilla was identified as Roberto Batz Chocoj, a construction worker from Patzún, Chimaltenango.'"[47]

Halfon's use of quotation marks, infrequent elsewhere in his works, here suggests that the citation incorporates an excerpt from an actual source commenting on the events of 1981. Of course, the specific name, profession, and origin of Batz Chocoj, as well as the quotation marks themselves, could have been invented or imagined; as we have seen, Halfon frequently insists on the fictionality of his works. But in fact, the name Roberto Batz Chocoj appears in *From Silence to Memory: Revelations of the Archivo Histórico de la Policía Nacional* (Historical Archive of the National Police). Volume 1 includes his name in Table III.4 of its report detailing the number of bodies found on July 7, 1981 at the house of the physician José Francisco Meneses in the Vista Hermosa neighborhood. "Three women and seven men, one identified as Roberto Batz Chocoj of 20 years of age" are described as casualties of the military's "Operations Against Guerrilla Safe Houses."[48]

Though the treehouse, the delight at classes being cancelled, and Rolando's handholding remind us that the unnamed narrator and his friend Oscar are still young children, the text they read and the photos they look at together represent real events that both sets of parents, in different ways, have hoped to prevent their children from witnessing. Initially unperturbed as violence rages outside his school ("Everything was always fine. What could be wrong?"), Eduardo's interaction with the news photos and accompanying text marks the start of a problematic process of reckoning for the narrator. The faces of the opposing sides in the struggle are indistinguishable to him: "I stared at the faces of the soldiers, as swarthy and indigenous as the face of the guerrilla with the guitar and the television. I didn't understand. The soldiers were indigenous too? Wasn't every indigenous person a guerrilla? So who then were the guerrillas?"[49] The process of sorting out this confusion implies his recognition of the evident contradictions in the official discourse circulating at the national level as well as at home in the family setting.[50]

From this point forward in the story, the narrator more explicitly foregrounds the indigenous protagonists in the memories relayed. A version of the indigenous figure in the newspaper even visits the boy in a troubled dream, in which "the guerrilla with the charred guitar" comes to his house, greets the security guard who continues to sip coffee as he enters, and then carries the boy's mother away over his shoulder, explaining "he wanted to take her with him to the mountains of Patzún, in Chimaltenango. My mother was calm, didn't seem to protest, didn't seem to mind. My father wasn't there."[51] The security guard's lack of resistance, the mother's unprotesting calm, and the father's absence, all seem to prefigure the distinct forms of engagement (or lack of it) that the boy must carry with him as part of his own "baggage" when he leaves Guatemala, only to wait perpetually for explanations that will help him comprehend these events. Nonetheless, he now understands that "indigenous" fails as a monolithic category, noticing that his piano teacher's face also looks like the face of the guitar-playing guerrilla as well as the face of the soldiers who have killed him.[52]

By reading the forbidden newspaper and identifying guerrillas killed by government forces, at least one of whom can be found by name in an actual chart of the AHPN, the child protagonists of "Tomorrow" reveal key details of the conflict their parents have silenced and from which they have attempted to shield their children. But "Tomorrow We Never Did Talk About It" also points to how these child protagonists still deal with that conflict as adults. And the improbability of simply remembering such a name or citing a source article word-for-word, many decades later from the perspective of adulthood—an improbability confirmed by the use of quotation marks—suggests the "memory" of the boys' treehouse discovery has been enhanced or recreated with verifiable supporting materials.[53] In fact, the newspaper account Oscar rescued from the trash, and the reiteration of certain details in the AHPN report offer two opposing accounts of the incidents, amidst which the narrator who experienced this moment must later navigate, subtly participating in a kind of "archival activism." For Ignacio

Sarmiento, the story functions, then, as part of the "constant reactualization" of the work of mourning by means of a permanent memory of trauma—not primarily the trauma of the bombing in Vista Hermosa or even of the family's flight from Guatemala, but more importantly, of discovering the contradictions of the official discourse around the armed conflict: "So, differently from a work of mourning that looks for closure, that would imply at its most basic level, moving beyond the trauma, Halfon presents us with a narrative in which trauma is constantly revisited. It is only through maintaining mourning as an active process, he believes, that we can interrupt the silence that seeks to impose itself regarding war atrocities."[54]

GUATEMALAN HOLOCAUSTS

A curious aspect of *Mañana nunca lo hablamos* is that it appears to feature no sustained engagement with the theme of Jewish identity, especially when placed side by side with earlier works such as *The Polish Boxer* or later books such as *Mourning*. There are only a few elements, such as the mezuzah on the doorframe in "El último café turco" ("The Last Turkish Coffee") that point explicitly to Jewish life in its pages. It seems the allusions to the Holocaust and religious difference so frequent in Halfon's fictions are absent from this collection. Or are they? Should the human toll of the Guatemalan civil war be read as a kind of holocaust, as the subtitle of Thomas Melville's *Through a Glass Darkly: The US Holocaust in Central America* suggests? And how should we consider this question within an ongoing discussion of the use of the term *holocausts* to refer specifically to the treatment of the country's Mayan populations? It is no accident that Melville's book includes a reproduction of an engraving from the 1598 version of Spanish Dominican priest Bartolomé de Las Casas's *Narratio Regiorum Indicarum per Hispanos quosdam devastatarum verissima*, or the *Brief Narrative of the Destruction of the Indies*. The engraving shows Spanish conquistadors murdering a naked child, while someone else lights a fire under the bodies of naked men and women hung from a crossbeam, their bodies riddled with wounds.[55] By including this engraving portraying torture and massacre during the period of Spanish conquest in his volume, together with a clandestine photo of massacre victims from Panzós piled into the back of a truck during the Guatemalan civil war, Melville decries a five-hundred-year history of Mayan genocide that for him merits the term *holocaust*.[56]

Within a fierce contemporary global debate over the acceptable use or misappropriation of such terms as "holocaust" and "concentration camps," several critics have shown its aptness for describing cases of internal state violence characterized by torture and genocide in Latin America. For Amalia Ran, for example, dictatorships in Argentina and elsewhere represent "Nuestra shoá," our Shoah:

> It's precisely the emergence of the Holocaust as the sum of a totality representative of the twentieth century that permits that its memory be attached to specific situations different from the original event historically and politically ... It's important to clarify that the modification of the Holocaust discourse does not imply the conversion of the original event in something banal, but rather, it opens a space of representation of other national and local traumas silenced up to this moment. Thus, the trope of the Shoah allows us to comply with the mandate to remember the past in order to not repeat it, especially as that refers to claims on the part of victims to recognize the injustices of the past and the rights of collective memory.[57]

The repetition of such moments in literature is thus for Ran a desirable act, as it simultaneously eliminates and reformulates silence into a different sort of national monument.[58]

Along similar lines, Ignacio Sarmiento finds that the use of the autofictional form (discussed elsewhere in this volume) allows Halfon to approach the Guatemalan civil war from a personal and reflexive prism, "without implying that the problematics which he develops can't be read in a broader fashion." At the same time, he finds Halfon to be one of the Central American authors who has best discovered how to use the silences within contemporary narrative, "which can be appreciated in his treatment of traumatic events such as the Jewish holocaust and the Guatemalan civil war" in *The Polish Boxer* and *Mañana nunca lo hablamos*, respectively.[59] In other words, rather than being radically different texts dealing with historical events distant from one another in time and space, Halfon's different works offer opportunities to read such events as somehow related to each other. Jasmine Garsd and Felix Contreras noticed this when they spoke with Halfon for *Alt.Latino*, a US-based public radio program, in 2013. Contreras begins the interview by asking "What does the number 69752 mean?" returning us to the focus on the Auschwitz tattoo on the forearm of the author's grandfather, explored in Chapter 1. Garsd noted in the same interview, "You parallel the Jewish Holocaust, and many, many years later, what happened in Guatemala. Guatemala had a civil war, a genocide, a genocide for which the genocide trials actually recently restarted, against the dictator Efraín Ríos Montt, and you parallel them in a way that is so logical. They're both based in this lexicon of horror." Halfon claims this "logic" was not intentional: "I can only write about one individual when I'm writing (in this case Kalel in 'Distant'), but one man is all of us, isn't he?" "When you see the horror of the Holocaust through one man's survival," he added, "and you see the horror of the genocide in Guatemala, it's the same horror. It's the same oppression, it's the same racism, it's the same thing all over again, whether it be a Jew or an indigenous person. The evilness of the actions, the meanness of the actions, are the same, and they are as appalling. So when placed side by side, they make sense. They're logical, even though they happened far apart in time, far apart in space, they are the same: as deep a wound in both cases."[60]

BETTER NOT SAY TOO MUCH

It seems important to bring into play here a journalistic text published by the *Guardian* in 2015, "Better not say too much: Eduardo Halfon on literature, paranoia and leaving Guatemala." Though a very different text from "Tomorrow We Never Did Talk About It" in terms of genre and venue, "Better not say too much" also takes up the theme of silence. Here, though, it is uncoupled from the idea of the unspoken as a product of memory gaps of a distant childhood, or as a tactic to avoid inconvenient truths. Here, silence is a survival tactic. When the *Guardian* included Halfon's text in its series "The Writing Life Around the World," they prefaced it by acknowledging "how a culture of silence and fear makes life creepily dangerous for writers in his country." Halfon begins by explaining that just after publishing his first book in Guatemala in 2003, his Salvadoran writer friend Horacio Castellanos Moya warned him, over beers, to leave the country as soon as possible. He refers to the "normal, everyday psychotic state" in which individuals live in the Guatemalan context.[61] By this point, the civil war had "ended" almost two decades earlier; yet Halfon still warned that

> Guatemalan writers, and Guatemalans in general, have lived for almost a century now in a climate of fear. If anyone dared to speak out, they either disappeared into exile, or disappeared literally. This fear is still prevalent, woven deep into the subconscious of the Guatemalan people, who over time have been taught to be silent. To not speak out. *To not say or write words that might kill you.* The first consequence of this, of course, is overall silence. Certain things in Guatemala are simply not spoken or written about . . . a second and perhaps more dangerous consequence of a culture of silence is a type of self-censorship: when speaking or writing, one mustn't say anything that puts oneself or one's family in peril. The censoring becomes automatic, unconscious. Because the danger is very real.[62]

The piece ends with an especially disturbing visit from someone he had known "before," ostensibly during his childhood. The person bearing the familiar face enters his house uninvited, places a big black gun on the living room table, and after some small talk, begins to talk about Hitler.

> I was lost. My head was reeling. I remember feeling the sweat rolling down my back. I couldn't keep my eyes off the gun, although I was trying my best to be discreet and not stare at it. And he just kept talking about Hitler—to me, a Jew. He said that Hitler was one of his heroes. He said that Hitler was one of the greatest of men. He said that he admired how Hitler always knew exactly how to dispose of his enemies. He said that we should all learn from Hitler.

Did this unnamed person who entered uninvited into the author's domestic space typically talk about Hitler in his efforts to intimidate those who said too much in the Guatemalan context? Or was Halfon getting special treatment as a self-proclaimed Jew?

The tensions and "paranoia" Halfon describes in "Better Not Say Too Much" may seem melodramatic viewed from a certain distance, but as Marileen LaHaije suggests in a 2020 article, "such narrative techniques lend themselves especially to capturing the alienating dimensions of violence in Central America where paranoia, rather than being a question of truth or exaggeration, constitutes a survival strategy."[63] Analyzing "Better not say too much" alongside the short fiction "Ningún Lugar Sagrado" (No Sacred Place) by fellow Guatemalan author Rodrigo Rey Rosa, LaHaije finds that they complicate an interpretation of paranoia in pathological terms, identifying it instead as a "normal" state and a form of being and surviving in contemporary Central American society: "Far from classifying a paranoid character as a pathological exception, the authors recognize the sociopolitical context of generalized violence in Central America that discharges paranoia."[64] And as we see in other works by Halfon, many of them dealing with settings distant from the region of his birth, his protagonists resolutely come down on the side of survival, whatever it takes. It is in this sense of keep quiet or leave—or even, keep quiet *and* leave—that "Mañana nunca lo hablamos" can be read as a story about exile, despite Halfon's ambivalence about never belonging to Guatemala in the first place.

Several critics read the Halfons' move to Florida as an "exile." According to Vanessa Perdu, *Mañana nunca lo hablamos* "is born of the experience of exile."[65] Browitt mentions it twice in his biographical sketch of the author, noting, "his life not only speaks of cosmopolitanism, but also multiple marginalities" that reflect experiences "from his country of birth through exile."⁶⁶ Pridgeon believes the experience of exile is one of the elements that places the author and his work in the Jewish tradition. But is the Florida experience an exile? There are several obstacles to this reading that merit our attention. First, the family already owns a house in the United States, one they've typically used on vacations, and is thus already familiar to them when they decamp there. Second, the condition of "exile" assumes an unsevered relationship of identification with the country left behind, and very often an even more intense identification with that country due to the forced separation from it. But we don't see that in "Tomorrow We Never Did Talk About It." The title itself suggests an investment in "moving on," in assimilating to the new culture, just as Halfon's immigrant ancestors had done before him. The family's diverse "roots" and transnational origins also complicate the notion of "exile." All four of Halfon's grandparents were immigrants, each from a different place, and his parents are first-generation Guatemalans. Does the departure to the United States constitute an actual exile, then, or is it just another stop on a peripatetic journey? With this multi-strand history, can any one place in the world permanently represent a *home*-land, and thus an exile? Whereas old meanings of exile and its very etymology in Latin refer to forced removal from one's country, banishment, no one has kicked out this family. Instead, adult members of the family choose to leave and return at will, though the child characters do not possess this choice.

Impending departure itself gives rise to a scene in which Guatemalans are united in their differences. As he sits with his indigenous piano teacher for his last lesson in an almost-empty house full only of echoes, he muses: "It occurred to me that his face resembled the face of the guerrilla with the guitar and the television and that it also resembled the faces of the soldiers, and then it occurred to me that his face in some way resembled any face, every face, my face." The teacher offers his hand to the student as a final farewell: "Looking at me, he reached out his long, earthy hand and held it in midair and I took a while to realize that he wanted me to stand up too and reach out my hand, that he wanted us to say goodbye, not as teacher and pupil, not as adult and child, not as indigenous and white, but as two men."⁶⁷ As Perdu observes, the scene stages the erasure of differences and the leveling of the characters as participants in the universal aspects of the human condition. For her, "exile is, symbolically, the entrance to the world of adults" and "from the experience of exile, writing is born."⁶⁸ While I also read this scene as a poignant coming-of-age episode, it strikes me as well as the most notable portrayal of equity in the story, and by extension of belonging to the *pueblo* or Guatemalan peoplehood. As to whether writing is born of exile, it's noteworthy that Halfon did not write during the thirteen years he spent in the US after the family's flight in 1981, and only took up the craft upon returning to Guatemala, where he studied literature together with philosophy, and consciously recovered his maternal language of Spanish as he embarked on a life as a writer.

FRAGILE RECKONINGS AND RECONCILIATIONS

Stephanie Pridgeon has argued persuasively that the experience of the Jewish child in *Mañana nunca lo hablamos* "is one in which he is marked by ethnic difference, yet he is young and vulnerable enough to be moved to affective identification with an ethnic other."[69] What are the possibilities, ultimately, for reconciliation with this other, whether for a child abruptly snatched from his childhood environment, or for the same character who returns to the country as a young adult? The chronicle "Dicho hacia el sur" (Spoken Toward the South) offers something of a continuation of the personal story portrayed in "Tomorrow." Though situated in the Florida landscape to which the protagonists have fled, the tale begins with the subhead "Días de disparos" (Days of shootings), obviously referring to the continuing presence of the Guatemalan conflict for Eduardo and his family. The story begins:

> The day after my tenth birthday, I was split in two. It was August of 1981. They were days of shootings. Guatemala was in political and social chaos. I remember machine gun fire, single shots, combat in the streets and ravines, and even a case in front of the grade school, with all the students sheltered inside. I remember the new security guard who arrived at the house each night and sat next to the main door wrapped in a poncho, with a huge shotgun on his lap and a lukewarm thermos of coffee in his hands. I remember when my parents announced that we were leaving the country . . . The day after my tenth birthday then, we fled with my parents and brother and sister to the United States, and I was split in two.[70]

The use of the anaphora "I remember" three times in this passage insistently draws our focus to scenes of explicit or implicit violence, whether of the machine gun fire in front of an elementary school, a shotgun on a guard's lap, or the parents' announcement the family will be leaving for the US. This latter memory is one of severing or splitting the child's sense of self; it foregrounds the attempts by Halfon and his adult narrator to later reconstitute this self and soothe this memory through writing. His work titled "La memoria infantil," (Childhood Memory), also published in 2011, similarly dialogues with "Tomorrow We Never Did Talk About It." Only a few pages long, it is divided into ten short untitled, enumerated sections preceded by a kind of introduction numbered "O." The text numbered zero is in fact the same text we hear (but don't see) Halfon reading aloud in the publicity video for *Mañana nunca lo hablamos* mentioned at the beginning of this chapter.[71] In my translation, the text begins, "Without setting out to, and almost without realizing it, I return time and again to the narratives of my childhood. The stories of my youth. As if, by writing them, I'd like to also recuperate something or remember something." The subsequent sections in "La memoria infantil" correspond to the ten *relatos* in *Mañana nunca lo hablamos*: Section 1 is a one-paragraph version of "El baile de la marea," Section 2 a recasting of the story "Polvo" about the 1976 earthquake, Section 3 a reframing of "El poder de la euforia," and so on. The perspective in this piece is noticeably different, however. In Section 2, the narrator recognizes that now he knows that 30,000 people died in that earthquake, that a million Guatemalans were left homeless; if he concentrates, he can even remember the smell and hear the silence of the trees without a single bird in them. He remembers the stories and testimonies others began to tell him about the earthquake and explains his relationship to the event from the later landscape of memory:

> I can write—I have written—from that place in my memory. A writer writes from there, after all. From what they have seen. From what they have heard. From the smells and sounds that flutter like black doves in their memory. They don't write their memory. They write only from memory as a starting point. Toward what's ahead. It's a poor memory, Lewis Carroll's queen says, that only works backwards.[72]

Like Carroll's Alice, who learns that memory can work in both directions, Halfon's narrator is also interested in memory as a motor that propels us toward what's ahead. "Narrative memory is not fluid," he declares in the third section of "La memoria infantil." "It's not continuous. Rather than as a film, it manifests as a series of fragmented images . . . I want to give them the flow they don't have . . . The thread that unites them is literature. Literature, weaving them together, imbues them with sense. The craft of the writer is no different from the craft of the tailor. Patches, mendings, seams, threads, remnants that with craft, create the illusion of a whole."[73]

In Section 4 of this rich reflection on childhood memory, "Muerte de un cácher" (Death of a Catcher), the narrator recalls a mysterious childhood head ailment for which he was hospitalized as a child. Immediately after returning home from the hospital where his parents and various doctors disputed the correct course of treatment, he learns of the death of his baseball hero Thurman Munson. Halfon brings these remembrances of childhood into the present, implying the dynamic and ongoing functions of memory:

> Still today I remember, or rather I perceive, deep inside, the sensation of loss, of absence. That's because in memory, sensations are more intense than facts, and absences occupy more space than presences. Something that we did not have, that we lost, that went away, leaves in us an irreparable permanent emptiness. Creating literature is the exercise of wanting to fill the empty spaces of memory, knowing all along it can't be done.[74]

The fifth section of "La Memoria infantil" recalls the narrator's relationship with Rol, a handyman of sorts who lived on the family property in Guatemala. Except here, the two meet after not seeing each other for twenty years, and the protagonist observes, "hearing him speak . . . was like feeling him pull a long, silky cord from the depths of my memory." He finishes the reflection by citing (in Spanish translation) Eudora Welty's contention that "writing fiction has developed in me an abiding respect for the unknown in a human lifetime and a sense of where to look for the threads, how to follow, how to connect, find in the thick of the tangle what clear line persists. The strands are all there: to the memory nothing is ever really lost."[75] Perhaps even more so than lived experiences themselves, the storehouse of memories *about* those experiences offers *materia prima* for Halfon's writing project, the tools for creating an unforgettable through-line.

Indeed, as the narrator concedes in the sixth section of "La memoria infantil," memory is mischievous, *caprichosa*; in the seventh, he contends that storytelling happens from a midpoint between remembering and forgetting. In the eighth, he finds in memory a sexual element, related not only to actual, tactile experiences, but in the pleasure derived from the pure act of remembering, the "delight we perceive upon remembering (finding) something we had forgotten (lost), of that we thought we had lost. The writer, in writing, in writing well, in rummaging around and finally finding the suitable words, experiences this same pleasure." In the ninth section, our narrator-guide declares that "fiction-making is the art of manipulating memory." The tenth and final section closely resembles "Dicho hacia el sur," also beginning, "The day after my tenth birthday, I was split in two." Here, though, he ends by adding, "My language was split in two. My memory was split in two. A piece of my memory, the first, the lightest and most diaphanous, remained suspended in the Guatemala of the seventies. From here, from each blank sheet of paper, I keep looking for it."[76]

As Halfon told an interviewer many years later, this process of reassembly had already begun in Guatemala: "In reality, I was torn even before we left. We fled, that's the way I say it, though my parents don't like me using that term. But it's true: they sold the house, they took us out of school, and we left with no intention of coming back. But even before that, I have this sensation of an identity torn asunder, because I grew up in one of the very few Jewish families in a country that was entirely Catholic." Halfon has also claimed, "I don't have any rootedness in any one plot of ground on any one corner of the earth. I don't feel that I belong . . . I travel with the hope of finding my piece of the earth. [Pause] And I never find it." When Gustavo Mota Leyva asked him what defined him as a Guatemalan, he replied with a smile, "the passport."[77] Paradoxically, the action initiated to help the family hold together, to survive the strife around them, is also the action that initiates a severing of the self, not just from a territory, but from a language and from the memories contextualized in that place and that tongue:

> Leaving in '81 only emphasized and made official this feeling of being torn apart, and there, I fractured into more pieces. Other parts of me begin to break: language, for example . . . So, in linguistic terms I also split. But I didn't become a North American. It's not that I abandon one homeland for another. I just simply go along adding other aspects to my identity. The sensation of tearing [*desgarramiento*] is one I've had as long as I can remember.[78]

This reference to sensations of tearing or splitting brings to mind Claudio Guillén's description of exile as situation of loss, impoverishment or "even a mutilation of the person in a part of themselves. . . . The I feels broken, and its own psychosocial nature fragmented."[79]

What is the work of "Tomorrow We Never Did Talk About It," finally? As Ortiz Wallner suggests, the volume in which it appears represents a postwar, post-conflict intervention in which there is no direct denunciation, but rather, violence is contained in indirect, submerged, and allegorical forms.[80] No sides are taken explicitly.[81] The focalization from a child's perspective, a child who is first sheltered and shielded, and then abruptly spirited away from that idealized scene and installed in a house on a golf course in a place called Plantation where he perpetually awaits the answers to his questions, produces a kind of mourning that is also perpetually incomplete. At the same time, the story rejects, at least implicitly, the official discourse of forced silence and forgetting as the correct tools for rebuilding the national community.[82] The pages of this text thus bear witness to the potential weaponization of silence as violence, as a dangerous suppression of the evidence recuperated in texts such as *From Silence to Memory*. While the narrator as an adult may recall the simplicity or purity in the "white space" of childhood, he also recognizes that superimposed on this white space is the black hole of what remains untold.

Indeed, the story begins and ends without explicitly mentioning a civil war or war of any kind. Halfon represents the Guatemalan internal conflict and genocide, like the Holocaust before it, less as a historical moment marked by beginning and end dates, and more as an ongoing engagement (or refusal to engage) with trauma, mourning, and memory at the level of the individual family and the state itself. In the final lines of "Tomorrow We Never Did Talk About It," the confused child is literally left in the dark, despite his father's declaration, "We'll talk about it tomorrow": "He left our room and turned off the white hallway light. Everything went back to being black and still."[83] With the triple repetition of "Tomorrow We Never Did Talk About It" as the title of the book's last story, the last words in that story and the final words in the book itself, as well as the name Halfon chooses for the book as a whole, it's left to the reader to continue grappling with this "it" that has been forcibly silenced in official discourse and around the family table but not expunged from intergenerational memory.

As we shall see, the author himself will also continue with this grappling. In an interview that coincided with the launch of his 2021 volume *Canción*, Halfon noted, "I felt that little by little I was getting closer not just to writing about my grandfather's life and his Lebanese identity, but also to writing about the recent history of my country, about the internal armed conflict."[84] For him and for us, the work of recounting the untold and ultimately uncountable traumas of Guatemala's violent legacies continues.[85]

CHAPTER 5

ACTS AND ARTS OF SURVIVAL

> *I see all literature as small prayers. A story, or a poem, or a novel, is a form of prayer, or should be written and read as such.*

FAMILY DRAMA IN THE PROMISED LAND

In Eduardo Halfon's *Monastery*, published in 2014, a family trip to Israel provides a theater in the round for a vexed interrogation of what it means to be Jewish, Guatemalan, a grandson, a son, a brother, a love interest, a tourist, and all these things at once.[1] The author has categorized the work as a "short novel" and an offshoot of *The Polish Boxer*: "It's a continuation of the story of one of its characters. It takes place in Israel and delves even deeper into my identity as a Jew who doesn't want to be one. Or something like that."[2] The reader is obliquely invited to accompany the protagonist through this "affective, emotional, subjective cartography" in which the narrator functions, as in earlier works explored in previous chapters, as a keeper of Jewish memories.[3] Only in the last chapter of *Monastery* will we discover that its un-Jewish title paradoxically alludes to various Holocaust-era efforts to hide or change one's identity, in order to survive, to stay alive.

In the opening salvo, "Tel Aviv was an Inferno," blood ties oblige the narrator to travel to Israel to attend his sister's wedding to an Orthodox Jew, though neither he nor his brother want to be there. Mercifully, almost miraculously, before he's out of the Tel Aviv airport he has a chance encounter with Tamara, an Israeli woman he'd had met years earlier in a faux-Scottish bar in Guatemala. That encounter, first described in "White Smoke" in *The Polish Boxer*, is renovated and recounted in this later volume. In the final story, which gives the book its title, Eduardo and Tamara will sunbathe by the Dead Sea and discuss the tricks of Jewish survival, including changing names, languages, religious beliefs, and even one's gender, by dressing or undressing for the occasion, by hiding in a monastery, by passing as the Other even when such actions might be read as disloyalty or betrayal to who one is as a Jew.

Beginning and ending *Monastery* with episodes set in Israel stages this excursion in a way that could hardly be more symbolic, incorporating stops at the emblematic *Kotel* or Wailing Wall, a Haredi Orthodox neighborhood, and the Dead Sea. While Eduardo expresses annoyance more often than amazement at these revered sites, the grumbling protagonist also finds that his Holy Land tour frequently jogs his memory, catapulting him to other moments and sites embossed in family and personal history. An unpleasant encounter with an anti-Arab taxi driver, for example, prompts him to review the migratory odysseys of his three Arab-Jewish grandparents as well as his Polish grandfather. When he touches the stones of the remaining wall of the Kotel, he feels little more than vertigo, but it reminds him of touching another history-laden wall on an earlier pilgrimage to Poland.

It's possible to read the first and last sections of *Monastery* as contrapuntal "love" stories that present starkly different encounters with this sacred ground. In the opening pages, the narrator explains that his sister has been living in Israel for almost two years, studying Torah at a women's yeshiva: "At first we all thought it was just a touch of Zion fever, or Hebrew fever, or some juvenile obsession with finding a deeper manifestation of our grandparents' religion, and that it would eventually pass." Despite the story being set in this holiest of Jewish geographies, the protagonist is skeptical of his sister's newfound fervor, for him generated from a too narrow view of Judaism. In fact, the story places the pending marriage in a context of loss—of his sister's given name, of others' enjoyment of her beauty, of her exercise of her own freedom—rather than a context of celebration of his sister finding her *besheirt* or soulmate. The protagonist laments the fact that in letters and phone calls, the sister's words "were no longer her own;" she has relinquished her given name and adopted one in Hebrew; she has sent photos to Guatemala in which her "lovely black curls" are hidden under a wig or scarf and her body is lost under "long baggy dresses that didn't reveal her shoulders, or her neck, or her arms, and certainly not her legs. As though she were a prisoner of her own attire." The protagonist remembers the one time she returned to Guatemala during her yeshiva studies in Israel, a moment when "the five us were sitting around the dining room table at my parents' house, when my sister announced coldly that, as far as she and the Orthodox rabbis and teachers saw it, the four of us were not Jews. My father yelled once or twice. My mother stood and stormed off in tears, and my brother went after her. Well, I replied, at least that's one thing we agree on."[4]

It's very clear from these first paragraphs of *Monastery*, with its Catholic-sounding title, that Jewishness, paradoxically, is in the balance and on trial. While the sister finds new religious and romantic fervor in rituals practiced in a separatist community, the narrator's parents and brother seem to define their Jewishness in a very different way, more as an established fact, confirmed in their bloodlines and long-term affiliations. The protagonist, for his part, defiantly agrees with his sister that he is no longer a Jew, not because he has failed to follow the rules of an orthodox practice, but because he has chosen, voluntarily, to "retire" from the condition.[5] But as we shall see in subsequent pages, *Monastery* often seems like a test to see if such a choice—that of fully rejecting one's Jewishness—is even possible.[6]

The erotic encounter between the protagonist and the Israeli woman he had first met in a bar in Antigua years earlier offers a stark counternarrative to the sister's upcoming marriage to an orthodox groom from Brooklyn. Waiting at baggage claim after the long flight, the protagonist spots Tamara, who first appeared in *The Polish Boxer*, now attired as a flight attendant for Lufthansa. In language reminiscent of a Petrarchan sonnet or the *Song of Songs*, though perhaps more cheeky here, the speaker recognizes Tamara by studying her lips and her pale freckled cheeks, noticing her blue Mediterranean eyes, and recognizing her timid smile and her copper hair, the latter now streaked with gray. "Would she remember me after all these years?" he wonders. "Would she hug me or kiss me or maybe even slap me?"[7] And indeed, Tamara, blushing, does recognize him; she is in fact the first character to identify the protagonist as Eduardo, using his name in a unique way that transports him back to the beers they shared in Guatemala, back to a "heart-shaped mouth and nipples that were to be bitten hard or soft, it all depended."[8] Tamara offers Eduardo her number and he promises to call, though he doesn't understand Hebrew well enough to determine whether her last words are a goodbye or an admonition.

Can either of these contrasting "love" stories be considered a romance? If so, we can anticipate a comic denouement in which marriage and unity prevail, rather than the classic themes of separation, disharmony, war, and destruction that characterize tragedy.[9] But like the principal protagonist, we never arrive at the sister's wedding, and the erotic charge of the reconnection between Eduardo and Tamara never detonates, at least not explicitly. Instead, readers witness a series of confrontations between Eduardo and other family members, as well as his own intensely mixed feelings about Israel and all it represents. If Eduardo has been iffy about his Jewish identity on other occasions, here his disenchantment comes to a head. The setting is important; it is one thing to be ambivalent about one's Jewish identity in Guatemala, where the Jews are few and sometimes invisible, and a different matter altogether to express such ambivalence in Israel itself. Instead of fulfilling its role as the sacred site of *aliyah* or return, instead of serving as the City of Peace, here Jerusalem is the scene of family feuds both petty and profound. Only at the end of *Monastery*, as Eduardo contemplates Tamara's contours as the two discuss the uses of salt on a secret beach along the Dead Sea, will the riddle of Jewishness be considered in a more positive light. But even before that, Tamara serves as a kind of harmonic opposite to the protagonist's sister, who Eduardo claims no longer speaks her own words and is a prisoner of the clothes that engulf her and hide her beauty. Just the thought of Tamara, on the other hand, produces in Eduardo a "a sense of well-being or optimism."[10]

TENSION AND INTENTION

Climbing into a taxi in this promised land rendered hellish by the heat, Eduardo confronts a driver who, upon ascertaining that his passenger is from Guatemala, wants to make sure he is on the right team: "But Jewish? he shouted, almost insolently. I smiled and said: Sometimes." The driver, for whom such fluid categories are unacceptable, demands, "What do you mean, sometimes? his eyes squinting, his question abusive, his voice abrasive and obstructed, as though he were talking with a mouthful of grapes." Clearly, Jewishness cannot be a part-time or hybrid identity for this character—"Arab? he asked, and I said no." Though Eduardo answers in the negative, this us-or-them choice is a kind of trick question for the protagonist, even a trap question, since by responding yes, he declares himself the default enemy, and by responding no, he betrays his three Arab-Jewish Sephardic grandparents, one from Syria, one from Lebanon, and one from Egypt. Upon hearing his "no," the driver unleashes his "homily of hatred," insisting, "Bad people, Arabs . . . very bad. We have to kill them . . . Filthy people . . . We must kill the Arabs, he shouted again into the rearview mirror. You don't think? he asked, observing me, perhaps challenging me."[11]

This tirade sets a dark tone, anticipating other behaviors that strike the protagonist as extremist, such as his sister's association with the ultraorthodox sect and its views toward women, his future brother-in-law's devotion to the religious leaders of Kiryat Mattersdorf, a Haredi neighborhood in Jerusalem, or the way the Orthodox faithful besiege him at the Kotel.[12] Rather than inspiring a new level of connection with Jewishness, as has occurred with his sister, Israel produces in the narrator disturbing associations and dark thoughts:

> It struck me then, watching my brother stand there in front of all the gray buildings of Kiryat Mattersdorf, that the discourse about Judaism being in the blood, the discourse about Judaism not being a religion but something genetic, sounded the same as the discourse used by Hitler.
> There are thoughts that jump up, dark and clammy, like little frogs.[13]

The protagonist's encounter with holy ground is so tense and so *intense*, we can't help but wonder if the author himself had a similar experience of displacement and distrust on a visit to Israel. Did the scene with the nasty taxi driver happen to Halfon himself or did he invent it for dramatic effect?

Such questions ultimately lead us to see that *Monastery*, like Halfon's other works, successfully interpolates recuperated memory and literary invention. Once again, Halfon builds in interplay between fact and fiction, employing a narrator that is not him, but who talks like him and travels to the same places. Just as choosing between "Jewish" or "Arab" involves a trap for his protagonist, given his multiply diasporic family history, so too does neatly dividing lived experience from textual representation produce a pitfall. Whether or not some part of the text occurred in real life ends up being a moot point, as even a story that hews true to what happened on the ground necessarily involves selection, reassembly, and creative refashioning.

Following his confrontation with the xenophobic taxi driver, the character Eduardo can't stop thinking about his "three parts Arab," which include a maternal grandmother born in Aleppo, with children born in Mexico, Panama, Cuba and Guatemala; a paternal grandfather whose seven brothers and sisters settled in Paris, Guatemala, Mexico, Cali, Lima, Havana, and Manhattan after the family fled Beirut; and his paternal grandmother, who at age seven boarded a ship in Alexandria destined for Panama, but from which the family disembarked in Guatemala "by accident."[14]

When he finds himself at the Kotel, "so solemn and biblical, that final vestige of the Temple of the Jews, of my ancestors," he is annoyed by the Orthodox adherents who tug at his clothes, stalking and circling like the buzzards in The Cure's "Wailing Wall." He touches the wall, but all he feels is stone, rather than the religious epiphany the typical Jewish traveler to the Holy City anticipates. As María Paz Oliver notes, unlike the religious tourist's traditional attitude of awe toward the landscape before him, Eduardo's reaction to the Jerusalem experience is marked by distrust and isolation.[15] Indeed, the protagonist's "Jerusalem Syndrome" seems the polar opposite to the phenomenon observed by Moshe Kalian and Eliezer Witztum, psychiatrists who studied the high frequency of religious claims of tourists hospitalized in the city. This trip that for many constitutes a sacred pilgrimage to the source of their religious tradition drives Halfon's protagonist to more vociferously insist on being a Jew only "sometimes."[16]

Nonetheless, the family trip to Israel ultimately triggers memories of a different trip to a different city where Eduardo had touched another wall, a remnant of the Warsaw ghetto. "I touched it several times, from several angles, at both ends, with both hands. And I didn't feel anything there either. Or maybe I refused to feel anything."[17] His European trip, recalled in the first and last stories of *Monastery*, reinscribes the sacred not in the Promised Land, but in the intimacy of family memory, reconfiguring the role of the pilgrim as a personal and emotive search for his Polish grandfather's past and his own.[18]

ON BEING GUATEMALAN

"Tel Aviv Was an Inferno" ends with Tamara appearing at Eduardo's hotel, dressed in short shorts instead of her stewardess uniform, inviting him to accompany her to an undisclosed location. Before arriving at the secret site to which she has invited Eduardo and the reader, however, there are six other narrative waystations to traverse in *Monastery*. While the volume's first story stages a testy encounter with Jewish identity, the protagonist alternately questions and defends his Guatemalan nationality in the quartet of stories that follows: "Bamboo," "The Birds are Back," "White Sand, Black Stone" and "White Smoke."

In "Bamboo," the first of the "Guatemala suite," we find the protagonist stretching his legs in Iztapa, on the country's Pacific coast. A street vender named Doña Tomasa has handed him a tortilla filled with cracklings and the spicy condiment chiltepe on a piece of newspaper, asking where he is from. He responds that he is Guatemalan, just like her, but suspects Doña Tomasa still has her doubts.

> I don't know why I always find it hard to convince people, to convince myself even, that I'm Guatemalan. I suppose they expect to see someone darker and squatter, someone who looks more like them, to hear someone whose Spanish sounds more tropical. And I never pass up any opportunity to distance myself from the country either, literally as well as literarily. I grew up abroad. I spend long stretches of time abroad. As though I were a perpetual migrant. I blow smoke over my Guatemalan origins until they grow dimmer and hazier.[19]

While this admission to feeling "no nostalgia, no loyalty, no patriotism" might suggest complete disengagement with the country of his birth, the protagonist's attitude is much more complex. Walking through town on his way to the beach, he sees a dark and narrow warehouse where the floor is covered with sharks, all of which "seemed to be floating in a mire of brine and guts and blood and more sharks. The stench was almost unbearable." As with his visit to Lake Amatitlán in *Mourning*, published several years later, the narrator-protagonist refuses to idealize the scene, boldly focusing on decay and stench. He notices that many of the sharks are missing their fins, suggesting the illicit slaughter of the fish in order to harvest only a tiny piece of their flesh. The image of the sharks is so arresting, Eduardo feels compelled to stop the car and write it down, to "capture it, share it through words. But words are not sharks. Or maybe they are," he thinks, adding an allusion to Cicero.[20] The dead and gutted sharks are not the only disturbing image on Eduardo's path to the shore. He also encounters a lurching, half-naked man lying in a puddle of mud in a bamboo cage, a prisoner "to some kind of evil, or alcohol, or dementia, or poverty, or something much bigger and more profound." Needing to feel the bamboo bars of that cage in his own hands, perhaps to counter his own indifference or that of the entire country, seems an apt metaphor for trying to break the spell of estrangement he feels toward Guatemala itself.[21]

The following story, "The Birds Are Back," finds the narrator on a steep hill in La Libertad, in the temperate highlands of Huehuetenango, just a few kilometers from the Guatemalan border with Mexico. He provides a microhistory of this "notoriously dangerous and violent part of the country," associated with the revolutionary wars fought against President Manuel Estrada at the turn of the twentieth century, with the military abuses and massacres of the Civil War in the late twentieth century, and with narcotrafficking in the contemporary era. In La Libertad, even the boy who offers to shine his shoes wonders about the visitor's origins. "Where're you from? the boy asked, and I said in my best Guatemalan accent that I was Guatemalan, same as he was. He smiled, not looking at me, incredulous. Don't look like it, he mumbled."[22] But Eduardo is not in La Libertad for a shoeshine. He visits the home of the Martínez family, who run a coffee cooperative and have a mustachioed cat named Hitler, a tragicomic detail suggesting this will be another dark tale, though tinged with humor.[23] The grief the Martínez family displays following the murder of their son and brother Osmundo prompts Eduardo to think about his own "sibling dance" with its quarrels and fights, the episode of his sister's Israeli wedding the "hardest and most silent" of them.

"White Sand, Black Stone" takes readers to another extreme of the Guatemalan territory, Melchor de Mencos, the last Guatemalan town on its northeastern flank before crossing into Belize. Here, the protagonist's Guatemalan bona fides are called into question once more, as he pleads with the border officials to overlook his expired Guatemalan passport. Somehow locating a Spanish passport amid his belongings, he holds it together with his Guatemalan passport and tells the officer, "I am many . . . But today . . . I am two."[24] As so often occurs in Halfon's works, a contemporary experience calls forth the memory of a past one. Toward the end of "White Sand, Black Stone," the protagonist remembers how his Polish grandfather, after a heart attack in his seventies, had taken up walking, only to be robbed on Guatemala City's Avenida de las Américas, right by the statue of Pope John Paul II: "They knocked him to the ground, he told us later, outraged. They gave him a blow to the head, he said, showing us where. They wanted to kidnap him, he said, perhaps now exaggerating what had been a simple robbery. They took everything he had on him, he said, now indignant, or almost everything, now proud." The black pinky ring, bought from a Jewish jeweler in Harlem in 1945, on the first stop of his grandfather's journey to Guatemala after being released from Sachsenhausen, was still on his grandfather's hand, though he would provide contradictory versions of all these events: "Which version he told depended on the passing of the years, or on his nostalgia, or on his mood, or on the character of the person who was asking him (my grandfather understood, maybe at an intuitive level, that a story grows, changes its skin, does acrobatics on the tightrope of time; he understood that a story is really many stories)."[25]

For Eduardo's maternal grandfather, the black pinky ring is worth defending above all other possessions because it represents his covenant of mourning for his parents, siblings, and friends exterminated by the Nazis in the ghettos and concentrations camps. Though it would later be stolen from an office safe after his grandfather's death, the ring retained such talismanic power, that there on the border of Belize, even if he knew it was impossible, preposterous, or absurd, Eduardo imagines that the ring he sees on the hand of the man before him holding a tortilla is the same ring.

Whoever the thief, and wherever the ring is hidden, even if in plain sight on someone's hand on the Belizean border, it remains a kind of magic "mood" ring or miniature diorama and site of memory, because

> in that insignificant and somber black stone, one could still see the perfect reflections of my grandfather's exterminated parents (Samuel and Masha), and the faces of my grandfather's exterminated sisters (Ula and Rushka), and

the face of my grandfather's exterminated brother (Zalman) and the faces of so many exterminated men and women and boys and girls and babies who were killed as they slept in the arms of their mothers, as they dreamed in the gas chambers.

Not only can the ring, wherever it is, provide the visual record of so many individuals erased or exterminated in the context of the Holocaust; it can also produce an oral or aural record for the generations that follow, as "in that small black stone it was still possible to hear the murmur of all those voices, of so many voices, intoning in chorus the prayer for the dead."[26] The black pinky ring, in which one can still see the faces of murdered relatives, and in which one can hear their silenced voices, is the closest we may come in Halfon's work to the "magical real." We note, however, that this most treasured family possession is tied, *not* to an exuberant Latin American natural environment, as with Gabriel García Márquez's yellow butterflies, for example, but to Holocaust memory and the recuperation of the semblances and voices of its murdered victims.[27]

Finally, in a reworked version of "White Smoke" which first appeared in *The Polish Boxer*, the protagonist finds himself in a Scottish bar or one that passes as such in Antigua, yet another stop on the Guatemalan national tour imbedded in *Monastery*. It's the faux Scottish bar where he meets Israeli tourist Tamara, the woman who will "later" reappear in the first story of the volume. They exchange words, some in English and some in Hebrew, and a few in Spanish, before she confesses, perplexed, that she had no idea "there was such a thing as Guatemalan Jews." "I'm not Jewish anymore," the protagonist explains, "I retired." But Tamara protests, "What do you mean, not Jewish anymore, that's not possible." The narrator confounds her further, claiming not to believe in God either: "You don't consider yourself a Jew and you don't believe in God? She asked reproachfully, and I just shrugged and asked what for and went to the bathroom before there was any chance to start on such a pointless topic."[28]

In this suite of stories set in different corners of the Guatemalan territory, a grouping in turn sandwiched between the book's beginning and endpoints in the so-called Promised Land, movement produces memory, and vice versa. Whether telling the story—however obliquely—of a violent murder in La Libertad, or of dead sharks and a man in a bamboo cage in a town on the Pacific coast, or of the seeming reappearance of a pinky-ring sized memorial to the Holocaust dead on a man's hand at the border of Belize, or of the existence of Guatemalan Jews, even one who says in a bar in Antigua with a smile that he isn't one anymore, all four stories re-collect individual lived experiences as crucial pieces of the puzzle of what it means to be Guatemalan. In all these passages, the narrator seems to be asking less who he is (indeed, he seems more intent on ascertaining who or what he is *not*), than asking who those around him are, and what is their truth. Moving between peoples and languages, from one tragic or tragicomic scene to another, he reveals the open wounds of the country of his birth. Through it all, Halfon seems to be on a perpetual quest to simultaneously question and acknowledge Jewish memory as a sacred source of creativity. If, as Jonathan Sarna contends, cultural forgetfulness is a tool of ideological consolidation, then this kind of remembering is an exercise of both personal and communal liberation, not just religious belligerence.[29]

WALL TO WALL

The final, titular story of *Monastery* transports us back to Jerusalem, to Tamara's Citroen waiting outside the Hotel Kadima. When Eduardo asks where they're going, she won't tell him, asking instead about his brother, who, given the resemblance, was the one standing next to him at the airport. She comments on how much they look alike, but Eduardo insists on their many differences. Tamara asks about his sister, and when the wedding will take place. The protagonist replies that he decided not to go, that he can't go or he doesn't want to go. As she rolls a joint of hashish, steering with her elbows, Tamara begins to tell Eduardo the different names for the West Bank wall that appears alongside the highway: "The Israelis call it security fence, or separation wall, or antiterrorist fence. . . . The Palestinians call it the wall of racial segregation, or the new wall of shame, or the apartheid wall. . . . The international media, according to their political slant, call it wall or fence or barrier, depends."[30] Though he doesn't particularly like hash, Eduardo partakes, and the drug affects his experience of the "immense" wall, so much longer, thicker, more imposing than he had pictured. "I felt a profound desire to touch it," he says.[31]

Though Tamara is driving fast, Eduardo thinks he sees an image flash by of a black Banksy painting of a girl with a braid, floating skyward with the help of a bouquet of balloons. The mention of the famous 2005 work by Banksy, titled "Flying Balloon Girl" or "Balloon Debate," seems like an innocent enough allusion, but implicitly calls attention to the way in which what's expressed *on* a wall, and especially on this wall, can assume its own significance and multiple meanings.[32] Illustrating this point, Anna Ball begins her 2012 essay "Impossible Intimacies: Towards a Visual Politics of 'Touch' at the Israeli-Palestinian Border," with an analysis of Banksy's "touching" image and its diverse meanings for the individuals and collectives positioned along the wall. If for some viewers Banksy's "whimsical portrait of childhood innocence" represents "a daring transgression of authoritarian boundaries, his physical and artistic touch upon the Wall serving as a form of transnational and experiential empathy," others have found it offensive. Banksy himself described how a Palestinian man approached him and told him his work made the Wall look beautiful. But when Banksy thanked him for this compliment, the man countered, "We don't want this wall to be beautiful, we hate it. Go home."[33] Despite Banksy's proximity to the Wall, it would seem that something eluded his grasp; not the ability to touch, but the ability to be touched by the border and its realities for those on both sides.[34]

Once again, this wall reverberates with other walls, especially "the brick walls of a ghetto, the walls surrounding an entire people imprisoned in a ghetto, starving in a ghetto, dying slowly and silently."[35] Despite the "delicious lethargy" of the hash, Eduardo perceives

> that a wall is the physical manifestation of man's hatred of the other. A palpable, concrete manifestation that attempts to separate us from the other, isolate us from the other, eliminate the other from our sight and from the world. But it's also a clearly useless manifestation: no matter how tall and thick the construction, a wall is never insurmountable. A wall is never bigger than the spirit of those it confines. Because the other is still there. The other doesn't disappear, never disappears. The other's other is me. Me, and my spirit, and my imagination, and my black balloons.[36]

This passage from *Monastery* signifies on several levels, some less obvious than others. While, as Nicolás Campisi argues, it may reflect Halfon's impulse "of tearing down nationalistic barriers (the emphasis on walls, or *muros*, is no accident) in order to create an affective community of compassion and solidarity with the victims of human struggles, particularly the Holocaust and the Israeli-Palestinian conflict," it also suggests that Halfon considers the limitations of his writing project as a Banksyan effort to express a common cause with such victims, only to realize that good intentions, and even good art, cannot on their own make amends for the injustices he witnesses.[37] It's also notable that Halfon's protagonist does not experience revelation or epiphany in the expected Israeli settings such as the Western Wall, but in alternate contexts like the imposing West Bank wall built around the Palestinian enclave near the Qalandia checkpoint where Banksy painted his balloon girl. And even if *Monastery* predates the most intense debate surrounding its fast-tracked construction and continuing controversial role in the twenty-first century, it's hard not to read Eduardo's definition of these Israeli walls in relation to the physical barriers constructed along the border of the United States and Mexico as well.

THE LAST PRAYER

"Monastery" finally deposits Tamara and Eduardo on a private beach along the Dead Sea. Tamara tells Eduardo to take off his clothes, and he ponders her bikini-clad body as she tells him about salt, how Egyptian priests believed it increased sexual desire, how the Romans referred to a man in love as *salax*, from which we get the word salacious, and about a host of Jewish customs also related to salt. This salty-spicy eroticism of the idyll at the seashore is attenuated, however, by Eduardo's recollection of his trip to Warsaw, of his reluctance to travel to Auschwitz, where his grandfather had been a prisoner, and by his recognition, finally, that his grandfather's history was also his, and that "our history is our only patrimony."[38] As he undresses, he feels in his pocket a slip of paper, one that will remind him of another slip of paper, a scrap of yellowed paper his grandfather had given him, inscribed with the address of the apartment in Łódź where Leib Tanenbaum was living when he was captured by the Gestapo in 1939 at age sixteen, setting in motion his long journey through several concentration camps and on to Guatemala. The narrator receives this paper from his grandfather's hands as "a mandate. An order. A dictate. An itinerary. A travel guide. A few coordinates on the mysterious and uneven map of our family. It was, in short, a prayer. His last prayer."[39] This textual testament will propel him forward to retrace whatever bits and fragments of his grandfather's history that can still be recuperated.

The number written on the yellow paper, together with the number written on his grandfather's forearm, are "artifacts of memory" that "prompt journeys to the site of traumatic origin but also to life before the rupture, the attempted fulfillment of the desire to recreate lives not defined solely by the trauma of the Shoah," notes Victoria Aarons in "Found Objects: The Legacy of Third-Generation Holocaust Memory." The narrator of "Monastery" grasps the yellowed paper "like a lifeline" and is "struck by both the inadequacy and the power of this material referent of the past to direct him to a legacy that he now anxiously and only tangentially bears." Even recognizing the sacred trust the address represents is not without its mixed feelings, as the narrator "both fears and desires this legacy, for its conditions set loose by his grandfather's deathbed gesture, provide an opening into a traumatic history, a past that, once given voice, is now uncontained."[40] Indeed, those in the third generation like Halfon and his Halfonesque narrator occupy a unique position toward history, as they "are likely to be the last to remember Holocaust survivors as living people," and they are the ones who will "carry these memories of survivors and their contemporaries into a future where one day there will no longer be anyone alive who remembers the atrocities of Nazi Europe and the lost world of pre-Holocaust European Jewry."[41] As the first quarter of the twenty-first century ends, marking as well eight decades since the end of World War II, this "future" is now upon us, further highlighting the role of those in the third, fourth, and subsequent generations. As Andrea Hepworth noted in an article published in 2017, "one could argue that the third—and in some cases also the fourth—generation is at a junction between communicative and cultural memory, able to combine, transform and thereby transcend both forms of memory before the loss of the survivor generation."[42]

Halfon has recognized his role as both a recipient of communicative memory and a transformer of cultural memory, though he acknowledges that this task is not always easy. In an interview with Dwyer Murphy conducted before *Monastery* was published, Halfon spoke of visiting Łódź, of finding his grandfather's home there, still standing, still in use, of going to Warsaw, Auschwitz, and even Block 11, the notoriously deadly section of Auschwitz where his grandfather was held. "That was the trip. But to go from trip to fiction is not an easy bridge to cross," he told Dwyer.[43] As in "The Polish Boxer" and other allusions to his grandfather's saga in the Nazi camps dispersed throughout Halfon's fictions, whatever he discovers or uncovers does not and cannot disclose a full history of those events or provide the protagonist or his readers with closure. Like the story recounted to him by his grandfather, his knowledge and understanding of the trauma that occurred at those sites "can only exist in outline, intimations of the truth, like all clues, imperfect, partial," returning to Aarons's analysis.[44] Processing this firsthand but after-the-fact experience in fact creates additional challenges, additional responsibility, and additional vulnerability.

Eduardo finally tells Tamara of a recurring dream he has, in which he is on a plane hijacked by Arab terrorists. He uses the few words of Arabic he knows from his Lebanese grandfather to try to convince the terrorists not to shoot him. He even resorts to claiming "I'm not a Jew" when an Arab is about to put a bullet in his head. Even in his dreams, it seems, Eduardo denies his roots, his tradition, his heritage, Tamara observes. Eduardo defends himself, claiming "it's the same as a Jew passing himself off as someone else, disguising himself as someone else to escape the Nazis . . . it's better to be a living liar than a dead Jew."[45] *Monastery* closes with Eduardo recounting the tales of Peter, a Jew in Guatemala who survived by assuming the name of a Polish lumberjack, and of a friend's great-grandfather who survived by disguising himself as a German soldier named Neuman, a name he carried to his grave in Argentina, and of Jerzy Kosinski and his family, who lived as Catholics, putting the Virgin Mary and crucifixes on the wall, and of a prisoner named Kasik who escaped from Auschwitz dressed as an SS lieutenant, and finally, of an old Polish Jew he'd met who had escaped the Nazis dressed as a little Catholic girl, hidden in a monastery.[46] The monastery, it turned out, had been both a prison and a refuge, the survivor a captive to "another language, other prayers, other clothing, another identity." "Everyone decides how to save themselves," Eduardo tells Tamara finally, whether as a lumberjack or a Catholic girl with braids or as an Orthodox Jew, like his sister.[47]

This list of survivor stories is not just a defense of lying to stay alive, whether in life or in dreams, however. Erotic energy frames their enumeration, presenting desire as an antidote to the humiliations and losses of personal and collective history. Before telling Tamara of Peter, her hair brushes Eduardo's thigh and he adroitly adjusts his swim trunks. Arriving finally at the story of the boy who escaped as a girl sequestered in a monastery, he tries not to look "at the slightly raised red mound between her thighs that might have been the gentle rise of her warm vulva." What does it mean, finally, to invest these scenes of deception in the interest of survival with an erotic charge? What does it mean to tell tales of Jewish survival together with that of Louis Réard, the French engineer who invented the bikini in 1946? For Halfon, eroticism is "an escape valve, almost a juxtaposition between two things that are apparently opposed, like talking to Tamara about salvation while playing with her leg at the same time."[48] For Francine Prose, by punctuating his preoccupations or obsessions with violence and mass murder in Europe and Latin America with the pleasures of food, sex, humor, cigarettes, beer, and the natural world, Halfon *consoles* us.[49] In *Monastery*, survival itself might be viewed as a sacred and miraculous act, and the recounting of such acts might be heard as a love song to life itself. The novel ends with Tamara's hand on his thigh, but we don't know where it will travel from there. As for the wedding to which we never arrive in *Monastery*, maybe the protagonist or the author ends up attending, or maybe he doesn't. In any case, the dedication page of *Monastery* is an olive branch of sorts, declaring, "for my sister, for my brother."

CHAPTER 6

MEMORY DUELS

*Convinced that photographs reflect the reality
of the past, we have entered the realm of fiction.*

WHAT'S IN A NAME

In April of 2019, Eduardo Halfon traveled to West Hartford, Connecticut to receive the 2018 Edward Lewis Wallant Award for his book *Mourning*, accompanied by the book's two translators, Lisa Dillman and Daniel Hahn. Established in 1963 by Dr. and Mrs. Irving Waltman of West Hartford, the Wallant award is "one of the oldest and most prestigious Jewish literary awards in the United States . . . presented annually to a Jewish writer whose published creative work of fiction is deemed to have significance for the American Jew."[1] Once more, it seems, Halfon had defied the rules, passing as an "American" writer (and an award-winning one at that), though he is not a US citizen and his literary production to date has been composed primarily in Spanish. Halfon treated the occasion as another opportunity to employ his prerogative to embrace or alternately reject the many aspects of his multilingual and multicultural self-definition: "In other words, there are all these parts of my identity that can be placed, or exalted—I'm all of them. I *am* an American Jew. I grew up here, I'm still here. Yet I'll probably reject that at some point, just because I wind up rejecting most of those impositions. You know?"[2] As if to prove the point further, *Mourning* and its counterparts in Spanish and French also garnered Halfon the Premio de Las Librerías de Navarra in Spain, the Prix du meilleur livre étranger in France, and the International Latino Book Award in the United States.[3] Given this talent for shape-shifting, perhaps it is not surprising then that a Spanish newspaper reporting on the publication of *Duelo*, the Spanish-language original of *Mourning*, dubbed Halfon the "Guatemalan Zelig." To wit, Halfon himself has described his own identity as "adaptable, a liquid thing, that makes me think about Woody Allen's *Zelig*."[4]

After the presentation of the Wallant award, Professor Avinoam Patt moderated a discussion with Halfon and translators Dillman and Hahn that was later published in the *Massachusetts Review* under the title "The Purest Form of Writing, the Most Intimate Form of Reading."[5] Halfon began by alluding to a question a Spanish journalist had asked him several years earlier, a question he would take up again in a January 2020 presentation at Columbia University's Institute for Ideas and Imagination in Paris, where he was a fellow: "What are the two books that you've never read which have influenced you the most?"[6] Halfon wondered if this was the dumbest question he'd ever been asked, or maybe the smartest. The answer, he explained in West Hartford and later in Paris (and earlier with the Spanish journalist), occurred to him immediately:

> The two books which have influenced me the most, and which I've never read. One: The *Popul Vuh*—the cultural narrative of the Mayan people. I am Guatemalan. I am from their land. This narrative comes from the K'iche, the people of the Mayan highlands. It is their Bible, their oral tradition, their history. Never read it. And two: the Torah. Never read it. Besides the phonetically memorized part for my bar mitzvah, I've never read the Torah. I've never read The *Popul Vuh* and I've never read the Torah. I don't want to. I refuse to. Yet I know that those are the two main pillars of my house. Everything I am rests on those two pillars. My Jewish identity. And my Guatemalan identity ... My house, then, is built on those two pillars. But a writer must begin by destroying one's house.[7]

Given this admission of (and perhaps rationalization for) having failed to read the two books that together form the architecture of his identity, it is all the more ironic that *Mourning* (and the Spanish original *Duelo* before it) starts with a chapter and verse citation from the Torah. Or, if one prefers a narrower definition of the Torah to mean only the first five books of the Bible, the author cites from the *Tanakh*, the canonical collection of Hebrew scriptures: "I will give them an everlasting name—Isaiah 56:5." The inheriting of names, the invention of names, the granting of names, the alteration and exchange of names, and the diverse destinies of those who share a name (or its variants) constitute a vital theme in Halfon's works. Nonetheless,

Mourning's epigraph remains cryptic, less a guide to the following pages than a tease. How did Halfon find it, if he's never read Torah? Why did he select this verse? Should we understand the "I" of the epigraph as divine or autobiographical? Should we consider the dedication page preceding the citation as a clue to interpreting the epigraph? It reads, "For you, Leo, who arrived before dawn, with a hummingbird." Maybe the fragment from Isaiah refers to Halfon's (and/or his protagonist's) condition as a father; maybe it represents a textual naming ceremony for his son Leo, whose name echoes that of Halfon's maternal grandfather: León in Spanish, Leib in Polish. But it's also possible that the reference from the *Tanakh* is tongue-in-cheek, that Halfon wants to question the very notion of an "everlasting" name, given that his fictions repeatedly stage the susceptibility of names to a variety of dangers: substitution with a number tattoo in "The Polish Boxer;" disappearance in "Monastery," where a Jewish child's name is written on his hand before he is disguised as a girl and deposited in a monastery where his "true" name will fade on his skin and in his memory in the interest of survival; unpronounceability, unintelligibility, and modification in "Signor Hoffman," "Oh Ghetto My Love" and "Mourning."

The inclusion of the stories "Signor Hoffman," and "Oh Ghetto My Love" in the English version of *Mourning* make it a very different book from its Spanish antecedent *Duelo*, first published a year earlier in 2017. Despite the expansion of that volume for the English-language edition with the inclusion of texts from other projects originally published in Spanish (*Signor Hoffman*, 2015 and *Oh gueto mi amor*, 2018), its title in English seems shrunken, semantically reduced from that of the Spanish original.[8] Halfon himself recognized this difference, explaining:

> It's a book about names. It's a book about mourning, as the title suggests, but the title in English is very tricky. It's not the same as the title in Spanish. The title in Spanish is *Duelo*, which has three meanings: *duelo* can mean "mourning," but *duelo* can also mean "duel," as in combat, and it can also mean "pain," *dolor, yo duelo*, "I hurt." These three ideas are very present in the book: the one book where finally, or ultimately, or profoundly, these two parts of my identity, the Guatemalan and the Jewish, come together. This is a very Guatemalan book—it's about going back to Guatemala—and it's also a very Jewish book. In sum, a search for what these identities mean for me: What does it mean to be Guatemalan, and what does it mean to be Jewish?[9]

In *Mourning*, then, grief, duel, and pain come together in a tug-of-war of balm and betrayal, triggered by memories both recent and distant, created on familiar or foreign ground, and drawing on the sensory landscapes of both childhood and adulthood.

THE FERRAMONTI THEME PARK

In "Signor Hoffman," a narrator named Eduardo Halfon finds himself on a southbound train from Rome, headed to Paola, a town in Calabria where he has received an invitation to speak, and has been "too much of a coward to say no."[10] At the station, a benign oddball grabs his arm and introduces himself as Fausto. He ushers the protagonist into his rattletrap car, insisting they must go at once *to the concentration camp*. On the way, Fausto points out a huge church, crosses himself, then advises again, "Now straight to the concentration camp" where the director awaits them. The narrator thinks he hears him say "Herr Director," perhaps even with a German accent, and "was ready to yell at him that, while driving to a concentration camp, that's not something you ever say to a Jew."[11] This madcap approach, both literal and figurative, to Ferramonti di Tarsia, Ex Campo di Concentramento, a structure bedecked with an "elegant spiral of barbed wire," is a tip-off that not every Holocaust-themed pilgrimage must be morbid or morose, even if going there reminds the protagonist of an earlier trip he made to Hiroshima, where the atomic bomb was dropped in 1945, and even if the volume in which the trip appears is called *Mourning*.

At the camp they meet Panebianco, a man the narrator presumes must be the aforementioned Herr Director, dressed as if he were "in mourning," together with a young woman, also attired in black, perhaps "in mourning" as well. Though previously unaware that Italy had concentration camps during World War II—fifteen of them, in fact, of which Ferramonti was the largest, though not an extermination camp—Halfon has agreed to appear at the annual Holocaust Memorial Day event at the site.[12] There is a problem, though. The Ferramonti concentration camp he visits is not the Ferramonti where several thousand Jews were held during World War II, but only a model, only a simulacrum of the original, which had been demolished in the sixties to build a new highway. Marina, the young woman in black, explains that everything he sees before him is thus a "reconstruction." Halfon begins to understand that he has stumbled upon a site and sight that "was no more than a replica . . . a kind of mock-up or sample or theme park dedicated to human suffering; and that I myself, at that very moment, standing on the threshold of that fake block, was a part of the whole performance."[13] As Ángel Díaz Miranda has observed, Ferramonti is "acting" as a concentration camp in this scenario, assuming a role, playing a part.¹⁴

Whether from exhaustion after his long trip by plane, train, and unreliable automobile, or from jet lag, or from not having eaten, or due to "the growing feeling of guilt or complicity with the whole farce," Signor Halfon begins to feel sick.¹⁵ His hosts take him to a cool, dark auditorium where three large screens project a short movie explaining the history of Ferramonti in Italian. Despite his imperfect command of the language, he can see that "the images were the usual ones" that one sees in concentration camp documentaries. The film's soundtrack also was unoriginal, and even the bench on which he sat had been artfully placed "so that the spectator might feel surrounded by light, immersed in the sensationalism of bitterness and wretchedness and death."¹⁶ He is then ushered onto the stage, where Panebianco, already in the middle of a lengthy speech to the large audience in attendance, hands him a sealed white envelope with "a wad of dirty bills, I guessed. A wad of bills, I guessed, that Panebianco himself, standing at the front gate, had received from the little hands of boys and girls from all over Calabria, as they entered his fake concentration camp." Finally, after a lengthy preamble, Panebiano introduces his Guatemalan guest, "Il Signor Hoffman."¹⁷

The text doesn't reveal what Halfon/Hoffman said to his audience or if there was a Q&A afterward. More important, it seems, is a dream the protagonist had following the talk, in which he, his brother, and his sister were all prisoners "in our own concentration camp."¹⁸ Fortunately, Marina wakes him from this scene and takes him to the only bar in town, where she explains that her nonno, her grandfather, was also in a concentration camp, though he was not Jewish. On the verge of falling asleep again over his beer, Eduardo hears that "Hoffman died." Hoffman died today, Marina repeats, and Halfon realizes that the television is broadcasting the news of Phillip Seymour Hoffman's death from a suspected heroin overdose.¹⁹ The narrator remembers the one time he'd seen Hoffman up close in a Greenwich Village café; he lists, in succession, many of Hoffman's memorable roles; he now laments his failure to tell the actor how much he admired him and followed his work. Then he thinks with a shudder of how Panebianco had called him Hoffman just a few hours earlier, perhaps at the same exact moment the actor was dying in his New York bathroom:

> Hoffman, Panebianco had called me, while Hoffman died. As though it were more than a slip, more than a coincidence. As though in dying he had liberated his name to float freely around the world, for anyone else in the world to be able to catch it in the air, and say it, and embody it. As though the names

of dead artists were butterflies. As though this was what always happened to men who, in their lives and in their art, gave voice to everyman, to all men. As though all of us men, at that exact moment, were named Hoffman.[20]

The Hoffman coincidence has a contradictory effect on the protagonist, leaving him simultaneously euphoric and dejected. Due bicchieri de gin, he yells to Luigi the bartender in his bad Italian. In the midst or mist of these mixed feelings and libations, Panebianco's "theme park" and Ferramonti itself gradually fade from view. Halfon/Hoffman asks Marina to translate his request to Luigi to keep bringing gins until there are no more dirty bills left on the table, or until he and Marina collapse drunk and naked onto the floor, or until "love kills us all."[21]

As often happens in Halfon's fiction, the protagonist indulges in drink and sexual fantasy as a defiant counterpoint to trauma, whether his own or that of his Polish grandfather or others. Does this strategy offer a type of healing balm or is it merely escapist? In "Signor Hoffman," which frames Ferramonti and Holocaust Remembrance Day as a site and occasion for manufactured mourning, ethical concerns around how to best remember and memorialize the Shoah remain unresolved. Exposing the Ferramonti of the twenty-first century as merely a fake in turn suggests a margin of misrepresentation or falsehood in all Holocaust memorializing. And yet, without such memory sites, the opposing argument goes, injustices perpetrated there and in other sites of detention, internment, imprisonment, torture, and extermination are too easily forgotten or erased. For one of its survivors, Ferramonti will forever be a site of rescue, a "story of Jewish survival thanks to the efforts of Italian soldiers and impoverished Italian villagers who worked together to save nearly 4,000 Jews," a place where Jewish children "learned Hebrew and practiced Jewish traditions," and where "two barracks were configured as synagogues."[22]

Italy's response to the advances of the Third Reich has long been framed in the national narrative as more anti-Nazi resistance and less Fascist complicity; "the industry of historical representation devoted to these events in Italy—the commercial films, the documentaries, the school lessons, the regular annual days of commemoration—draws attention not to the many thousands of Italians directly involved in the murder of Italy's Jews but to the courageous few who took risks to try to save them," claims Simon Levis Sullam.[23] Steering clear of a definitive position on this question, "Signor Hoffman" deliberately leaves open the question of Italy's true role in the operation and administration of concentration camps such as Ferramonti. The real mourning in "Signor

Hoffman"—if indeed there is any—is arguably reserved for Hiroshima and Seymour Hoffman himself.

PHOTOGRAPHIC MEMORY

The themes of the Shoah as spectacle, entertainment, as an intergenerational family tragedy that can be seized upon for economic or political ends, and as a historical apogee of antisemitic expressions and actions whose effects continue into the present, are also on display in "Oh Ghetto My Love," the second tale in *Mourning*. Memory has many faces, some that console the characters, some that betray them. This range of functions is vividly apparent in a seemingly minor detail: the story's incorporation of that quintessential prompt for memory, the photograph.

"Oh Ghetto My Love" begins in the lobby of the famed Hotel Savoy, where the protagonist meets Madame Maroszek, a polyglot Polish woman known to many outside the country for assisting second and third generation Holocaust survivors find their roots, their property, and their dead.[24] Before helping the narrator search for signs of his grandfather's life in Łódź, Madame Maroszek had already helped a French friend find the graves of two siblings who died of typhoid in the Łódź ghetto, she'd helped a Chilean poet recover family property on the outskirts of the city, and she'd helped an American professor unravel the mystery of her grandparents' death in Chelmno and Treblinka. Madame Maroszek's motives for rendering these services are not exactly clear, however. Though not Jewish herself, she helps the children and grandchildren of survivors, one version has it, in memory of her parents' brave efforts, parents "who had been executed during the war for helping Jews." Another, seemingly contradictory view claimed she has aided second- and third-generation survivors in order to atone for these same parents' *denunciation* of the Jews, perhaps even "handing them over to the Gestapo at the much-feared Rote Haus, or Red House." The American professor, an expert on the subject, had uncovered testimonies supporting both views, suggesting Madame Maroszek or her parents had both helped *and* betrayed Jews. How is it possible, the narrator asks the American history professor, that someone could simultaneously help and betray, save some and send some to be executed? But the historian, nonplussed, explains that everything in war was incoherent.[25]

How much should the protagonist share with his guide, then, when she asks about the previous stops on his itinerary? Should he admit to his own ambivalent feelings about his trip? Should he confess he "felt nothing" as he touched the bricks of the last vestige of the Warsaw Ghetto wall, outfitted in a pink coat bought in a secondhand store after the airlines lost his luggage? Should he tell her he wavered, wondering whether to even visit Auschwitz, dressed in his rosy "Polishwoman disguise"? Should he admit to Madame Maroszek that he had ultimately "paraded through Auschwitz with all the other tourists," entering Block 11, where his grandfather was held prisoner and where his grandfather got his number tattoo and where his grandfather had met the Polish boxer who trained him one night "to defend himself and deliver jabs with his words"?[26] He was on the verge, in fact, of telling her about the two teenage tourists, probably American, who were groping each other in a cafeteria opposite Auschwitz "with all the imprudence and indiscretion of that which is forbidden, their hands lost in each other's clothes, their faces flushed and smoldering with the blinding fire that excites for the first time," even though he himself has on other occasions indulged in erotic distractions from the unpleasantries of Holocaust remembrance and other difficult subjects.

The main character refrains from sharing all these confidences, however, opting instead to present Madame Maroszek with an envelope containing two photos, the first portraying his Polish grandfather as a young man riding a bike on a Berlin street after being freed from the Sachsenhausen concentration camp in 1945, the second an earlier family portrait of his grandfather with his parents and siblings before their family life was interrupted by the Nazi advance. In hindsight, viewing it from some six decades later, the subjects in the family portrait seem "serious, concerned, almost frightened, as if they realized that this would be the last image of them together, as if they knew what was about to happen to them, and their gray faces foretold the whole tragedy."[27] These two photographic keepsakes, somehow miraculously preserved throughout the entire war and the grandfather's life in Guatemala, provide three generations of family members with the material evidence of an alternate identity to that of WWII victims of antisemitism and genocide. As we soon discover, the two portraits provide a sharp contrast to another set of photos that also figures prominently in this tale, pointing us to the crucial and varied roles photography plays in the complex exercise of Holocaust memory.

In the last supper the narrator would have with his Polish grandfather before his death, his Oitze had once more warned him against traveling to the country in which the pre-tragedy family portrait was taken, shouting that "a Jew must never go to Poland." He had pulled a newspaper clipping from a credenza, a clipping that he'd kept in that drawer for years and that he'd shown his grandson several times already "as evidence, as a warning," saying, "Look, Eduardito." The most important feature of the clipping seems to be the three large black-and-white photos that confirm the continuity of antisemitic sentiment in Poland, convincing the grandfather that its dangers remain, even for his adult grandson:

> The first was of a wall on a Łódź street, graffitied with a game of hangman, in which the hanged man was not a man, but a Star of David. The second showed a policeman holding up a confiscated t-shirt outside the stadium of Widzew Łódź, the city's soccer team, bearing an image of crosshairs, like from a shotgun, beneath which was written: We hunt Jews here. The third showed a stand full of Poznán hooligans, who the caption said were chanting at the Łódź team: Move on Jews, your home is at Auschwitz, back to the gas chambers. Before the war, the article explained, the population of Łódź was one-third Jewish. That is, there were two hundred fifty thousand Jews in Łódź. Fewer than ten thousand survived.[28]

No date is provided for the clipping the grandfather has preserved along with the photos of himself and his family, but the larger point is clear: graffiti and other public expressions of anti-Jewish sentiment have continued to appear in Poland and elsewhere for three quarters of a century following the war's end, even though the Jewish population itself was reduced by about ninety percent. However complicit the Polish populace in aiding and abetting Nazi genocide of Jews and other victims of the Shoah, much of the rhetoric propelling those actions seems to remain.[29] As Helen Sinnreich writes, "antisemitic texts on the walls of the city of Łódź include phrases such as 'Ż˙ydzi gaz!' (Jews to the gas chambers!), 'Hitler wro´c´ i wykon´cz Z˙ydo´w' (Hitler come back and finish off the Jews!), 'Jude raus'! (Jew out! ([Written in German]), and the transformation of the name of one of the soccer teams into the word Jew; from Widzew to Z˙ydzew . . . The symbols depicted include the swastika, the star of David hanging on a gallows, and Jewish stars adorning the name of a team or as a replacement for some of the letters in the name. The plain textual reading of these words and symbols is violent and antisemitic."[30]

Other sources confirm encountering scenes like those in the grandfather's clipping during their own travels to Poland. One second-generation Holocaust survivor, commenting on "extensive" antisemitic graffiti during a 2001 visit to Łódź, claims "it was impossible to go a block without seeing a Star of David on a hangman's scaffold or a 'death to Jews' proclamation sprayed on a wall." His tour guide urged him to hide his Star of

David necklace under his shirt, despite the fact that he was touring "the new Poland." In his memoir, Mark Biederman also speaks of visiting Jedwabne, the site of a 1941 massacre of more than 340 Jewish men, women, and children—most of whom were herded into a barn that was then set ablaze. Perhaps non-Jewish Poles were only following directives from Nazi military police in facilitating this massacre, as many have argued; nonetheless, the continued expression of anti-Jewish vitriol in contemporary times complicates the presumption of innocence for subsequent generations. Biederman includes in his text a photo he took of the monument marking the immolation of the Jews, itself defaced with a swastika. That photo shows a text on the monument, recently changed to acknowledge the role of ethnic Poles in perpetrating the massacre, painted over in adamant rejection of this version of events.[31]

What should we make of these different photos? How does writing *about* photos (only a very few of Halfon's publications include actual photos) reflect and enhance Halfon's stated goal of writing on the threshold of fiction and reality, especially in relation to his Polish grandfather's Holocaust experience? In *Photographing the Holocaust: Interpretations of the Evidence*, photographer Janina Struk considers the wide range of purposes cameras and the images made with them served during World War II. At one end of the spectrum, portraits and snapshots of Jewish family members like those the narrator hands to Madame Maroszek in "Oh Ghetto My Love" frame a miraculous survival, whether of the subjects themselves, or of the memories such documents trigger in the face of their death and the large-scale atrocity of mass murder. Struk's examination of photos at the other extreme of this spectrum, including the thousands of Holocaust-era photos that recorded executions and the humiliations preceding them, shows how photography was a potent tool for inciting, committing, and then celebrating such crimes. Whereas prewar family portraits and snapshots of individuals who later died invite the viewer to engage in nostalgia, mourning, or remembrance of someone as other-than-victim, at this other extreme of representation "the horrific nature of a picture can prevent rational or critical thought being applied to it. It can be easier to recoil from it rather than confront it."[32]

A photo of several naked men and a child, surrounded by fully dressed and armed soldiers, provided the starting point for Struk's study. Two of the naked men stand at the edge of an open pit, trying to shield their bodies from the camera's frontal view. On the righthand edge of the shot, a soldier, positioned closer to the camera, points to the pit with an outstretched arm, his face turned toward the photographer with anticipation. Though a caption reading "Sniatyń—tormenting Jews before their execution," now accompanies the photo held by the Polish Institute and Sikorski Museum, Struk first encountered it without this information. She wondered how to categorize or understand such a photo. Could it be considered a war photo, if there was no sign of resistance from those who awaited their execution? Were this and thousands of other existing "atrocity" photos from World War II merely "propaganda" from Poland, the Soviet Union, and elsewhere, as the British and US governments contended as they refrained from publishing them? Could such a photo even be considered germane to the genre of photography?[33]

As the narrator of "Signor Hoffman" contends while watching the documentary at Ferramonti, it has become "usual" in contemporary times to see certain images of the Holocaust and its torture and genocide of Jews and other maligned groups. "Signor Hoffman" acknowledges the mundane quality that has attached itself to many photos exhibited in Holocaust museums and memorials around the world, including at internment and death camps themselves. Struk's work radically challenges this numbness to photography's complex role in the Nazis' campaign against non-Aryans, explaining that "besides photographing round-ups and executions, for some German soldiers, police or SS men, to be photographed mocking or humiliating Jews was a popular activity." Of a photo that shows soldiers smiling and laughing as they flank an Orthodox rabbi with scissors, poised to cut his sidelocks, she notes,

> This was not a clandestine photograph. The scene had been organized, considered and set up. The perpetrators had proudly arranged themselves in front of the camera in the same way friends on a holiday might pose for a group picture. Photographing the enemy was equal to possessing or conquering it. Publicly to humiliate, degrade and possibly kill the "real" Jew was metaphorically to destroy the image of the mythical Jew. Taking photographs was an integral part of the humiliation process; in a sense it completed the violation.[34]

Such humiliation photos staged the "absolute mastery" of the German over the Jew and the destruction of Jewish manhood, visually staging racial superiority in ways that continue to influence contemporary attitudes in Poland and elsewhere, Struk observes. Past and present converge as Nazis and later their followers exploit "male group activity" to render apprehension, humiliation, and execution sport-like. During their occupation of Poland, for example, Nazis and their collaborators exhibited photos of public hangings in Łódź and elsewhere as "trophy" pictures in the way a hunter might boast about his recently killed prey; such photos were hung in military barracks so that other soldiers could order copies, and they were collected and preserved in elaborate photo albums. Though a personal activity, such photo collecting "was part of a wider collective responsibility. It gave individuals an opportunity not only to order their own experiences and decide how the past should be remembered and preserved, but also to express a commitment to National Socialist ideals."[35] As already mentioned, two of the news photos the protagonist's grandfather keeps presenting to Eduardo as evidence that perhaps too little has changed in post-war Poland, despite the march of time, retain this association of antisemitic activity with sport: in the first, a t-shirt photographed outside a soccer stadium in Łódź contains the message "We hunt Jews here" emblazoned over an image of a hunter's crosshairs; the other shows sports fans chanting at the Łódź team, "Move on Jews, your home is at Auschwitz, back to the gas chambers."

The miraculously preserved portraits of his grandfather that the protagonist hands to Madame Maroszek in "Oh Ghetto My Love" reference the human experiences and relationships of his Polish family members in the face of an antagonistic photographic history of the Jew as a hunted animal. Despite his ambivalence about how much to share—or even what to think—about his visit to Łódź, Auschwitz, Sachsenhausen, and other stops on the Holocaust tourism circuit, the family photos preserve the possibility of remembering unique individuals whose lives supersede victimhood and even death. If "Oh Ghetto My Love" has a happy ending, it is that the two photos of Leon Tenenbaum as a young man outweigh and triumph over the photos documenting ongoing antisemitism in Poland that the grandfather also has been zealously guarding. His testimony to survival has proved stronger than his trauma and fear of antisemitism's persistence. For despite his shouted admonitions to not go back to Poland ever, Eduardo's grandfather, in their last dinner together, finally writes down and hands him the address of the apartment where he was living when the Nazis picked him up, extending the yellow paper with his implicit blessing. Reading "Oh Ghetto My Love" after "Signor Hoffman" leads us to conclude that the family photos, one of which appears on the cover of a 2019 reprinting of *El boxeador polaco*, can also triumph over the "usual" photos and film images the protagonist views at Ferramonti.

HOFFMAN REMIX

In Poland's storied Hotel Savoy, the Halfonesque protagonist of "Oh Ghetto My Love" again morphs into Hoffman. This time it is of his own doing.

The hotel's ancient elevator operator introduces himself in Polish as Mr. Kaminski, and Halfon attempts to introduce himself as Halfon, but Kaminski's hand cupped around his ear indicates his inability to hear or process such a name.

> I repeated my name, louder and slower, but he simply shook his head and leaned in toward me, as though asking me please to assist him. And suddenly, seeing him there, helpless and hunched over, it struck me that it wasn't that he couldn't hear my name, but that it sounded too foreign to him, too unfamiliar, that my reality, in fact, did not mesh with his. So I banged my fist on my chest and assumed a voice that was forceful and booming and no longer my own, and said: Hoffman . . . That's right, I said on my way out. Signor Hoffman.[36]

The mistaken identity theme is not just a running joke, then, but a traveling joke, one in which the protagonist himself now indulges. The joke serves as a bit of buffoonery, a buffer as the narrative cuts abruptly to a scene of the protagonist and his well-attired Polish guide standing before "six enormous graves, gaping and empty" at the city's Jewish cemetery. In August of 1944, the narrative explains, the Germans had made some 840 Jews dig their own mass graves in preparation for their final liquidation of the Łódź Ghetto, a task the German soldiers had to abandon in their flight from the city, permitting the survival of the remaining Jews. Though Łódź is described as little more than a ghost town, a site where there is now no history, not even longing, these graves remain as a testament, as an open wound.

Madame Maroszek also takes her visitor to Anatevka, the sole restaurant in town "that still served Jewish food."[37] Borrowing its name from the Sholem Aleichem tale that was later recreated as the blockbuster film and soundtrack *Fiddler on the Roof*, Anatevka advertises itself as "a place where you can experience the unique and enchanting flavors of Jewish cuisine. Welcome to Lodz, where each of the four cultures has left its legacy and unforgettable atmosphere of the Promised Land."[38] The restaurant website features a list of "recent guests" that includes such disparate names as Umberto Eco, Joe Cocker, Lech Wałęsa, KENZO, and PRADA—"Live music every day! To keep you amused, there is a 'fiddler on the roof' playing for you in the first room, while in the other one you can listen to a pianist playing on the 19th-century piano!"[39] Are Madame Maroszek and her guest enjoying the continuation of a tradition, then, or participating in another simulacrum?[40] Eating, smiling, perhaps teasing him, she tells Halfon of another Signor Hoffman, the German writer and composer E. T. A.

Hoffman, who besides inventing the storyline of the Nutcracker, set to music by Tchaikovsky, was also the public official in charge of naming Polish Jews, creating "names that became real simply by virtue of being spoken and taken down in a register, and once real they were propagated throughout the world."[41] Halfon itself, the protagonist rejoins, is only a partial name, a fragment of an original name mangled by an immigration officer at Ellis Island, though retaining a meaning from ancient Hebrew or Persian of "he who changes his life." "Like the engineer who becomes a writer," the Polish-woman whispers, prompting the narrator to think that "a name, any name, is that transcendent, and arbitrary, and fictitious, and that all of us, eventually, become our own fiction."[42]

Throughout the remainder of his time with Madame Maroszek in Łódź and elsewhere in his travels in Poland, Halfon will continue to wonder why he had come, what he thought he would learn from his grandfather's apartment, why he needed to trace his forbear's footsteps, to "rummage through the last remaining bones and fossils of a truncated family history."[43] In *Textual Silence*, Jessica Lang proposes an answer to queries such as these:

> Third generation stories, both fictional and nonfictional, emerge from a need to design a connective web intended to draw closer together the eyewitness (first) generation and the third generation. I argue here that this connective web is established both imaginatively, through a process that involves third-generation authors developing a version of testimony (I call it post-testimony) that attempts to uncover the unknown and physically, through visiting and finding meaning in specific sites that played a role in their family's history.[44]

Indeed, just before they part, Madame Maroszek presents her visitor with an unexpected gift of three books that offer distinct Jewish voices from Łódź. Together, they recount life in the ghetto, including such details as Yankele Herskowitz's satirical songs of resistance, like the one that provides the title of this tale: "Geto getunya. Getokhna kokhana, went the Yiddish refrain. Ghetto, little ghetto, oh ghetto my love." Another mysterious text offers a compendium of diary entries written on loose pages at Auschwitz, "words that survived the internment and the gas," though by the time of their discovery, two-thirds of the pages were illegible.[45]

The gift leaves the protagonist both euphoric and unnerved. What does one do with such a gift? The lesson to be learned, he concludes, isn't about "where we write our stories but that we do write them. Tell them. Leave testimony. Put our whole lives into words."[46] For Halfon and his Hoffman doppelgangers, the denouement suggests, the purpose of the Poland trip, and its role in the entire itinerary of memory, is to link the testimony of his grandfather and other eyewitnesses to the contemporary moment, to both experientially and imaginatively establish a way to know this history. Though the simulation, simplification, and commodification along his path are sometimes deeply disturbing, the narrator's physical and narrative progress through the diverse landscapes of Holocaust remembrance create new pathways to individual and collective comprehension.

MEMORY DUELS

The title story in *Mourning*—the last and by far the longest of its three sections—introduces us to a new source of family mourning: the mysterious death of Salomón, the brother of the protagonist's father, the uncle he never knew. Whereas the lost and dead and souls of the Holocaust are grieved—sometimes explicitly, sometimes implicitly—as victims of war, genocide, starvation, and dehumanization, Salomón represents a broken branch of the family tree for which grieving has been purposely silenced. When he was a mere boy of five, Salomón had died in Guatemala's Lake Amatitlán, or at least, that's the story the protagonist remembers hearing as a child, though "no one in the family talked about Salomón. No one even spoke his name."[47]

Salomón's absence represents a distinct type of mourning, one associated with Guatemala instead of Nazi Europe, but nevertheless a mystery that exerts a strong pull on Eduardo across a period of many years. The story begins with the adult narrator making a return pilgrimage to his grandparents' house, sold in the 1970s, long before Amatitlán's designation as a "dying" lake due to long-term pollution from nearby Guatemala City.[48] The first thing to assail him is the "smell of humidity, of sulfur, of something dead or dying. I thought that what was dead or dying was the lake itself, so contaminated and putrid, so mistreated for decades."[49] He sees on the asphalt road before him "a horse. An emaciated horse. A cadaverous horse."[50] The scene is triply dead or deathly, with the tale of the drowned Salomón (submerged in mystery if not in Amatitlán) framed by a dead lake and a cadaverous horse, the latter an "off-white apparition amid all the green."

The protagonist seeks out Don Isidoro Chavajay, an employee of the family who had remained through a succession of subsequent owners of the lake house. When he introduces himself to the young woman who answers the door as Señor Halfon, as the grandson of Señor Halfon, he is met with skepticism and silence. In order to be recognized, worlds away from Ferramonti or the Hotel Savoy, he must introduce himself, yet again, as Señor *Hoffman*, even with Don Isidoro, who has known three generations of the family. "Sometimes I feel I can hear everything," the protagonist says, "save the sound of my own name."[51]

The narrator remembers how he and his siblings, as kids, had trusted all the things Don Isidoro said to them, even when the stories contradicted each other. They believed "that the ever more frequent gunfire and bomb blasts in the mountains were only eruptions of the Pacaya volcano" and that "the two bodies that turned up one morning floating by the dock were not two murdered guerillas tossed into the lake, but two normal boys." They even believed the conflicting explanations Don Isidoro provided for the meaning of the word *Amatitlán* in the language of his ancestors, whether "place surrounded by amates" or ficus trees, whether "city of letters" due to the glyphs carved into the trees around the lake by those ancestors, or whether none of these versions.[52] The children's acceptance of these varied truths suggests a willingness to acknowledge multiple versions of reality and multiple ways of naming and remembering that reality. But by the time of his reencounter with Don Isidoro, the protagonist's confidence in his belief that Salomón died in a Guatemalan lake has been shaken together with his confidence regarding his own Guatemalan identity.

> I don't know anything about that, Don Isidoro said to me when I finished recounting my memory—possibly false—of a boy drowned right there, by the dock. Young man, I didn't even know that your grandparents had had another boy, he whispered, combing his white hair with one hand... Tell me, young man, you and your siblings grew up outside the country, right?... and I said yes, we had, that we'd left the country as children, gone to the United States, and spent many years there. So many years, I told him, that at times I feel I'm no longer from here... Young man, he said, you will always be from here.[53]

Finding Salomón thus reveals itself to be a task about finding oneself and explains why a dead uncle the narrator has never met has produced such curiosity across so many latitudes at so many moments of his life.

As "Mourning" intersperses incremental revelations concerning the shadowy Salomón with the narrator's observations as he visits the sinister scenes of his Polish grandfather's journey through many years of war and concentration camps, it also stages a duel between different kinds of memory, different forms of grief, and their respective representations. Unsolved mysteries around Salomón's death, together with the outright prohibition from the father figure (whether fictional or flesh and blood) to write about the matter, conspire to drive the forbidden story forward, staging different, competing explanations of Salomón's death. The suppression attached to his Polish grandfather's survival of the Holocaust on the one hand, and

Salomón's tragic death on the other—both stories involving alternate versions—forces to the surface questions about how or even whether to remember and mourn such events. "Mourning" complements the already long list of ways that memory functions on several levels in the family's history, including grandfather Leon's own memory of his wartime experiences, of which he almost never speaks; the subterfuge used by the Polish grandfather to avoid remembering such experiences out loud, claiming his Auschwitz prisoner tattoo was a telephone number; the adult narrator's memory of the ways he tried to fill in those silences with scenes from his own imagination, once he understood what the tattoo truly signified; the memorializing—yet another kind of memory—associated with objects such as the two surviving family photographs of the Tenenbaums and a "black-stone ring (a symbol of mourning for his parents and siblings murdered in concentration camps)," so valuable to his Polish grandfather that he ended up in a Guatemalan hospital after defending himself from two thieves who attempted to steal it from him.[54]

Two key questions seem to drive all these troubled forms of memory and their relationship to "Mourning." First, which elements of family trauma should be remembered openly or collectively, and which should be silenced? Which should appear between the covers of a book, and which are verboten in those pages? A text included on the back cover of *Duelo*, the Spanish original of *Mourning*, suggests a duel of wills around grief and memory at the very heart of "Mourning:"

> You aren't going to write anything about this, my dad asked or ordered me, with his index finger lifted and his tone halfway between appeal and command. I thought of answering that a writer never knows what he will write, that a writer doesn't choose his stories but that they choose him, that a writer is nothing more than a dry leaf in the wind of its own narrative. But luckily I didn't say anything. You won't write anything about this, my dad repeated, his tone now stronger, almost authoritarian. I felt the weight of his words. Of course not, I said, perhaps sincere, or perhaps already knowing that no story is imperative, no story is necessary, except those that someone forbids us from telling.[55]

In 2018, Halfon told an interviewer that *Mourning* arose from this prohibition, and that even *The Polish Boxer* was not meant to circulate outside the family.[56] A metatext designed to turn the reader inward, the prohibition text on the back cover of *Duelo* heightens the suspense around Salomón's story while also further confounding the lines between lived experience and invention, author and protagonist, events and their fictional recreations.

Whether or not details such as the date of Salomón's birth (1935), the date of his voyage with his mother to the United States aboard the United Fruit Company vessel *Antigua* from Guatemala's Puerto Barrios (1940), or the confirmation of his death in a New York clinic (date unknown) are veridical, they make "Mourning" more credible, and the problem of memory more complex.[57]

Salomón's story serves as a through-line across temporal, spatial, and cultural landscapes as the narrative circulates between scenes from the protagonist's childhood in Guatemala, his youth in suburban Miami, his reintroduction to the Guatemalan reality and its Indigenous cosmovision as an adult, and travels beyond these varied iterations of "home." The narrative spiraling around Salomón makes "Mourning" something of a ghost story, too, muddling the distinctions between the physical and the metaphysical. "We used to spend every weekend at my grandparents' house on the lakeshore, and I couldn't look at that water without imagining the lifeless body of Salomón suddenly appearing. I always imagined him pale and naked, and always floating facedown by the old wooden dock." The protagonist had even invented a secret prayer, one he could still remember as an adult, that he and his brother would whisper before diving into the lake "as if it were a magic spell. As if to banish the ghost of the boy Salomón, in case the ghost of the boy Salomón was still swimming around."[58] Or did they have this incantation? Toward the end of the tale, the protagonist, now an adult, calls his brother in France, asking him about his memories of the lake house and mentioning their secret prayer to ward off Salomón's ghost. Not only can his brother not recall the brothers' prayer of protection against their dead uncle, but he seems to have forgotten the very existence of Salomón. "Our father had an older brother?" he finally asks.[59]

"Mourning" thus reveals how unreliable memory can be, even those remembered episodes we hold most dear and whose representation of lived experience we defend most staunchly. A photograph he finds as a child prompts the protagonist's first spate of unsteady footing as to the true story of his father's brother Salomón. That moment, like so many others, occurs in the context of impending displacement. The narrator recalls how his "Lebanese" grandfather had left his home country (not yet Lebanon at the time) for the Americas in 1919, spending several years in New York in route to Guatemala while other members of his extended family sought to establish themselves in far-flung locales including Haiti, Peru, and Mexico, where one cousin had reportedly served as Pancho Villa's arms dealer. In his grandfather's house, a few days before his own family's move to Florida, on the eve of his tenth birthday, Eduardo had discovered a black-and-white photo with the words "Salomón. New York. 1940" on the dorsal. What happened to the drowned boy in the lake, he wondered? How could he also appear in a photo taken in New York in 1940? Later, asking his father about his relatives for an assignment at his new school in Florida, the protagonist learns that both his great-grandfathers on his father's side, one from Aleppo and the other from Beirut, had also been named Salomón. "The king of the Israelites," his father proclaimed, prompting his son to deliver an account to his classmates in which his father's brother Salomón, king of the Israelites, had died from drowning in a Guatemalan lake where the body and royal crown both remained.[60] Even in childhood, it seems, the protagonist had a strong penchant for embellishing family memory with fantastical images drawn from his imagination.

Salomón's ghost reappears at other junctures along the roads of boyhood and adolescence, his dramatic story of drowning becoming ever more nonsensical or suspect. On a Florida highway, his mother tells Eduardo that a letter they've received from a funeral home is about his father's brother. "Salomón, I said quickly, and she turned to me and half-smiled, perhaps surprised I remembered that name, so seldom spoken. That's right, she said, Salomón." But his mother corrects him as to the place of death; it was not in the lake, but in New York, where he was buried when he was a boy, as the letter indicates.[61] His specter also resurfaces at the moment the protagonist is transitioning from boy to man. "Sitting between my two grandfathers, the Polish one and the Lebanese one, I was dying of hunger," the protagonist remembers. The occasion was the first Yom Kippur after his thirteenth birthday, the first time he observed the twenty-four-hour fast forbidding all food and drink during the Day of Atonement. That morning, he had barged in on his grandfather still in his pajamas, his false teeth in a glass on the table. "It had never occurred to me that on his arrival in Guatemala in 1946, when he was barely twenty-five years old, after the war, after being a prisoner in several concentration camps, my Polish grandfather had already lost all of his teeth."[62] The grandson's intense hunger and thirst on a single fast day stand in contrast to the terrible privations the grandfather endured along with his brother, also named Salomón, who had died of hunger in the Łódź ghetto.[63] The grandfather's reaction of covering his mouth and "stammering something in Spanish" as the adolescent observes "in horror" his false teeth on the table beside him suggests the shame and embarrassment of both generations at this permanent sign of trauma.[64] The "false" teeth are another clue to the true history and long-term effects of the grandfather's experience, suppressed and silenced by the survivor himself and others in the first and second generations.

The narrator's participation in the religious ritual of fasting for the first time as a "man" frames his coming-of-age story as bracketed by mourning. Amid the intonation of a long list of names to which both grandfathers contribute a number each time the rabbi extends his yad toward them, Eduardo clearly hears his Lebanese grandfather pronounce the name Salomón. After the prayers have finished and the congregation has dispersed to the lobby, he asks his dad in English what all this listing of names and numbers was about. Responding in Spanish, his father says the names were spoken as part of *yizkor*, the prayer to honor the memory of the dead, and the numbers his grandfathers pronounced represented *tzedakah*, the donations given in honor of them. "Names of dead family members?" the teenager asks. "Yes," his father replies after a silence, "but also dead friends, and dead soldiers, and the dead six million, and that number, for a Jew, even a Jew who's just a boy, needed no further explanation." He knows that when he asks, "Also the name of your brother Salomón, then, the one who drowned in the lake?" it is an illicit, even dangerous question, but post-bar mitzvah, he is emboldened by his new condition as "all man." But his father stammers that he doesn't know what he's talking about, leaving these questions unanswered and the true story of Uncle Salomón still hidden from view.[65]

RELUCTANT TOURIST

The protagonist's travels in Europe as an adult will bring him closer to his Polish grandfather's story and its dark details. In Poland, as we have already seen in "Oh Ghetto My Love," he even enters the apartment where León Tanenbaum lived. In the course of these travels, however, he also becomes increasingly suspicious of the ways in which Holocaust memory can be exploited, commodified, or converted into tourist attractions devoted to human suffering. In some cases, the mere accumulation of signs of trauma and violent death makes continued remembering difficult or impossible. In Berlin, a friend offers to accompany him to Sachsenhausen, one of the camps where his grandfather was held. But before Berlin, he had seen the *stolperstein*, the markers placed between the cobblestones on streets where Jews had lived "before being captured and murdered by the Nazis," plaques that functioned "like little bronze gravestones" for those denied a proper burial. In Frankfurt, he had given a talk at Goethe University, which before serving as a university, had once been the headquarters of IG Farben, the principal manufacturer of Zyklon B gas, used by the Nazis to exterminate humans, though originally designed to eradicate plagues of insects.

I tried to tell my friend in Berlin that I'd already seen too much on my travels around Germany, that I was starting to lose the scope of the tragedy, that I wasn't interested in visiting concentration camps, not even one of those where my grandfather had been a prisoner, that to me every concentration camp was nothing but a tourist attraction dedicated to profiting from human suffering. But finally I gave in. In part because I'm weak and find it hard to say no to women. In part because that entire trip was a sort of tribute to my Polish grandfather, who had arrived in Guatemala after surviving for six years—the entire war—as a prisoner in concentration camps. . . . My grandfather never spoke to me of those six years, or of the camps, or of the deaths of his siblings and parents.[66]

Of course, the grandfather has spoken, if only cryptically and at the end of his life, an abbreviated account that, as we have seen, provided the impetus for *The Polish Boxer* and the texts that rippled out from it, also studied here.

Once at Sachsenhausen, the narrator is most struck not by the concentration camp but by the unperturbed attitude toward daily life of those in the residential neighborhood just across the street. "I have always been more appalled by man's apathy in the face of horror than by the horror itself," he reflects. Almost against his will, he takes the tour of the camp, which includes a torture device known as the Rack, a gas chamber, the crematoria, a cafeteria, and a small shop. But then he and his friend discover the Sachsenhausen Museum and Memorial Archive, where after a few fruitless hours looking for records of Leon Tenenbaum, the protagonist remembers his grandmother always called him Leib, and with that, his grandfather's list of prisoner numbers and imprisonment in several different concentration and forced labor camps comes to light.

Following Dora Apel's lead in *Memory Effects*, we can see that Halfon provides us with a "third frame" for considering the events of the Holocaust. If the first frame is the lived experience of the survivors themselves, and the second the journey of the secondary witness in retracing that experience, the resulting representation provided by this secondary witness "takes on an independent life and creates its own effects, especially on those who know little of the events."[67] Here and elsewhere in Halfon's writings, the unfinished business of mourning is part of an "epicurean epistemology," in which "if there exist several possible explanations to explain a phenomenon, you must retain them all."[68] The narrator recalls this as he considers the possibility that his long-tended memory of a boy named Salomón who drowned in Lake Amatitlán might be one version of the past among many, just as *duelo* itself refers to several different actions and reactions, of which mourning is only one piece.

HOFFMAN AND THE HUMMINGBIRD

Don Isidro finally remembers hearing of a boy dying on the lake years earlier, perhaps after falling into the water from a boat in the middle of the lake with no one noticing, and the lake itself returning his body to shore. But that had occurred near the village of Tacatón, on the other side of the lake.[69] In Tacatón, Eduardo meets Doña Ermelinda, next to an altar for the Maya deity Maximón, a trickster figure.[70] Doña Ermelinda tells him she has already dreamed of him sitting under the very tree where she finds him waiting for her. To his questions about Salomón, she responds with a litany of tales about boys who drowned in Lake Amatitlán, none, unfortunately, named Salomón. Instead, she serves him a potion of herbs and roots. "It will help you see your truth," she explains. He wants to ask her what truth, or which one of all truths, or whose truth exactly: "Not the truth of the drowned boy, the old woman said. Your truth of yours, she said, with that double possessive so common among indigenous speakers." She tells him about Tz'unun, the hummingbird, who in Maya cosmogony, was created from a piece of jade to carry people's desires and thoughts from one place to another.[71]

The next morning, he remembers images from the night before, though his memories are disjointed and chaotic, and he can't tell which parts were real, dreamed, or imagined. He recalls black candles, of Doña Ermelinda laughing and dancing with the figure of Maximón, of her holding a small hummingbird in her hand and rubbing it all over his body and telling him it would help him have a child, that life was senseless without a child. Amidst these heightened sensations, he feels something that could be euphoria or grief. This is where *Mourning* ends, seemingly back at its point of departure, where the first piece of text beyond the copyright page reads, "For you, Leo, who arrived before dawn, with a hummingbird." Just as the epigraph from Isaiah brings the Hebrew Bible into play, though the author claims to have never read it, Doña Ermelinda's hummingbird, harbinger of Leo's birth, suggests an affinity with the Popul Vuh as well.

CHAPTER 7

ECHOES AND REFRAINS

*I'm interested in secrets, in the taboo,
prohibited stories, in what's not said.*

PLAYING THE PARTS

"I arrived in Tokyo disguised as an Arab," declares the first line of "The Conference," the first story in *Canción*.[1] This opening, equal parts chutzpah and cheekiness, suggests yet another escapade or escape act from a protagonist who's already taken us to unexpected places along a mostly accidental itinerary. Capitalizing once more on the element of surprise, this bold entrée immediately transports us to a hybrid, extranational space. Why does a conference of Lebanese writers take place in Tokyo? What is a Jewish writer from Guatemala doing at such a conference? And what could this event have to do with a work dubbed Halfon's "kidnapping novel," centered on the story of his Lebanese grandfather's kidnapping in Guatemala City, several years before the author was born?[2] These are questions *Canción* may never answer completely; its author believes literature is about the questions, not the answers.[3] Nonetheless, in Halfon's creative universe, it might be amusing or bemusing, or even surreal, but not entirely illogical, that a trip to Japan where he "passes" as a Lebanese writer could provide a suitable story frame for the kidnapping of his Syrian-born grandfather in 1967. *Canción* offers us a surprising new fictional world which "feeds voraciously on the factual, the biographical, or the truthful."[4] As we advance in its pages, which begin and end in the same city, it will become ever clearer that Tokyo is not a random setting, but a unique "memoryland" that, like other memorylands in Halfon's itinerary or repertoire, prompts yet another reckoning with lived history and its afterlives for subsequent generations.⁵

Halfon considers *Canción* another installment in a series that began with *The Polish Boxer* and spawned other books in an unplanned way. "When I wrote the stories of *The Polish Boxer*, what presented itself was a voice, the voice of another Eduardo Halfon, a voice which is not my voice, with a temperament very much his own."⁶ Or, as one compatriot put it, *The Polish Boxer* "became an earthquake, and its ripples can still be felt today."⁷ The return of this other Eduardo Halfon is just one of the structural and thematic echoes and refrains readers will find in *Canción*. Others include, obviously, the preoccupation with disguises, evident in the novel's first line; the obsession with names, nicknames, and the untrustworthy semantics of both; the reappearance of characters from previous stories; and in the same vein, the reworking of entire narrative episodes from earlier volumes. *Canción* advocates for reading Halfon's works as an itinerary of memory by calling our attention to the intertextual relationships between his works, even as it offers new twists, turns, and invitations to join the journey.

The protagonist's reception at the Tokyo airport soon reveals he can't even manage a conversation in Arabic, suggesting his performance as an "Arab," even in Japan, even after insisting on his three Arab-Jewish grandparents in *Monastery*, may be the most outlandish of the identities he has assumed thus far. He glibly admits that "playing an Arab for a day at a conference at the University of Tokyo seemed a trivial matter if it was going to enable me to see the country" (with the word "trivial" standing in for the even more frivolous sounding "poca cosa" of the Spanish original).⁸ But this is the beginning, not the end, and the rest of the book will prove that this superficiality might itself be a cover-up. Halfon explains, "the disguise appears from the first phrase of the book . . . but it's a disguise that later one embodies. One becomes the character. It's a disguise linked to identity. Or identity through a disguise."⁹

The narrator will later explain to his Tokyo audience that he is in fact the grandson of a Lebanese grandfather who was not, *stricto sensu*, Lebanese, given that his progenitor, also named Eduardo Halfon, had left Beirut in 1917 when it was still Syria, three years before it became part of Lebanon.¹⁰ The younger Halfon, the Guatemalan-born Halfon, was himself surprised to learn this detail about his grandfather's life, as in his recollection, his grandfather had always identified as Lebanese (*libanés* in Spanish), never as Syrian, and thus for him, always *was* Lebanese.¹¹ This new thread regarding his own grandfather's previously unquestioned origin story only feeds his conviction that "our identity is nothing more than a collection of masks."¹² The name Eduardo Halfon thus circulates between author and protagonist, and between grandfather and grandson, just as the younger character's decision to "play the part" of the Lebanese writer echoes and expands on his grandfather's lifelong practice of emphasizing a Lebanese identity that was itself dubious. Halfon queries, "So, what is being Lebanese, if it has nothing to do with a country or a nationality? And on another level, what does it mean to me to be Lebanese, as the grandson of a Lebanese person who wasn't Lebanese? . . . Is identity, then, a disguise I can put on and take off when they ask me to, or when I most need to?"[13]

Canción insists once more that we approach personhood not as an essentialist uniform but as an entire wardrobe of options, options one might try on, wear for a while, or cast off when they don't respond to the needs of the moment or the climate. In the case of Halfon's characters, the puzzle of identity appears as a tug-of-war between the given and the chosen elements of being, between the immutable and undeniable fact of being born into a Jewish family in Guatemala, on the one hand, and the ongoing assertion of individual choice on the other. One can choose to be a writer, work in a given language or languages, adopt a nomadic lifestyle, elect fatherhood, or even decide they are or are not Jewish, at least in Halfon's world. Readers familiar with his body of work over two decades have come to expect and even count on this testy approach to the topic; one review of *Canción* goes so far as to claim that "the impossible alloy of identity is Halfon's great subject, the anxiety that undergirds his compulsive restaging of the past."[14] Another review summarizes *Canción* as "another minimasterpiece by a master of the form" (which form, we might ask), noting that Halfon employs an "understated conversational style" to draw us into this nightmarish world.[15]

Despite its protagonist who at times seem self-serving, even arrogant, "The Conference" introduces *Canción* as an homage or memorial to Eduardo Halfon, grandfather—not the one who survived six years in the Nazi camps immortalized in *The Polish Boxer*, *Monastery*, and other texts, but the one who arrived in Guatemala decades earlier, established himself as a successful businessman over a half-century, and then was kidnapped for ransom during the Guatemalan civil war. "Canción" was the nickname of a member of the Guatemalan guerilla group that carried out the 1967 kidnapping during the early stages of a conflict that would last another thirty years, though its effects continue to be felt in contemporary Guatemala. Occurring more than two decades after the end of World War II and the maternal grandfather's experience of that war, the 1967 kidnapping occupies a similar terrain of family history marked by shadows, secrets, and unresolved questions.

To provide some context for this incident that occurred before he was born, Halfon turns to material from his 2011 collection *Mañana nunca lo hablamos* for the second story in *Canción*.[16] In the earlier text from *Mañana* titled "El último café turco," he had already described his paternal grandparents' home as a "palace;" that same description reappears here in a story now titled "The Bedouin." The home is full of complex and elegant aromas and "fragrances and spices that emanated like souls from the kitchen." The Guatemalan cooks, trained in the arts of Arabic and Israeli cuisine (if in fact there's a difference between the two) prepare falafel, kibbe, sambouseks, mujadarra ("jadarra, my grandfather called it"), yapraks, hamin, yogurt, and baklava. But their culinary repertoire also includes Guatemalan delicacies such as hilachas, jocón, tamales, pepián, kak'ik, and a "miraculously thick corn atol." One of these remembered aromas or perfumes is that of the Turkish coffee his grandfather drank every night, serving as "a rite, a cadence, a spell, an end point to things both sweet and bitter."[17]

The narrator recalls a large gathering when he was a child, at which members of the far-flung family were arrayed around the table waiting for Uncle Salomón, a well-dressed man with the face of a Bedouin, to read the coffee residue, to have it "tell us something." The inverted cup in the narrative signals the insertion of an ancient form of knowledge or futurology into the Guatemalan dining room, but as in earlier texts such as "Tomorrow We Never Did Talk About It," this revelation or interpretation will be interrupted. The extended family, with relatives visiting from as far away as Argentina, suddenly hears footsteps. Soldiers invade the house, one of them "pawing the bronze mezuzah nailed to the doorframe." Even when an aunt explains that it is a Jewish talisman, that it contained a scroll of parchment with verses from the Torah, that people put them on their doorframes for good luck, the soldier continues to bang at it, hoping to remove it and carry it away as a trophy "so that he, too, could have good luck."[18]

With all these soldiers "prowling through the house like wild beasts," the big house suddenly seems too small, and the narrator can remember "thinking that I wanted to be deaf. I wanted to put my fingers in my ears and be deaf and so not have to hear those voices that I, in a very childlike way, understood were not entirely good, were out of place, did not belong to my world."[19] The soldiers are there, apparently, to tell the grandfather they've located one of the men who kidnapped him in 1967. But their visit brings no solace; this news brings no closure. Uncle Salomón continues to silently read the coffee's imprint in the uncomfortable company of the soldiers but does not share his interpretation with the family around the table, perhaps seeing in the residue something he dares not say out loud. The unstated, unrecounted message is also part of what the narrator remembers of this traumatic moment. What's left unsaid ominously foreshadows deeper military incursions and traumas yet to come, both in this book, and in the lives of those who will experience them.

RESEARCH AND REMEMBERING

The third story in the English version of *Canción* is "Beni," a piece that only later would appear in Spanish in Halfon's subsequent work, *Un hijo cualquiera*. With this inclusion, *Canción* represents an unprecedented engagement with the "real" in Halfon's fictional works. In an interview conducted soon after the book appeared, fellow *chapín* José García Escobar commented that it was the first time he'd seen Halfon "address Guatemalan history so thoroughly in a book," featuring it in both the background and foreground of the narration. Halfon, for his part, acknowledged that he conducted significant research and used a variety of resources such as the CIA file on his grandfather's kidnapping. He insisted, though, that for him the historical record never takes precedence over fictionmaking: "It's just a feeling of what should be where on the stage. What should be in the foreground. What should be in the background. It's a very natural process of selection and placing . . . I'm not interested in the facts, but in the smell and taste that the facts leave behind."[20]

However ingenuous this focus on sensations over facts, Guatemala's twentieth-century history plays a role in *Canción* unseen in earlier works, to some extent taking up where the unanswered questions of "Tomorrow We Never Did Talk About It" left off. In the earlier work, an adult narrator ponders the unspoken tensions that permeated his family's sudden flight to the United States in 1981, on the eve of his tenth birthday. The same protagonist returns in "Beni," but here recounts what happened when he was called back to Guatemala from his first semester of university studies almost a decade later to attend his paternal grandfather's burial. Guatemala's internal conflict has continued to rage through those years, but Eduardo for the most part has been protected from its truths and consequences.

Even though his parents had chosen to flee the country when Eduardo and his siblings were children, now it seems they have reestablished their residence as well as a certain posture in the country's still-tense conflict. Eduardo's father will insist that his oldest son fulfill his obligation as a Guatemalan by enlisting in the country's military ranks and receiving his military ID card. As father and son stand at the grave of Eduardo Halfon, *abuelo*, while a rabbi chants "some Jewish prayer," the protagonist is assured it will be a simple bureaucratic procedure, even an empty gesture. "It doesn't mean anything, my father whispered. And it's also your duty. Whether you like it or not, whether you live in Guatemala or not, you're still a Guatemalan, and every Guatemalan man who turns eighteen has to enlist in the military and receive his official military ID card."[21] Upon his return to his birthplace and nuclear family, Eduardo must attend to the duties of being both Jewish and Guatemalan.

Enter Beni, a former soldier from the Guatemalan special forces known as the *kaibiles*, who will assist Eduardo in this formality. More precisely, the story starts with the two of them en route to the Matamoros General Barracks, on their way to comply with this task that on the one hand means nothing, and on the other, means something terrible and defiled.[22] "I'd wanted to ask him if he'd really had to eat his own dog," Eduardo wonders in the first line of the story, though with Beni he keeps quiet, finding the question "almost unutterable."[23] As they make their way to the barracks through the dystopian urban landscape of the capital (buildings that look unfinished, potholes in the asphalt streets, broken windows, idlers on the streetcorners), Beni asks Eduardo about his life in the United States, whether he likes it there, whether he's working. Beni tells him how he himself once tried to leave the country, not on an airplane like Eduardo, but on foot, by land, reaching Mapastepec before Mexican police dumped him and other hopeful migrants back on the Guatemala side of the border.

The privileges of race and class are newly revealed as the family turns to an inside contact to assist Eduardo in the task of complying with a military directive, no doubt providing Beni with an economic incentive. Eduardo vaguely remembers that Beni had been a longtime associate of the family, though he can't recall if he was his grandfather's employee, or his father's employee, or just had helped with odd jobs. Whatever this personal history, Beni's handholding during this ostensibly bureaucratic act will signify both salvation and perdition. He helps Eduardo fulfill his patriotic duty, but at the same time draws him into a space of dread, a loss of innocence, and a new consciousness of a horrific national history in which he will now become complicit.

Later, the protagonist will discover an obituary with Beni's full name: Benito Cáceres Domínguez, "or let's just say that was his name. Here, for security reasons, that will be his name." He thinks he remembers seeing Beni among the soldiers who swarmed his grandfather's house at the family dinner where Uncle Salomón was preparing to read the coffee dregs, but his father emphatically denies this.[24] "Beni, before, he said, had been a Kaibil.

When I asked him what a Kaibil was, my father said a soldier. But given his expression, or perhaps given his insistent yet nervous tone, I understood at once that a Kaibil was more than just a soldier."[25]

Along with finding Beni's full name in a newspaper obituary, the protagonist will with time fill in other details about the Kaibiles, elite commando forces of the Guatemalan army who engaged in counterinsurgency tactics during the civil war, sometimes with the help of the U.S. Marines. He will learn that the Kaibiles borrowed their name "from the Mayan prince and warrior Kaibil Balam (he who has the strength and astuteness of two jaguars, in the Mam dialect)."[26] He will learn that the Kaibiles trained in warfare and other tactics at a site in the Petén jungle known as the "Inferno," enduring psychological humiliation, sleep deprivation, semi-starvation, and a final test called Dismembering the Mascot in which the soldier had to dismember the puppy he was given at the start of the training, drink its blood, and eat its flesh.[27] Such training, the text explains, was designed to make the men into "killing machines."[28] Even though the Kaibiles were later tied to "numerous massacres, widespread rape, and acts of genocide against Guatemala's indigenous population," a fact sheet from the Guatemalan Human Rights Commission claims there is little evidence to suggest that Kaibil training has changed significantly since the end of the thirty-six-year internal armed conflict, as "Guatemala continues to train Kaibiles and their role is expanding to include combating organized crime." The GHRC also found that despite a congressional ban restricting direct funding to the Guatemalan army due to its involvement in these forms of violence, the United States had continued to support, train, and collaborate with the Kaibiles into the second decade of the twenty-first century.[29]

Along with the personal, family tale that "Beni" restages, it also references an actual event that occurred on December 5, 1982, when fifty-eight Kaibiles, disguised as guerrilla fighters and armed only with the weapons typically used by their guerrilla opponents, left their base at Santa Elena Petén and travelled to a small village where they interrogated the fifty families there, demanding the location of a stash of weapons their commanders erroneously believed was hidden there. The next morning, reporting to their superiors their failure to find any weapons or communist propaganda, they received the order to "vaccinate them all."[30] The narrative describes some of what followed: a three-month-old baby was dropped in a well; children were killed with a sledgehammer or a gunshot wound to the head, or by smashing their heads against a wall; girls and women were raped before falling dead or alive into a well; men were tortured, beaten and shot before being tossed in the same well; and a grenade was finally dropped into the well to silence the "sounds of agony and sobbing" still emanating from it.³¹

The date, the location, the number of Kaibiles who participated, the information sought in the interrogations, the types of murder used, the ages of the victims, the numbers of bodies recovered, and even the euphemisms used to order the notorious Massacre at Las Dos Erres, all mark this section of the text as referring to an actual historical event. The quintessential detail at the center of the story, though, is the one-sentence paragraph that confirms that "one of the fifty-eight Kaibiles, according to testimony, was Benito Cáceres."³²

Halfon deals with historical data in a new way here, folding in a whole series of verifiable details including Beni's full name. Although there's no mention of a particular source, the use of the term "killing machine" and other descriptions strongly suggests that the author drew on the United Nations High Commission for Refugees report of the massacre, in which the language is strikingly similar to his own.³³ "Beni" doesn't just smell of facts, then, it serves them up, blurring the lines of story and history. Nonetheless, for Dustin Illingworth in his review of *Canción*, "the novella exists primarily in the borderless zone of memory."³⁴ How should readers navigate this paradox, this bloodied threshold of fact and fiction? In an article on the strategies certain contemporary Latin American writers use to narrate the real, Ana María Amar Sánchez points to parallels between Halfon's strategies and those of certain Southern Cone writers who are the children of survivors of national dictatorships. Like them, Halfon is a "son" of one of the most violent historical periods in his country. In both cases, the writers choose to distance themselves from the genre of testimony preferred by their parents' generation, and from writing as an overt form of political practice.³⁵

Despite this distancing from testimonial-style narration, tracing the arc of Guatemalan history remains a central task of *Canción*. Within this broader context, "Kaibil" emerges as a contradiction in terms, a name with many faces. Historically, Kaibil Balam (Two Jaguars) was a sixteenth-century resistance leader of the Mam people in the Maya kingdom of western Guatemala who together with his warriors, repelled the attacks of the conquistador Gonzalo de Alvarado for several months until hunger forced him to surrender. With this feat, Kaibil is remembered together with a cohort of indigenous leaders with mythological status in Latin America and the Caribbean famous for resisting the Spanish conquest and its agents, including the Taíno leader Hatuey in the Caribbean, the Aztec Cuauhtemoc in current-day Mexico, Tupac Amaru in the Incan Andes, and the Mapuche hero Caupolicán in what is today Chile.³⁶

In the context of the twentieth-century civil war in Guatemala, the military misappropriates and weaponizes the name and fame of the Maya leader with an alternate, ulterior meaning, attaching it to its special forces—many of whom were themselves of indigenous descent—tasked with committing rape, torture, and genocide in largely indigenous villages accused of harboring resistance leaders and "communist" ideology.[37] "Kaibil" thus becomes a Janus-faced figure with two opposing expressions on the same head, returning us to the confusion of the child in "Tomorrow We Never Did Talk About It" who can't tell the difference between the faces of the two opposing sides in the conflict: "I stared at the faces of the soldiers, as swarthy and indigenous as the face of the guerrilla. . . . I didn't understand. The soldiers were indigenous too? Wasn't every indigenous person a guerrilla? So who then were the guerrillas?"[38] In fact, the Kaibils' ability to "disguise" themselves as guerrillas by merely changing their clothes and weapons confirms the physical interchangeability of the two sides, suggesting, ultimately, that the crimes of the civil war were committed by brother against brother, or as Halfon himself put it, "compatriota contra compatriota."[39]

Beni himself inhabits more than one face, incarnating many paradoxes and incongruities in the story. There is Beni the trusted associate who babysits Eduardo through the process of enlisting in the army, a "simple bureaucratic procedure" rendered increasingly sinister and terrifying as the eighteen-year-old waits on a chair at the barracks. As his anxiety grows, he thinks he hears "moans, like those of a dying animal," sounds that echo those of the victims of Dos Erres, still alive when they were tossed into the well, in a massacre in which Beni his "protector" may have participated. "These were the last days of 1989 and the country was still in the midst of the civil war and it wasn't implausible to think that somewhere inside—above or below or behind me—there were prisoners of war," the narrator explains.[40] Indeed, when Eduardo finally panics and opens the door behind which Beni had disappeared earlier, he doesn't recognize the man on the other side of it, disheveled, his face flushed, his breath reeking of rum: "He was now someone else entirely. His face was someone else's. His body was someone else's. His demeanor was someone else's. His two jaguars were now ferocious and vivid and perfectly tattooed. It was as if when he crossed the threshold of the black door, he'd also crossed another darker and more metaphysical threshold and once again transformed into a Kaibil."[41]

Though he was not an eyewitness to the massacre at Dos Erres or to other atrocities committed in the context of the civil war, thanks to finding a safe haven far away in the United States, Eduardo nonetheless becomes a witness to its ongoing terror at the Matamoros barracks. Watching Beni cross the "darker and more metaphysical threshold" into the Kaibil world and worldview, he himself becomes a witness after the fact to the horrors recounted. By complying with his father's "meaningless" mandate to enlist in the military, the narrator implicates himself in the gruesome history that runs from Kaibil the Mayan hero defending his people from the notorious cruelty of the Alvarado brothers to Beni the Kaibil, converted into a killing machine capable of committing acts strikingly similar to the most heinous crimes of the colonizing project.[42]

"Beni" thus reenacts and interweaves personal and historical memory, directly engaging with the grim details of the civil war and the military's role in that war in ways we have not seen previously in Halfon's writing. His protagonist's claim to innocence is weaker here than in "Tomorrow We Never Did Talk About It" as he's no longer a child who depends on his parents for knowledge or understanding of what's happening in his country. In the here and now of the narration, Eduardo himself enters this world as Beni hands him a military ID card and tells him, soldier to soldier, to follow him into the world behind the black door.

PURSUING PERCY

Texts like "Better Not Say Too Much" and "Beni," while representing the protagonist's family as less susceptible to the range of terrors experienced by the "masses of poor Guatemalans" during and after *La violencia*, also call into question Jeff Browitt's contention that Halfon's Guatemala is an idealized space or paradise lost.[43] If in the U.S., the protections the family enjoys might be classified as white privilege, that term doesn't necessarily corelate to the racial composition and politics of Guatemala.[44] And despite possessing the resources and power to leave Guatemala at the peak of the violence, the characters in Halfon's stories end up experiencing the war in their own skin and the skin of their family members in a number of ways. The titular episode that constitutes nearly half of the pages in this volume recounts the kidnapping of the protagonist's Lebanese grandfather by the Rebel Armed Forces (FAR in the Spanish acronym), in the process demonstrating that a character like Canción may be as conflictive, unresolved, and reflective of a commitment to defend national interests as is Beni the Kaibil.

Halfon's attempts to pursue the facts of this kidnapping that predates his birth is evident, perhaps most obviously with the character of Canción himself. The perpetrator's nickname provides a deceptively lyrical title for the episode and the book itself, in line with the author's fondness for jostling readers' expectations.[45] At the same time, *Canción* reintroduces the semantic power and richness of names and nicknames seen in earlier works such as

The Polish Boxer and *Signor Hoffman*. The author's use of a single word in Spanish for the title across editions in several languages reminds us of the extralinguistic number of the grandfather's Auschwitz tattoo in "The Polish Boxer," as well as the incongruous title of *Monastery* (and its title story), about a Jewish boy who survives the Holocaust thanks to his parents' willingness to relinquish him to a new identity, a new religion, and even a new gender identity, hidden in a Catholic monastery.[46] The melodious-sounding moniker of the primary character Percy Amilcar Jacobs Fernández turns out to be illogical, even a bit nonsensical: "They called him Canción because he used to be a butcher. Not because he was a musician. Not because he was a singer (he couldn't even sing)." The explanation that "his nickname, then, stemmed from the alliteration between the words in Spanish for butcher (carnicero) and song (canción)" hardly resolves the problem of names and their meanings, and in fact creates more problems for the translator, who now must include the words in Spanish to show how this works. There are other theories for the name, too, such as Canción's tendency to say too much, to *cantar*, to "sing" or snitch.[47]

Despite all these possible meanings of the name and the important contextual and intertextual considerations around them, the most important thing to know about Canción and the book named after him, though, is that he has a real-world counterpart. The name is most arresting, most surprising, because it is the nickname of the real person Percy Amilcar Jacobs Fernández. We find the name in viable sources such as Mario Monteforte Toledo's 1971 essay on the violence of that moment in Central American history, published the year *Canción*'s author was born. In the introduction, Monteforte Toledo notes,

> Perhaps the most amorphous, but best ambushed group of the rebels is that of the FAR-3, in which lumpen proletarians participated. It is directed by Percy Amilcar Jacobs Fernández, a former university student, son of blue-collar workers and insider of the underworld. Since the end of 1967, the resistance began in the capital, not only with its own actions, but also as a source of support for commandos in other areas.[48]

Percy Jacobs's name also appears in more recent sources, such as an article by Jaime Barrios Carrillo published in 2020, that associates Canción with a half-century of bloody history, noting that it was in prison that he acquired his nickname.[49]

As with Beni and the Kaibiles, Canción and his fellow rebels create their own language, replete with alternate meanings, code names, and euphemisms. The most fluent speaker was Canción himself, who had a manner of speaking and way of expressing himself "in short, cryptic, almost poetic phrases:"

> He would rarely utter a long or even a complete sentence, and rarely was the meaning of his words in fact their literal meaning. It's not that he spoke in slang, but in his own idiolect. I beheaded a rooster, Canción would say when he killed a high-ranking military officer. My armadillo, he would say when referring to his weapon, his machine gun or rifle ... And this here is my prayer, he'd say with pride and ownership, which meant this here is my prey, my hostage.[50]

Canción and his forces use code names like "Operación Tomate" for the kidnapping operation, "El Espinero" for the house prison where his grandfather was held and "El Turco" for the grandfather himself, as "at that time, in Guatemala, all Jews and Arabs were called Turks regardless of their religion or country of origin."[51] Leaving the names in their original Spanish form further confirms their historicity and veracity.

Though the kidnapping of his grandfather happens before the protagonist is born, the focus on the character of Percy/Canción allows the narrator to carry the event both backward and forward in time, highlighting key moments. He tells us that only one of the four men who forced his grandfather into the Tiburón, the police car used to kidnap him, would survive the civil war, which ended in 1996.[52] He explains how the Guatemalan guerrilla movement had begun in the 1960s, and how, before that, his grandfather Eduardo Halfon had helped a business partner leave France in April of 1940, thanks to his connections with Jorge Ubico, Guatemala's former president and dictator, the "Little Napoleon of the Tropics," the "Hitler of Guatemala."[53] The narrator explains how in 1968, when US ambassador John Gordon Mein was assassinated, the Guatemalan government peppered the city with notices bearing the photos of three youths, offering ten thousand quetzales for information leading to the capture of the purported assassins, one of whom was Canción, alias "The Butcher." He mentions March of 1970, when Canción pulled German ambassador Karl von Spreti into a blue Volvo in another kidnapping in which the guerrillas hoped, unsuccessfully, to pressure the military government into releasing seventeen political prisoners.[54]

All of these verifiable names and chronological events create a context of actuality for the kidnapping of Eduardo's grandfather, endowing it with historical gravitas. Details of "Operación Tomate" itself also suggest that fact weighs more heavily than fiction in the account. The protagonist remembers that his grandfather claimed he had been kidnapped by a beauty queen, a beautiful and refined woman who always treated him with respect, who he believed was Rogelia Cruz, though he never heard her name. This real or imagined "perk" in his grandfather's kidnapping alludes to a unique chapter in the country's civil war, as Cruz was a well-known personality before her involvement in the Rebel Armed Forces and remains an icon today. Mary Jane Treacy explains:

> Although Guatemalan women and girls participated in street riots, student groups, even guerrilla organizations, most of their names and activities have been occluded or lost. The one exception is Rogelia Cruz Martinez, Miss Guatemala of 1959, who was abducted and killed in 1968 for her ties to the FAR ... Ironically, it is her femininity (but not her politics), and the beauty of her body (along with its destruction), that has preserved her name for over forty years. Her image, which blends the youthful promise of a beauty queen with that of a defiled victim of the state, has turned Rogelia into an icon that may be evoked in attempts to understand Guatemala's recent past.[55]

Halfon's narrator notes that "La Roge" had been elected Miss Guatemala in 1958, and that in the competition for Miss Universe, dressed in typical Mayan dress, "she criticized the U.S. government for their intervention in Guatemala in June 1954, when they had orchestrated and financed the toppling of president Jacobo Arbenz, only the second democratically elected president in the country's history."[56] Later, the narrative fills in other details regarding Rogelia Cruz following her return from the Miss Universe competition in California, such as her collaboration with the revolutionary movement, her stint at the Santa Teresa women's prison after authorities found bomb-making materials on the family property, and in January 1968, "exactly one year after my grandfather's kidnapping," her rape, torture, mutilation, and murder at the hands of the military, when she was three months pregnant.[57]

Canción also explains, in a style that seems surprisingly dry or straight for Halfon, how Arbenz—also known as "El Chelón" or "El Suizo"—began to introduce agrarian reform in 1952 with Decree 900, how in 1953 he expropriated uncultivated land from the United Fruit Company, and how a CIA operation called Operation PBSuccess led to a series of repressive governments, "genocidal military men and almost four decades of civil war (while John Foster Dulles, in 1955, was named Time magazine's Man of the Year)."[58] In an interview with Xavi Ayén, Halfon acknowledged that he conducted substantial research on the stories of Cruz and Arbenz, and recognized the relationship between *Canción* and Mario Vargas Llosa's novel *Tiempos Recios*, also focused on the US–Guatemala relationship.[59]

Finally, the narrator returns to the summer of 1981, already recounted in "Tomorrow We Never Did Talk About it," when his parents left him and his siblings in his grandfather's house during a trip to the U.S. to prepare for the family move there. This time, though, it is "not a house, not a palace, but, in fact, an alcázar: magnificent, ostentatious, enveloped in an air of eucalyptus and grandeur." Musicians, celebrities, ambassadors, and presidents had stayed as guests; there's even a photo of Golda Meir, prime minister of Israel, smiling under a black screen with gold dragons.[60]

LADY IN A RED COAT

The biographical and political information about Percy Jacobs, Rogelia Cruz, and Jacobo Arbenz that emerges in the first half of this "novella" insistently marshals the reader of "Canción" toward the topic of the Guatemalan Civil War: its causes, its contradictions, a few of its key personalities. The actual event of the grandfather's kidnapping is not just inserted within a larger theme of national violence, then, but superseded by other events, such as what happened at Dos Erres or what happened before Rogelia Cruz's body was found at the Culajaté bridge. And even with this tale of family history, the narrator can't be sure of the details, whether to trust his grandfather's boast that during his captivity he interacted with no less a personage than the beauty queen Rogelia Cruz. Maybe his grandfather, who rarely saw his captors' faces, was confusing her with "the lady with the marimbas and the red coat."[61]

The lady with the red coat has already appeared in the sixth story of the 2011 collection *Mañana Nunca Lo Hablamos*. At first, she seems to reemerge here mostly intact. The narrator recreates the episode in which his family went out for their typical Sunday midday meal at El Rodeo on Séptima Avenida; Eduardo remembers how he and his brother got permission to watch the musicians play the big marimba, and how his father whispered during the meal that the woman with the red coat was one of the guerrillas who had kidnapped his father, Eduardo's grandfather. But the woman with the red coat hardly fit with the nine-year-old's idea of villains as "smelly, fat, hairy, with oily faces covered in warts and pimples and scars;" certainly a kidnapper could not look like the beautiful lady dressed to the hilt in her red coat, could she?

In *Canción*, however, the earlier version of the story is called into question. During a visit from his father while the writer is living in Paris, Eduardo starts to share his recollections of the Sunday in which the lady with the red coat appeared, only to hear "no, that's not how it happened," that he has the details all wrong: wrong day, wrong restaurant, wrong color coat. Whose memory is at fault? "My father's memory used to be remarkable, particularly for rumor and gossip, but I think when it came to this recollection, he was mistaken," the narrator ventures. "Impossible, unacceptable, that the scene with the guerrilla woman all decked out in red could have happened in a seafood restaurant owned by a Jew."[62] Reluctant to relinquish his own view of the past, to put his own memory on trial—especially as those memories have now been set down in text, Eduardo clings to his version. There's an implicit condemnation in representing his father's memory as especially "remarkable" when it came to rumor and gossip, as these genres are inevitably associated with embellishment, distortions of the truth, and harm to the subjects. In Jewish thought, gossip constitutes *lashon hara* or evil speech that damages not only the subject of the gossip, but also the one who speaks it and the one who hears it.[63]

Now, more than thirty years after those events, in the bar in which the protagonist has been anxiously waiting since the first page of "Canción," the lady he remembers wearing a red coat in the long-ago family meal reenters the story. He recognizes her at once, and she him. "You're Halfon," she says.[64] Their date with history, if not destiny, has begun. Before conveying their conversation, however, the narrative takes yet another detour to the Guatemalan Book Fair and a motley crew of attendees. The director of the Guatemalan Muslim Association, a fan of the author's work, presents Eduardo with a Qur'an. Another man calls him an asshole, and a third grips his arm and tells him, "You're no longer kidnappable." Halfway through his memorized speech in Kaqchikel about how Guatemalan ladinos need to find common cause with their Mayan compatriots, Eduardo realizes that the last man, the one who has downgraded him from kidnappable, is El Sordo, the deaf one, another of the guerrillas involved in his grandfather's kidnapping. As he goes on with his own speech, he can't help but be disturbed by El Sordo's remark, unsure if he's unkidnappable because of his politics, or his paltry bank account, or for some other reason.

Finally, protagonist and reader sit down with Sara the guerilla kidnapper, a woman who once wore a coat that might have been red, a woman who had lived in exile for many years in several countries, a woman from a prominent family of artists and intellectuals who agrees to talk to Eduardo about his grandfather because she feels she owes it to his family, a woman who insists that under no circumstances should he write anything about whatever they discuss.⁶⁵ Of course, we already know from other warnings not to write about certain things (such as the one that adorns the back cover of *Duelo*) that our author-protagonist believes such matters are outside his control.

More than fifty pages into "Canción," finally, the text reveals some of the possible reasons that Eduardo's grandfather was kidnapped in January of 1967, including the guerrillas' contention that he treated his employees poorly (despite the grandson's recollection of him as proper and upright), and due to their urgent need for funds. But at the bar, amid tequila and smoke, he will learn of another secret, more sinister reason:

> my grandfather's name was given to the guerrilla forces by another Jew. By one of his friends from the synagogue. By one of his companions in Saturday prayers. By somebody who knew him very well, and who knew the value of the name he was handing over, and who probably received something in exchange. A Jew wrote another Jew's name on a slip of paper and handed that slip of paper over to his torturers. Eduardo Halfon, barely legible, in pencil.⁶⁶

Another slip of paper appears in *Canción*, one that flutters down to cover the yellow fragment bearing León Tenenbaum's Polish address in *Monastery*, one in which the theme of betrayal resounds, but this time from within the tribe. This fragment of paper symbolizing the sacrifice of Eduardo's grandfather to the FAR by someone from within his tiny Jewish community seems to cut even deeper than the betrayal ascribed to all Poles by his grandfather the Holocaust survivor, suggesting a crime of greed or selfishness, malice at the hands of one's own. The details that follow—of his grandfather's thirty-five days in captivity, of how his grandfather's accountant, Señor Elías, negotiated with the kidnappers for a month, of how his secretary Mery Ramírez waited on a streetcorner with the ransom money, of how his grandfather was finally dumped in a vacant lot, from which he walked home to his house on Avenida Reforma—all seem to constitute less of an injury than this betrayal, especially taking into account that the captors had treated him with decency.⁶⁷

LEVELING BLAME

Whether a fictional device or not, the appearance of a paper on which a member of his own congregation had written Eduardo Halfon's name and proffered it to Canción or another guerrilla readjusts the orientation toward the crime committed against the narrator's Lebanese grandfather. Who is responsible for that crime? Who's to blame, finally? Later, readers learn, Canción meets with an unsavory end after a return to his previous profession as a butcher, this time in Mexico City. Someone fires a single bullet into his forehead, whether the Mexican police, the Germans avenging his involvement in the death of the ambassador Karl von Spreti, the CIA avenging the death of the U.S. ambassador John Gordon Mein, someone in the FAR itself who believed he had betrayed them, or perhaps a hit man for the family of one of his victims.[68] The unresolved nature of Canción's death suggests that who's to blame for the kidnapping of the protagonist's grandfather might also be unsolvable and unresolvable. Whether or not Eduardo has in his possession all the documentation relating to the case, together with the memories and accounts of those directly involved, the secret contents of his conversation with the lady in red, and even the skeletons in the family closets and congregations, can he hold any one character accountable?

As "Canción" ends, the kidnapping of Eduardo Halfon is now long past, the protagonist who shares his name has been told he's no longer kidnappable, and his sleuthing has paid off: he's discovered important information and uncovered at least one crucial secret. But will Eduardo ever be able to step out of this story or this history as he steps out of the bar in which he meets with Sara, who now hardly seems his archenemy? Is the villain Beni the Kaibil, someone who hoped to escape the country's violence like Eduardo's family, only to be returned to Guatemala and forever marked by the physical and psychological training of the killing squads in a training ground dubbed "The Inferno"? Is Canción the primary criminal, as a member of the resistance forces that stood up to the military government's bloody terror, but were themselves sometimes perpetrators of violence? Is there an end to this story or to this conflict? A 2011 *Time* magazine article suggests that while the war may have officially ended, the violence has not.[69]

The Kaibiles, whatever their disturbing connections with the past, remain a highly revered force in Guatemalan society. A 2018 YouTube video shows several Kaibiles in full uniform, war paint, and camouflage, traipsing through jungle terrain with their weapons raised as they share personal messages with their mothers, ostensibly on Mother's Day. "The sacrifice is temporary, but the glory is eternal," says one. Comments below the video offer respect and blessings to the soldiers, honoring the Kaibiles as the best special forces in Central America and perhaps in the US as well. A few comments contest this glorious heroism, alluding to the Kaibiles' murder of unarmed villagers or the commando forces' contemporary ties with drug cartels. At least one viewer recommends incorporating the Kaibiles in a video game, suggesting the ultimate interpolation of fact and fiction.[70]

Given the ongoing support for this form of Guatemalan patriotism and heroism, it's not surprising that in the bathroom of this bar, Eduardo and the reader find the warning to "be careful."[71]

TOKYO REFRAIN

The last story in *Canción*, "Kimono on the Skin," brings the volume full circle, returning the protagonist and reader to Tokyo, to the implausible site of the conference of Lebanese writers and the participation of a Guatemalan Jewish author in that event. Some characters display their disguises, others their hardened countenances. Even the reviewers seem torn: while one attests that Eduardo "all but falls in love with a conferee named Aiko, whose own grandfather also suffered wartime brutality," another reviewer finds the novel to have "compelling scenes but scant emotional resonance."[72]

Though certain readers seem unaware of her earlier cameo, Aiko has reappeared from an earlier text, whether *Signor Hoffman* in the original Spanish, or the version in English of "Signor Hoffman" that appears in *Mourning*.[73] This recurrence is one more proof that *Canción* is anything but "scattershot" or random, as the *Publisher's Weekly* review characterizes it. In the earlier text, a visit to Ferramonti, an Italian concentration camp, has Eduardo "thinking about other bombs, thinking about Hiroshima, dreaming about Hiroshima," remembering that a Japanese girl named Aiko had taken him to the Fukuromachi primary school, located half a kilometer from the site where an atomic bomb was dropped on August 6, 1945, where all 160 teachers and students had died instantly.[74] García Escobar recognizes the return of Aiko in *Canción* as strategic, asking Halfon in an interview how important it is to the him to "build bridges into the future." Halfon describes this process as sowing seeds: "When Aiko first appeared, she was a one-page character in *Signor Hoffman*, and I didn't know who she was. I didn't know she would appear later. I didn't know her story. I didn't know her grandfather's story—which now, years later, I finally tell in *Canción*. Back then I just knew I had to place her in there, perhaps with the hope of seeing her later."[75] "Kimono on the Skin" accomplished this desire, filling in details of a visit to Hiroshima that is only hinted at in the earlier text. Ironically, Eduardo doesn't at first recognize Aiko, until she puts back on the mask she had been wearing the night before; he adjusts his own disguise as well.

In this last story of *Canción*, we learn that Aiko is, like the principal protagonist himself, a study in contrasts: "Everything about her was a contradiction. For instance: she wore a short plaid skirt, schoolgirl-style, but at the same time had antique reading glasses hanging from her neck, like a grandmother. For instance, the skin on her face was taut and rosy as a teenager's, but at the same time one silvery gray strand sparkled in her hair, almost lost in the black expanse."[76] Aiko, though Japanese, knows something about the Lebanese diaspora because she's married to a Lebanese man; she is also a 3G survivor of World War II, her grandfather a survivor of an atomic bomb dropped in Japan.

Back at the conference with which *Canción* started, it's Eduardo's turn to read from several of his works, in English, with simultaneous translation into Japanese. He launches into the first text, about El Tumbador, a Guatemalan coffee farm his grandfather had sold at the start of the civil war. But because "the image of that farm (or that civil war) ricocheted and activated the image of another farm," he gets sidetracked, and begins to talk about a Guatemalan dairy farmer of Italian descent names Azzari who had also experienced loss and displacement in the internal conflict after helping the indigenous villagers of San Juan Acul: "He told me that several members of the community had visited him one afternoon to warn him that the military were coming to look for him. A figure of speech, he said, meaning something worse. Be careful, they told him."[77] Following their advice, Azzari leaves with his entire herd, somehow managing to reach safety with his milk cows, only to learn that more than a hundred soldiers had arrived the day after his escape, and an indigenous man dressed in a ski cap had served as an executioner in the town square, deciding who would go to heaven, and who to hell, that is, who would receive a single bullet to the head that would topple them into a black hole. Despite the mask, everyone knew this man was a friend of Azzari's son, that they had played together as boys.

The story of Azzari and his milk cows, which some of the conference attendees will complain is irrelevant, bears eerie similarities to other scenes in other settings in Halfon's works. The fact that Azzari's father was an immigrant who arrived from Italy at roughly the same time as Eduardo's grandfather ties the story to the protagonist's own family history, and of course, the Italian setting is also where Eduardo met Aiko and learned that there had been concentration camps in that country as well. Other elements of the story resonate in more disturbing ways: the masked executioner's decision regarding who lives and who dies recalls the separation of Jews at Auschwitz and the *gnadenschuss* or single shot to the head; the black hole at San Juan Acul recalls the empty tombs Eduardo visited in Warsaw with Madame Maroszek took Eduardo, or closer at hand, Dos Erres' well of horror recalled in "Beni." The final element of Azzari's story—or at least Azzari's story as retold by Eduardo, is that the soldiers had burned down his farm. Thus, fire will also connect this episode to several others in Halfon's "fictions": the destruction of other indigenous villages in Guatemala during the Civil War, the gas chambers of the Holocaust, and the fire of the atomic bomb that left the kimono of Aiko's grandfather imprinted on his skin.

Aiko remembers seeing her grandfather's bare back only once, when he took her swimming as a child. She saw that a trace remained on the skin itself, the trace of a traditional kimono passed from generation to generation. She explains to Eduardo that such survivors rarely showed their scars in public, not wanting to reveal that they were "Hibakusha" or bomb survivors, as together with their children and grandchildren, they were disdained and feared, due to the possible effects of the radiation. "I was going to tell her that I very much understood the silence of a grandfather survivor, that I very much understood the marks they even wear on their skin for the rest of their lives," the protagonist muses.[78]

So it is that the narrator in *Canción* moves, sometimes subtly, sometimes abruptly, through several periods and places, from the dark room where his grandfather's kidnappers held him, to the bar where, decades later, he meets a woman who was one of those kidnappers. In its portrayals of social and political violence, this narrator avoids easy answers and rarely passes judgment on any specific person (the fellow congregant who betrays his grandfather to the kidnappers might be an exception), as that's not the role of literature. At the final session of the conference of Lebanese writers in Tokyo and the end of "Kimono on the Skin," the protagonist's Lebanese disguise begins (begins?) to unravel, to lose its shine. His critics start to circle. An old novelist from Tripoli accuses him of being an imposter, to which he responds that "every writer of fiction is an imposter." A jacketed journalist wants to know what a Guatemalan farmer and his herd of cows has to do with the Lebanese writers conference. A literature professor defends (defends?) him, explaining "that Halfon did the same thing in his writing, that all his stories seemed to lose the thread and never go anywhere."[79] A perturbed poet from Beirut wants to know if Eduardo has ever tried to visit Beirut, to which he responds that it's not an easy jaunt for a Jew (here suggesting that in matters such as these, at least, Jewishness is not so optional). To a Japanese woman who discreetly asks why the participants aren't all equally Lebanese, and what criteria was used to invite them, someone else responds with a discourse on the diversity of Lebanese identity. Eduardo stops paying attention as the arguments accelerate and proliferate, but slowly begins to feel a need to clear his name. He finally takes the microphone and matters into his own hand, returning to the theme of his grandfather. He talks about his Lebanese grandfather's house (or palace, or alcázar), his grandfather's siblings, his grandfather's businesses, his kidnapping, his death, even details about his grandfather made up on the spot, all in an attempt to prevent his colleagues from accusing him of being an imposter or a traitor.[80] In this last act of verbal or verbose self-defense, the protagonist once again demonstrates that his creator is not a documentarian but a storyteller, or as Halfon himself puts it, "I explain things that happened while at the same time confusing the matter, it's an emotional explanation, not the act of a notary."[81]

FUTURE WORLDS

To what new or familiar thresholds of history and fiction will Eduardo Halfon's forthcoming works introduce us? At what crossroads, and in what game of literary hopscotch will he situate his future fictions? What new characters or communities will we meet? What sensual commonalities with these new fellow travelers will he accentuate? Will his name-sharing protagonist traverse those pages as well? Will his homework for these projects include, finally, a reading of the Torah and/or the *Popul Vuh*?

In these pages exploring his primary works published thus far in English, I've tried to demonstrate David Ulin's contention that "what Halfon finds particularly compelling is memory and how it may or may not accrue."[82] His fictions offer examples of how to put memories to good use, whether we've recovered or inherited or even invented them, whether painful, partial, or pleasant. On this point, Lawrence Langer reminds us that engaging the imagination in this work can be potent medicine for indifference or the assumption that other generations' histories are ancient and irrelevant: "A statement like 'to understand, you have to go through with it,' however authentic its inspiration, underestimates the sympathetic power of the imagination. Perhaps it is time to grant that power the role it deserves."[83]

Perhaps there's an implicit promise in Halfon's description of writing as a kind of music-making, undergirded by the responsibility to "to keep writing, to keep riffing, or the music will stop."[84] In his case, this task will likely continue to feature a defense of the most diverse forms of survival over acquiescence to victimhood or death, always acknowledging that whether in the first or subsequent generations of events such as the European Holocaust, the bombing of Hiroshima, or the Guatemalan Civil War, to "survive as a witness," is an endlessly complex and vexed task.[85] When we accompany the author through these diverse terrains, it serves as its own kind of memory work, as "listening to a witness makes you a witness, in reading these words, you the reader, have become a witness too."[86]

No doubt, "History is always a fantasy with no basis in science, and when anyone tries to raise an invulnerable platform and place on it anything of consequence, they run the risk that a fact will change and the whole historic structure comes tumbling down," as Pío Baroja argued.[87] Nonetheless, Halfon's excursions into the historical events and memories alluded to in these texts demonstrate how fiction can contribute to deeper truths concerning these moments and more expansive understandings of the people who experienced or continue to experience them. Within each text and in the aggregate, his works reach for an ecstatic truth, and point us to "a future for which we yearn."[88]

NOTES

INTRODUCTION

Epigraph. Franco Chiaravalloti, "Eduardo Halfon: 'La incomodidad es un sentir judío,'" *Revista de letras*, June 16, 2014, https://revistadeletras.net/eduardo-halfon-la-incomodidad-es-un-sentir-eminentemente-judio. Though the citation can be translated literally as "I think I'm making a sort of hopscotch," it also alludes to Julio Cortázar's 1963 novel *Rayuela* (*Hopscotch*, 1968), which can be read in different sequences and is sometimes referred to as an experimental counter-novel.

1. Eduardo Halfon et al., "The Purest Form of Writing, the Most Intimate Form of Reading," *Massachusetts Review* 60, no. 3 (2019): 448–63, 457.
2. Eduardo Halfon, *Monastery* (New York: Bellevue Literary Press, 2014), 109, 112.
3. See the video archive of this interview with Gustavo Moto Leyva: "Desde el 'no sé': Eduardo Halfon," *El País*, Dec. 12, 2015, https://elpais.com/cultura/2015/12/15/actualidad/1450207763_402437.html, 0:40.
4. Eduardo Halfon, *Canción* (New York: Bellevue Literary Press, 2022), 13–14.
5. Juan Camilo Rincón, "El grandioso universo de Eduardo Halfon," *El Tiempo*, Nov. 17, 2020, https://www.eltiempo.com/cultura/musica-y-libros/eduardo-halfon-el-autor-guatemalteco-habla-de-su-universo-literario-549379.
6. Halfon, *Monastery*, 150.
7. Julia Johanne Tolo, "We Become the Mask That We Wear: An Interview with Eduardo Halfon," Electric Literature, Nov. 10, 2015, https://electricliterature.com/we-become-the-mask-that-we-wear-an-interview-with-eduardo-halfon.
8. Alexandra Ortiz Wallner, "Una escritura más allá de las fronteras," *Hispanorama*, no. 144 (2014): 34–38, http://otrolunes.com/35/wp-content/files/2015/01/OrtizWallner_EHalfon.pdf, 35.
9. Gabriela Stoppelman, "Tizas blancas sobre humo negro," El Anartista, Sept. 29, 2020, https://www.elanartista.com.ar/2020/09/29/tizas-blancas-sobre-humo-negro.
10. Interviewer: "Tus personajes viven permanentemente en conflicto con sus orígenes, desarraigados, como en una nada territorial." Halfon: "Soy yo el que se siente desarraigado. Lo traigo de fábrica. Me fui de Guatemala cuando era pequeño, y eso hizo que no solo me quedara sin tierra sino también sin lenguaje, ya que el inglés reemplazó al español. Para mí el desarraigo es un estado normal, no siento desasosiego en ello.

Cuando encuentro a personas con el mismo dilema me siento atraído, y me acerco a ellos a través de la literatura." Chiaravalloti, "Eduardo Halfon."

11. "I was born in a Jewish family in Guatemala, which is very different from being born in a Jewish family in Argentina." Stoppelman, "Tizas blancas."

12. Moto Leyva, "Desde el 'no sé.'"

13. Eduardo Halfon, "Dicho hacia el sur," in *Sam no es mi tío: Veintidós crónicas migrantes y un sueño americano*, ed. Aileen El-Kadi and Diego Fonseca, 133–41 (Buenos Aires: Aguilar, Altea, Taurus, Alfaguara, 2012), 135.

14. Halfon, *Mourning*, 79.

15. Eduardo Halfon, "Better Not Say Too Much," *Guardian*, November 4, 2015, https://www.theguardian.com/books/the-writing-life-around-the-world-by-electric-literature/2015/nov/04/better-not-say-too-much-eduardo-halfon-on-literature-paranoia-and-leaving-guatemala.

16. Dan Reiter, "Remembering as Deconstruction: Eduardo Halfon's *Mourning*," The Rumpus, Sept. 25, 2019, https://therumpus.net/2019/09/mourning-by-eduardo-halfon.

17. See Judy Bolton-Fasman, "Novelist Eduardo Halfon Wins Edward Lewis Wallant Award," JewishBoston, April 9, 2019, https://www.jewishboston.com/novelist-eduardo-halfon-wins-edward-lewis-wallant-award.

18. Halfon, *Monastery*, 23.

19. Halfon, *Monastery*, 105. Alan Astro finds Halfon to be "a bit sophomoric in his attitude toward Jewishness, writing for example that his recurring narrator is 'not Jewish anymore' or is Jewish 'sometimes.'" See Alan Astro, "Avatars of Third-Generation Holocaust Narrative in French and Spanish," in *Third-Generation Holocaust Narratives: Memory in Memoir and Fiction*, ed. Victoria Aarons (Lanham, MD: Lexington Books, 2016), 103–30.

20. "Jews get very pissed off. Anything I say about Judaism, I'll piss somebody off. Either I didn't explain enough, or I said too much, or whatever. Jews are very, very touchy, when you're speaking about Judaism, especially when speaking about Israel, as I do in *Monastery*. So that's tricky. And I know it's going to be, and I'm fine with that. Jews are really susceptible, but they're not offensive. They're not going to go on the offense. They're not going to put a gun on the table." Marilyn Miller, interview with Eduardo Halfon, July 22, 2022, author's residence, Guatemala City.

21. While such doubt is—undoubtedly—ubiquitous in many if not all faith traditions, Jewish skepticism has been a subject of inquiry from at least medieval times forward. "A Conversation with Eduardo Halfon on *Monastery*." Bellevue Literary Press, accessed May 16, 2024, https://blpress.org/author-qas/conversation-eduardo-halfon-monastery. See also the *Yearbook of the Maimonides Centre for Advanced Studies*, 2018, devoted to the topic of Jewish skepticism across time. Bill Rebiger, ed., *Yearbook of the Maimonides Centre for Advanced Studies* (Boston: De Gruyter, 2018).

22. Erika Dreifus, "A Special Kind of Kinship: On Being a '3G' Writer," in *Third-Generation Holocaust Narratives: Memory in Memoir and Fiction*, ed. Victoria Aarons, 1–16 (Lanham, MD: Lexington Books, 2016), 11. Astro similarly notes in "Avatars" that "Holocaust fiction itself is a self-conscious trope of Halfon's." Astro, "Avatars," 120.

23. JTA and Emily Burack, "Why Is Holocaust Fiction Still So Popular?" *Haaretz*, April 24, 2019, https://www.haaretz.com/jewish/holocaust-remembrance-day/2019-04-29/ty-article/why-holocaust-books-continue-to-be-in-high-demand/0000017f-e732-da9b-a1ff-ef7f075f0000.

24. In Eduard Aguilar, "Eduardo Halfon: 'Nada les gustaría más a mis editores que una

novela larga,'" *Alicanteplaza.es*, July 28, 2018, https://alicanteplaza.es/eduardo-halfon-nada-les-gustaria-mas-a-mis-editores-que-una-novela-larga.

25. Halfon, *Monastery*, 2014, 145.
26. Moto Leyva, "Desde el 'no sé.'"
27. "Si te faltara algo o quisieras puntualizar lo que sea, te doy permiso para que inventes todo." Gras explains, "Eso me dijo **Eduardo Halfon**, con ligera pero meditada picardía, sorbiendo un té cuyo sabor ya no recuerdo, en la librería **Laie** de Barcelona. O eso quisiera pensar yo que me dijo, pues en los tiempos que corren uno no puede estar seguro de nada, menos teniendo enfrente a un escritor que también es personaje, a un personaje que es, al mismo tiempo, escritor. Halfon vs. Halfon. Y vuelta a empezar. Lo cierto es, si me preguntan, que mejor inventarse todo, inventarnos todos. Porque todo puede ser. Todo se resume en eso: *Peut-être*." (That's what Eduardo Halfon told me, lightly but with premeditated mischievousness, sipping a tea whose flavor I no longer remember, in the Laie bookstore in Barcelona. Or that's what I would like to think that he told me, since these days you can't be sure about anything, least of all having in front of you a writer who is also a character, a character who is, at the same time, a writer. Halfon vs. Halfon. And back to the beginning. What's certain is, if you ask me, it's better to invent everything, invent ourselves completely. Because anything is possible. Everything can be summarized in this: *Peut-être*.) In "Permiso para que inventes todo: Unas breves notas sobre Eduardo Halfon," *Iletradoperocuerdo* (blog), May 26, 2015, https:// iletradoperocuerdo.com/2015/05/26/permiso-para-que-inventes-todo-unas-breves-notas-sobre-eduardo-halfon.
28. Daniel Alarcón, "A Roundtable Discussion with Daniel Alarcón + Eduardo Halfon + Santiago Vaquera-Vásquez," *Believer Magazine*, no. 69 (Feb 1, 2010), https://www.thebeliever.net/a-roundtable-discussion-3.
29. "A Conversation with Eduardo Halfon on *The Polish Boxer*," Bellevue Literary Press, accessed May 16, 2024, https://blpress.org/author-qas/a-conversation-with-eduardo-halfon.
30. Des Barry, "Eduardo Halfon and *The Polish Boxer*: Des Barry interviews Eduardo Halfon," *3:am Magazine*, May 29, 2013. https://www.3ammagazine.com/3am/eduardo-halfon-and-the-polish-boxer.
31. José García Escobar, "'Ch'ayonel almost means boxer, in Kaqchikel': Translating Eduardo Halfon into a Mayan Language," *Asymptote*, Feb. 24, 2020, https://www.asymptotejournal.com/blog/2020/02/24/chayonel-almost-means-boxer-in-kaqchikel-translating-eduardo-halfon-into-a-mayan-language.
32. In my July 2022 interview with the author, we discussed how publishers often call his distinct works novels, even though he may not. Regarding *Canción*, for example, he noted that, "the English edition has chapter titles. And I tried to take that off, and the publisher said, no no, let's keep that, because we've done that in the two previous books and your readers expect that." Miller, interview with Eduardo Halfon, July 22, 2022, author's residence, Guatemala City.
33. While pieces of these works have appeared in English, no work of those listed has appeared in its entirety in English except "Oh Ghetto My Love" (in *Mourning* [New York: Bellevue Literary Press, 2018]), but without the wonderful illustrations of David de las Heras. See Halfon, *O gueto mi amor*, illustrated by David de las Heras (Primera edición, Páginas de Espuma, 2018).
34. Barry, "Eduardo Halfon and *The Polish Boxer*."
35. "Quería narrar en el lindero mismo que divide la historia y la ficción." Eduardo Halfon, *De cabo roto* (Barcelona: Littera Books, 2003), 9.

36. On the differences between *cuento* and *relato*, see "Relato y cuento corto": "El cuento es una narrativa en prosa de hechos imaginarios, el relato por su parte admite hechos no ficticios." "Relato y cuento corto: Diferencias," Las letras del alba, accessed May 18, 2024, https://www.lasletrasdealba.es/diferencias-entre-relato-y-cuento-corto.
37. See Benjamin Veschi, "Etimología de relato," Etomologia.com, Jan. 2019, https://etimologia.com/relato. I used Google Translate to render this description into English as a way to highlight the shortcomings of the literal rendering in English.
38. Halfon, *Canción*, 154.
39. "Creo que la clave allí es que no son memorias, no escribo memorias, no es autobiografía, es ficción. Todo lo que escribo es ficción." "Eduardo Halfon, mi obra es una novela en marcha," YouTube, posted by Casa de América, June 7, 2018, https://www.youtube.com/watch?v=oc4I1rMPV6w, 0:18.
40. Müller-Funk, "On a Narratology of Cultural and Collective Memory," *Journal of Narrative Theory* 33, no. 2 (2003): 207–27: "If one gives up the concept of memory as storage, in which nothing gets lost, you also have to relinquish the idea of a strong and stable subject," 208.
41. Eduardo Halfon, *The Polish Boxer* (New York: Bellevue Literary, 2012), 76 and Halfon, *Monastery*, 108–9.
42. Eduardo Halfon, "Tomorrow We Never Did Talk about It," trans., Anne McLean. Working Title 1.3. (Hadley, MA: Massachusetts Review, 2016). All publication dates are for the English translations of the works cited.
43. Ortiz Wallner has suggested the notion of "writerly mosaics" in relation to Halfon's fictional worlds. Ortiz Wallner, "Una escritura," 35.
44. See Erica Durante and Maude Havenne, "La obra en 'matryoshka' de Eduardo Halfon: Un proyecto literario global." *Revista Iberoamericana* 87, no. 274 (2021): 265–88.
45. See for example, "Eduardo Halfon, mi obra es una novela en marcha" and José García Escobar, "'Literature is not about answers. But questions': An Interview with Eduardo Halfon, Author of *Canción*." *Asymptote*, Oct. 12, 2022. https://www.asymptotejournal.com/blog/2022/10/12/literature-is-not-about-answers-but-questions-an-interview-with-eduardo-halfon-author-of-cancion.
46. While Eduardo Halfon's *Un hijo cualquiera* (Barcelona: Libros del Asteroide, 2022), was released while I was working on this book, it had not been translated into English at the time of publication.
47. Jhumpa Lahiri, Eduardo Halfon, Ilan Stavans, "Three Authors Leave, Stay, Dream, and Long for Elsewhere: Jhumpa Lahiri, Eduardo Halfon, and Ilan Stavans in Conversation." LitHub, Aug. 24, 2020, https://lithub.com/three-authors-leave-stay-dream-and-long-for-elsewhere.

CHAPTER 1

Epigraph. Ariel Burger, *Witness: Lessons from Elie Wiesel's Classroom* (New York: Houghton Mifflin Harcourt, 2018), 34.

1. The international team included Ollie Brock, Thomas Bunstead, Lisa Dillman, Daniel Hahn, and Anne McLean. Hahn and Dillman have continued to work with Halfon on subsequent translations into English.
2. "Entonces, sin yo planificarlo, y sin saber que esto iba a pasar, aquella primera edición de *El boxeador polaco* ha ido funcionando como una especie de libro gestor, o como libro madre, o como un sol, si se quiere, para todos los libros siguientes que circulan alrededor de él y que forman parte de un proyecto o quizás de un solo libro, escrito por entregas. Nunca sé cómo seguirá. Ni tampoco cuándo termina. Quizás sólo

lo sabe ese otro Eduardo Halfon." In Aloma Rodríguez, "Entrevista a Eduardo Halfon: 'Nuestra identidad no es más que una colección de máscaras,'" *Letras Libres*, Feb. 24, 2021, https://www.letraslibres.com/espana-mexico/libros/entrevista-eduardo-halfon-nuestra-identidad-no-es-mas-que-una-coleccion-mascaras.

3. Rodríguez, "Entrevista a Eduardo Halfon."
4. See "The Polish Boxer," Bellevue Literary Press, accessed May 18, 2024, https://blpress.org/books/the-polish-boxer.
5. Author email communication with Eduardo Halfon, December 19, 2022.
6. "De hecho, pese a que los títulos mantengan exteriormente la ilusión de la equivalencia entre las ediciones en castellano y las versiones en otros idiomas, el pacto de fidelidad que usualmente define el vínculo entre un original y su traducción se halla traicionado por este autor, quien se burla borgianamente de la noción de autoría, entregando una obra proteiforme y concéntrica." Erika Durante and Maude Havenne, "La obra en 'matryoshka' de Eduardo Halfon: Un proyecto literario global." *Revista Iberoamericana* 87, no. 274 (2021): 265–88.
7. "Author Eduardo Halfon in Conversation with Daniel Medin," Center for Writers and Translators, American University in Paris, Dec. 12, 2019, https://www.aup.edu/news-events/news/2019-12-12/author-eduardo-halfon-conversation-daniel-medin.
8. An audio version of the Spanish original is available. "Lejano – Eduardo Halfon (Audiolibro)," YouTube, posted by Audioclásicos, April 1, 2020, https://www.youtube.com/watch?v=dGYSjxoKHK8.
9. Eduardo Halfon, *Polish Boxer*, 9. A version of Piglia's 1986 "Tesis sobre el cuento" (Thesis on the short story) can be found at the University of Sao Paolo's E-Disciplinairies, https://edisciplinas.usp.br/pluginfile.php/2544967/mod_resource/content/1/RicardoPigliaTesissobreelcuento.pdf. The English translation of Piglia's first thesis that "un cuento siempre cuenta dos historias" erases the difference between *cuento* and *historia* and the respective nuances of fiction and history associated with the two terms. Despite the reference to Piglia and Latin American theory on the short story, Halfon has indicated elsewhere that English language writers such as James Joyce, Ernest Hemingway, John Cheever and Raymond Carver all are important models: "But before all of them, and after all of them, there was Chekhov." In "A Conversation with Eduardo Halfon on *The Polish Boxer*," Bellevue Literary Press, accessed May 13, 2024, https://blpress.org/author-qas/a-conversation-with-eduardo-halfon.
10. Halfon, *Polish Boxer*, 9.
11. Halfon, *Polish Boxer*, 12–13.
12. Halfon, *Polish Boxer*, 36.
13. See Aurelio Auseré Abarca, Luis Miguel Estrada Orozco, and Eduardo Halfon, "Eduardo Halfon: Identidad en construcción: Una conversación con Aurelio Auseré Abarca y Luis Miguel Estrada Orozco," *Latin American Literature Today*, May 2018, https://latinamericanliteraturetoday.org/es/2018/04/eduardo-halfon-identity-under-construction-conversation-aurelio-ausere-abarca-and-luis. "Eduardo Halfon: ¿Qué guatemalteco? El guatemalteco de cierta clase social y capitalino es un tipo, del cual vengo. Pero también está el guatemalteco indígena, que es el 80% del país y al cual me acerco a veces. Como Juan Kalel, en *El boxeador polaco* (2008). Ese cuento me gusta tanto por la inversión que se da entre alumno y maestro. Kalel se vuelve aquél que guía al que era su profesor hacia otra Guatemala, la Guatemala rural e indígena adonde mi narrador Eduardo Halfon lo va a buscar. Por eso el título es 'Lejanía,' la distancia que existe entre esas dos Guatemalas y la necesidad de Juan Kalel para guiar al profesor en un mundo que le es desconocido y donde se siente inseguro. Del mismo modo que Juan

Kalel se siente en la vida universitaria en la capital. Son dos mundos en el que cada cual es un extranjero en el territorio del otro."

14. The story order is different in the Spanish versions, with "Twaineando" appearing third in both the 2008 and 2019 editions of *El boxeador polaco*.
15. Halfon, *Polish Boxer*, 45.
16. "UFM.edu - Libro El Boxeador Polaco por Eduardo Halfon: entrevista con Luis Figueroa." YouTube, posted by Newmedia UFM, Feb. 27, 2009, https://www.youtube.com/watch?v=AYfqh6CbmG4.
17. As Arlene Stein points out, "to draw fragments of an experience into a coherent narrative is a potentially devastating process if the experience was so overwhelming as to have been shattering. Therefore, to protect the individual from reexperiencing terrible events, trauma is often 'banished from consciousness.'" Arlene Stein, "'As Far as They Knew I Came from France': Stigma, Passing, and Not Speaking about the Holocaust." *Symbolic Interaction* 32, no. 1 (2009): 44–60, 45. The disjointed nature of the grandfather's account recalls a description in Nadezhda Mandel'shtam's *Hope Against Hope: A Memoir* (New York: Atheneum, 1970), 379, that recounts camp life in Russia during the Stalinist regime: "Most accounts of life in the camps appeared on first hearing to be a disconnected series of stories about the critical moments when the narrator nearly died but miraculously managed to save himself. The whole of camp life was reduced to these highlights, which were intended to show that although it was almost impossible to survive, man's will to live was such that he came through nevertheless. Listening to these accounts, I was horrified at the thought that there might be nobody who could ever properly bear witness to the past. Whether inside or outside the camps, *we had all lost our memories*" (my emphasis). See also Dora Apel's chapter "Appropriating the Testimonial Form" in *Memory Effects*, where she notes, "If we recognize that secondary witnesses also may suffer forms of secondary trauma, it is reasonable to inquire into their relationship to these testimonies and the testimonial format as a form for secondary witnessing. While identifying with survivors, secondary witnesses also resist and reject the pathos and abjectness that are associated with victimhood, often constructing the survivor in ways that create a tension between the horror of the past and resilience to it that has brought them into the present." Dora Apel, *Memory Effects: The Holocaust and the Art of Secondary Witnessing* (New Brunswick, NJ: Rutgers University Press, 2002), 93. Apel also notes there that "a great deal of weight has been given to survivor testimonies as a form of representation closest to the historical truth. Yet the role of the interview-artist is of considerable importance in how the work is shaped and perceived." Apel, *Memory Effects*, 95.
18. Dora Apel, "The Tattooed Jew," in *Visual Culture and the Holocaust*, ed. Barbie Zelizer, 300–20 (New Brunswick, NJ: Rutgers University Press, 2001), 308.
19. Shoshana Felman and Dori Laub, *Testimony: Crises of Witnessing in Literature, Psychoanalysis and History* (New York: Routledge, 1992), 57.
20. Halfon, *Polish Boxer*, 80.
21. "Origin Stories: Dwyer Murphy interviews Eduardo Halfon," *Guernica*, April 15, 2013, https://www.guernicamag.com/origin-stories.
22. Halfon uses the term "mosaic of episodes" in his 2013 interview as guest DJ with NPR's *Alt.Latino*: Jasmine Garsd, "A Braid Of Words: Guest DJ Eduardo Halfon, Author of 'The Polish Boxer.'" *Alt.Latino*, NPR, May 10, 2013, https://www.npr.org/sections/altlatino/2013/05/04/181136776/a-braid-of-words-guest-dj-with-eduardo-halfon-author-of-the-polish-boxer.

23. Janet Liebman Jacobs, *The Holocaust across Generations: Trauma and Its Inheritance among Descendants of Survivors* (New York: New York University Press, 2016), 41.
24. Halfon, *Polish Boxer*, 78. Halfon confirms the number was his grandfather's own number in his interview with *Alt.Latino*. Garsd, "A Braid of Words."
25. Tanja Schult, "From Stigma to Medal of Honor and Agent of Remembrance," in *Entangled Memories: Remembering the Holocaust in a Global Age*, ed. Marius Henderson and Julia Lange, 257–91 (Heidelberg: Universitätsverlag Winter, 2017), 268.
26. Victoria Aarons, "Found Objects: The Legacy of Third-Generation Holocaust Memory," in *Translated Memories: Transgenerational Perspectives on the Holocaust*, ed. Ursula Reuter and Bettina Hofmann, 231–50 (Lanham, MD: Lexington Books, 2020), 238–39.
27. "The Polish Boxer by Eduardo Halfon. (book trailer)." YouTube, posted by Polish Boxer, Sept. 5, 2012, https://www.youtube.com/watch?v=kq1UzG_wmIs.
28. The lyrics can be found on Wikipedia, s.v. "Tumbalalaika," last updated June 4, 2024, https://en.wikipedia.org/wiki/Tumbalalaika.
29. Halfon, *Polish Boxer*, 78–79.
30. Halfon, *Polish Boxer*, 91.
31. "The first experiments in tattooing used a metal stamp, which perforated the skin (on the left breast), and ink was rubbed into the wound. This developed into a more sophisticated system of needle tattooing (on the left arm). At least 400,000 people were tattooed in this way." Imogen Tyler, *Stigma: The Machinery of Inequality* (London: Zed Books, 2020), 139.
32. Reeve Brenner, *The Faith and Doubt of Holocaust Survivors* (New Brunswick, NJ: Transaction Publishers, 2014), 90, 37 (emphasis in the original).
33. Halfon, *Polish Boxer*, 89. See also Maurice Lamm, "The History, Meaning, and Significance of Kaddish," Chabad, accessed May 13, 2024, https://www.chabad.org/library/article_cdo/aid/281617/jewish/The-History-Significance-and-Meaning-of-Kaddish.htm.
34. Schult, "From Stigma to Medal," 259.
35. Aarons, "Found Objects," 241.
36. Primo Levi, *Survival in Auschwitz: The Nazi Assault on Humanity*, trans. Stuart Woolf (New York: Touchstone, 1996), 27, 26.
37. Nina Fischer, *Memory Work: The Second Generation* (New York: Palgrave Macmillan, 2015), 115.
38. Halfon, *Mourning*, 89.
39. *Numbered*, dir. Dana Doran and Uriel Sinai, documentary film (Israel, 2012).
40. Lisa Costello, *American Public Memory and the Holocaust: Performing Gender, Shifting Orientations* (Lanham, MD: Lexington Books, 2020), 132.
41. See producer Neta Zwebner-Zaibert's synopsis for the film at "*Numbered*. Plot." Imdb, accessed May 13, 2024, ttps://www.imdb.com/title/tt1921040/plotsummary?ref_=tt_ov_pl.
42. "The number was rarely openly displayed and remained a personal item of memory.... Most know the number by heart, but some refused to say it in Hebrew, only referring to it in German, the language of the perpetrators. Some could not recall the number etched on their arm but believed that this was a conscious act of suppression. Others, who throughout the years had been asked the question why they did not remove the tattoo, answered that it was the perpetrators not the survivors who should be ashamed." Schult, "From Stigma to Medal," 262.
43. Arlene Stein, "As Far as They Knew," 53–54.
44. Tyler, *Stigma*, 139.

45. Schult, "From Stigma to Medal." Schult begins with the case of Marina Vainshtein, who "turned her body into a living Holocaust memorial by covering large parts of her skin with scenes showing ghettoization, deportation, the extermination by gas, the burning of corpses in the crematoria, and placed an Auschwitz serial number on her right arm," 256. Dora Apel discusses Vainshtein's case in "The Tattooed Jew," noting, "to demonstrate her belief that the postwar generations must carry on the memory of the Holocaust, she places her own body between the past and future as a barrier to forgetting," Apel, "The Tattooed Jew," 308. Vainshtein's extensive tattoos can be seen in this trailer, beginning at 1:26: "Tattoo Jew Documentary Trailer," YouTube, posted by Andy Abrams, Dec. 13, 2011. https://www.youtube.com/watch?v=nLszeZgvU5s.
46. Primo Levi, *The Drowned and the Saved* (New York: Summit Books, 1986), 105.
47. Schult, "From Stigma to Medal," 259.
48. Fischer, *Memory Work*, 118.
49. Costello, *American Public Memory*, 132.
50. Daniel C. Brouwer and Linda Diane Horwitz, "The Cultural Politics of Progenic Auschwitz Tattoos: 157622, A-15510, 4559," *Quarterly Journal of Speech* 101, no. 3 (2015): 534–58, 538.
51. Marianne Hirsch, "Surviving Images: Holocaust Photographs and the Work of Postmemory," in *Visual Culture and the Holocaust*, ed. Barbie Zelizer, 214–46 (New Brunswick, N.J.: Rutgers University Press, 2001), 220.
52. Brouwer and Horwitz, "Cultural Politics," 540.
53. Brouwer and Horwitz, "Cultural Politics," 536–37.
54. Brouwer and Horwitz, "Cultural Politics," 537–38.
55. Halfon et al., "The Purest Form of Writing, the Most Intimate Form of Reading," *Massachusetts Review*, 60, no. 3 (2019): 448–63, 451.
56. Halfon, *Polish Boxer*, 76.
57. Eduardo Halfon, *Monastery*, 108–9.
58. Halfon, *Polish Boxer*, 89–90. Many firsthand sources confirm the presence of boxers at Auschwitz, including at least one Polish boxer. Hermann Langbein notes that boxing was the sport "the SS most consistently supported" and that "Teddy Pietrzykowski, a Polish amateur, was probably the best-known boxer in the main camp" of Auschwitz. Prisoners were sometimes provided with boxing gloves and received incentives of food and better work assignments in exchange for boxing. See Hermann Langbein, *People in Auschwitz* (Chapel Hill: University of North Carolina Press in association with the United States Holocaust Memorial Museum, 2004), 130. Other volumes dedicated to the experience of boxers in the Nazi camps include Alan Scott Haft, *Harry Haft: Auschwitz Survivor, Challenger of Rocky Marciano* (Syracuse, NY: Syracuse University Press, 2006); the graphic novel by Reinhard Kleist, *The Boxer: The True Story of Holocaust Survivor Harry Haft* (New York: Harry N. Abrams, 2014); and Robert Sharenow, *The Berlin Boxing Club* (New York: Balzer and Bray, 2012). Other boxers "forced to fight for the entertainment of their Nazi captors" include Jacques Razon and the Greek-Jewish Salamo Arouch, the latter of whom inspired the 1989 film *Triumph of the Spirit*, directed by Robert Young and starring Willem Dafoe as Arouch. Though it had the distinction of being the first feature film to be shot on location at Auschwitz, Peter Travers called it a "woefully misguided film" in his review. Peter Travers, "Triumph of the Spirit," *Rolling Stone*, Dec. 8, 1989, https://www.rollingstone.com/movies/movie-reviews/triumph-of-the-spirit-252966. In the 1980s, Razon and Arouch sparred with each other in the California courts over issues of intellectual property rights related to their experiences in

Auschwitz: "California. Court of Appeal (2nd Appellate District). Records and Briefs. B062757, Petition for Rehearing," Google Books, Nov. 23, 1992, https://www.google.com/books/edition/California_Court_of_Appeal_2nd_Appellate/r3F8tmZEsaMC. The Tunisian world champion boxer Jung Perez was also deported to Auschwitz. See Hayim Azses, *The Shoah in the Sephardic Communities: Dreams, Dilemmas and Decisions of Sephardic Leaders* (Jerusalem: Sephardic Educational Center in Jerusalem, 2005), 285. The French boxer Sim Kessel reportedly avoided death many times, including when the rope intended to hang him broke: "it was the support of the boxing fraternity that saved him on two critical occasions." Sim Kessel, *Hanged at Auschwitz: An Extraordinary Memoir of Survival* (Lanham, MD: Cooper Square Press, 2001), 1.

59. Chaim Potok, introduction to *Last Traces: The Lost Art of Auschwitz*, by Joseph P. Czarnecki (New York: Atheneum, 1989), xii.

60. Czarnecki, *Last Traces*, 104–10. Pietrzykowski was reportedly transferred to the camp at Neuengamme in 1943, where he continued to box, knocking out a German heavyweight named Schally Hodemach in a famous fight that would later become the subject of the 1962 Slovakian film *The Boxer and Death*, based on Pietrzykowski's experience, though the boxer is given a different name. Czarnecki, *Last Traces*, 175n27.

61. Potok, introduction to *Last Traces*, xiii.

62. Ángel M. Díaz Miranda, "'El boxeador polaco': Operaciones mnemónicas e identitarias en la obra de Eduardo Halfon," *Cincinnati Romance Review*, no. 50 (Spring 2021): 44–65, 47.

63. Steffi Hobuß, "Silence, Remembering, and Forgetting in Wittgenstein, Cage, and Derrida," in *Beyond Memory: Silence and the Aesthetics of Remembrance*, ed. Alexandre Dessingué and Jay Winter, 95–110 (New York: Routledge, 2016), 105.

64. Levi, *The Drowned and the Saved*, 172. See also Daniel Schwarz's discussion of this passage in *Imagining the Holocaust* (New York: St. Martin's Press, 1999), 76–77.

65. Halfon, *Polish Boxer*, 78.

66. Schult, "From Stigma to Medal," 267.

67. Jacobs, *Holocaust across Generations*, 92.

68. The most obvious example of this preoccupation is *Signor Hoffman*, still untranslated into English in its entirety. On the topic of Jewish names in the context of the United States, see Fermaglich, who argues, "historical debates about immigration, antisemitism and race, class mobility, gender and family, the boundaries of the Jewish community, and the power of government all look different when name changing becomes a part of the conversation. . . . Rather than a step on the way to forgetting the past, name changing was a part of Jews' ethnic networks, strategies, and values." Kirsten Fermaglich, *A Rosenberg by Any Other Name: A History of Jewish Name Changing in America* (New York: New York University Press, 2018), 4.

69. Halfon, *Polish Boxer*, 84. The narrator hears the reference to the *lagerleiter*'s elegant hands with recognition, as an explanation of why his grandfather always took great care of his own hands.

70. Halfon, *Polish Boxer*, 90.

71. Halfon, *Polish Boxer*, 78.

72. Halfon likely read *Tropic of Cancer* in English, as the translation does not match that of other translations to Spanish. James Goodwin notes, in relation to Miller's work, "As a genre, autobiography combines discourse and history, the two axes of temporality and subjectivity in prose. In discourse, temporality is defined by the act of writing itself, which is the point of origin for the writer's identity. Discourse situates subjectivity within the moment of expression. In history, temporality is defined by past events

arranged in a narrative order; in strict application, as in standard histories, it excludes signs of the writer's intervention with the material." James Goodwin, "Henry Miller, American Autobiographer," in *Critical Essays on Henry Miller*, ed. Ronald Gottesman, 297–313 (New York: G.K. Hall, 1992), 302.

73. Halfon, *Polish Boxer*, 82.
74. Aarons, "Found Objects," 234.
75. Halfon, *Polish Boxer*, 78. For more on the connection of food and memory to the Shoah, see Fischer, who notes that "familial Holocaust memory is also evident at the dinner table itself." *Memory Work*, 160.
76. Fischer, *Memory Work*, 185.
77. Halfon, *Polish Boxer*, 78.
78. Halfon, *Polish Boxer*, 81.
79. Halfon, *Polish Boxer*, 82–89. Other terms specific to life in the camps can be found at "The Language of the Camps." JewishGen, accessed Sept. 16, 2023, https://www.jewishgen.org/ForgottenCamps/General/LanguageEng.html.
80. Nina Sankovitch, *Tolstoy and the Purple Chair: My Year of Magical Reading* (New York: Harper, 2011), 71.
81. Schwab distinguishes between memories that "often bear the traces, gaps, and lacunae of trauma like raw scars" and fiction, poetry, and film, that "can create a more protected space to explore the effects of violence from within multiple voices embedded in imagined daily lives." Schwab, *Haunting Legacies: Violent Histories and Transgenerational Trauma* (New York: Columbia University Press, 2010), 5.
82. Halfon, *Mourning*, 97–98. Lang writes, "third-generation authors invest a remarkable amount of time in recovering documents, artifacts and places." Jessica Lang, *Textual Silence: Unreadability and the Holocaust* (New Brunswick, NJ: Rutgers University Press, 2017), 92.
83. Brouwer and Horwitz, "Cultural Politics," 538.
84. Lang, *Textual Silence*, 90.
85. Lang, *Textual Silence*, 93.
86. Brouwer and Horwitz, "Cultural Politics," 538.
87. Lang, *Textual Silence*, 89.
88. Melvin Jules Bukiet, ed. *Nothing Makes You Free: Writings by Descendants of Jewish Holocaust Survivors* (New York: W.W. Norton, 2002), 16.
89. "Es difícil resistir la tentación de convertir en literatura el pasado familiar si, como le sucede al guatemalteco Eduardo Halfon, se tiene un abuelo polaco que se libró de morir en Auschwitz gracias a un boxeador que le enseñó las palabras exactas para poder sobrevivir. Y más difícil aún si ese abuelo llevaba tatuado en el antebrazo el número 69752 y, cada vez que su nieto le preguntaba por ello, se limitaba a responder que era su teléfono y que se lo había tatuado para no olvidarlo." Ana Mendoza, "Eduardo Halfon: 'La ansiedad de vivir es algo muy judío,'" Zenda, June 27, 2018, https://www.zendalibros.com/eduardo-halfon-la-ansiedad-vivir-algo-judio.
90. Jacques Derrida's concept of cryptonomy, "that is, a traumatic designification of language to ward off intolerable pain," seems relevant in this context. "For Derrida, cryptographic writing is fractured writing that always 'marks an effect of impossible or refused mourning.'" Schwab, *Haunting Legacies*, 4.
91. Sida Dekoven Ezrahi, "Representing Auschwitz." *History and Memory* 7, no. 2 (1995): 121–54, 122, cited in Lang, *Textual Silence*, 97.
92. Lang, *Textual Silence*, 92.

NOTES TO PAGES 38–44   161

93. See Brouwer and Horwitz, "Cultural Politics," 538; and Pritika Chowdhry, "What Is Counter-Memory?," Pritika Chowdhry (website), July 15, 2021, https://www.pritikachowdhry.com/post/what-is-counter-memory.
94. "The Polish Boxer," *Publishers Weekly*, July 9, 2012, https://www.publishersweekly.com/978-1-934137-53-6.
95. Dreifus, "A Special Kind of Kinship," 11–12.
96. Halfon, *Polish Boxer*, 180.
97. Halfon, *Polish Boxer*, 181. "Lech lecha" represents a central tenet of the Jewish faith, in which God makes a covenant with Abraham and tells him to "go forth" to see the covenant fulfilled and the Jewish people established. Some scholars consider the encounter the moment when God shifts God's focus from the collective to the individual.
98. Halfon, *Polish Boxer*, 182–83.
99. Halfon, *Polish Boxer*, 183. See the prologue in Rena Kornreich Gelisson and Heather Dune Macadam, *Rena's Promise: A Story of Sisters in Auschwitz* (Boston: Beacon Press, 1995), for details of Rena's tattoo removal and the preservation of the piece of skin in formaldehyde.
100. "Characters Who Are Looking for Their Roots: Q&A with Eduardo Halfon," *Sampsonia Way*, March 15, 2013, http://archive.sampsoniaway.org/blog/2013/03/15/characters-who-are-looking-for-their-roots-qa-with-eduardo-halfon.
101. "Origin Stories."

CHAPTER 2

Epigraph. NPR Staff, "Questions For Eduardo Halfon, Author of 'The Polish Boxer,'" National Public Radio, May 10, 2013, https://www.npr.org/2013/05/10/182258778/questions-for-eduardo-halfon-author-of-the-polish-boxer.
1. While *Roma* is often preferred to the term *Gypsy*, considered offensive to some, *gitano* and *Gypsy* are the terms that Halfon and his character Milan Rakić use in the texts in the Spanish original and its English translations, respectively.
2. Mark Forsyth, *The Elements of Eloquence* (New York: Berkeley Books, 2014), 92–97.
3. For information on the Mesón Panza Verde's restaurant, hotel, and art gallery, see https://www.panzaverde.com.
4. Halfon, *Polish Boxer*, 53.
5. Halfon, *Polish Boxer*, 55–56.
6. Halfon, *Polish Boxer*, 54. To peruse David Beidenbender's score for "Melodious Thunk," a jazz composition itself inspired in Monk's signature style, see "Melodious Thunk," David Biedenbender (website), accessed May 15, 2024, https://davidbiedenbender.com/work/melodious-thunk.
7. Halfon, *Polish Boxer*, 57.
8. Robin Kelley, *Thelonius Monk: The Life and Times of an American Original* (New York: Free Press, 2009), 69.
9. See, for example, Kelley, *Thelonius Monk*, 302, on always closing with "Epistrophy"; and Rob Van der Bliek, *The Thelonius Monk Reader* (Oxford, UK: Oxford University Press, 2001), 222.
10. Kelley, *Thelonius Monk*, 76.
11. Thelonius Monk, *Thelonious Monk Quartet with John Coltrane at Carnegie Hall*, produced by Michael Cuscuna, recorded November 29, 1957 (Blue Note, September 27, 2005).
12. David Dicaire, *Jazz Musicians, 1945 to the Present* (Jefferson, NC: McFarland, 2006), 23.

13. Tony Bolden, *Afro-Blue: Improvisations in African American Poetry and Culture* (Urbana: University of Illinois Press, 2004), 57.
14. Timo Müller, *The African American Sonnet: A Literary History* (Jackson: University Press of Mississippi, 2018), 79–80.
15. Brent Hayes Edwards, *Epistrophies: Jazz and the Literary Imagination* (Cambridge, MA: Harvard University Press, 2017), 7, 20, 212.
16. Halfon, *Polish Boxer*, 58–59. Martha Argerich's recording of the sonata can be heard on YouTube: "Martha Argerich plays Franz Liszt—The Piano Sonata in B-Minor S.178," YouTube, posted by ArgerichHD, May 24, 2013, https://www.youtube.com/watch?v=no4GkRTC_Lo.
17. Halfon, *Polish Boxer*, 60.
18. Halfon, *Polish Boxer*, 61.
19. Halfon, *Polish Boxer*, 62.
20. See, for example, "Sebald, Wittgenstein, and the Ethics of Memory," which considers Wittgenstein's ideas in relation to W. G. Sebald's *Austerlitz*, whose protagonist is a double for the philosopher: "Sebald's initiation of the reader into Austerlitz's life story through visual and verbal references to the philosopher suggests certain Wittgenstein themes and problems," including "the relation of ethics to aesthetics and of both to memory, of propositions to truth-making, and of the verbal to the visual arts." Nina Pelikan Straus, "Sebald, Wittgenstein, and the Ethics of Memory," *Comparative Literature* 61, no. 1 (2009): 43–53, 43.
21. Halfon, *Polish Boxer*, 54–56.
22. Halfon, *Polish Boxer*, 63.
23. Halfon, *Polish Boxer*, 64.
24. Halfon, *Polish Boxer*, 64.
25. Halfon, *Polish Boxer*, 65.
26. Halfon, *Polish Boxer*, 67.
27. Halfon, *Polish Boxer*, 68–69.
28. Halfon, *Polish Boxer*, 71. For a chart on the different meanings and uses of *Gypsy*, *Roma*, and other terms associated with the same group in the context of the Holocaust, see "Their Name: 'Roma'? 'Sinto'? 'Gypsy'?" USC Shoah Foundation, accessed May 14, 2024, https://sfi.usc.edu/education/roma-sinti/en/conosciamo-i-roma-e-i-sinti/chi-sono/da-dove-vengono-il-nome/il-nome-rom-sinto-zingaro.php.
29. Halfon, *Polish Boxer*, 71.
30. In Halfon's "Domingos en Iowa," a brief story published in the Colombian journal *El malpensante*, "a father and his two-year-old son go to classical music concerts to get to know each other in silence." Eduardo Halfon, "Domingos en Iowa." *El malpensante*, no. 210, Aug. 2019, https://elmalpensante.com/articulo/4224/domingos-en-iowa.
31. According to Christian Gerard, the song recalls a trip band member Robert Smith made to Jerusalem with Siouxsie and the Banshees, and further describes "Wailing Wall" as an exploration of "the intense devotion of those who hold religious devotion to their core, consuming their very being, permeating the pores of their skin and the tangled threads of their psyches." Christian Gerard, *The Cure FAQ* (London: Backbeat Books, 2021), 144. Jeff Apter groups "Wailing Wall" with other "epic downers" in The Cure's repertoire and classifies it a "Middle East-flavoured dirge that came to Smith when he was touring Israel with the Banshees." Jeff Apter, *Never Enough: The Story of the Cure* (London: Omnibus Press, 2005), 201–2. The song references a scene in which the narrator complains of being "besieged" by Orthodox Jews.

32. Eduardo Halfon, *Monastery*, 38–39.
33. The reader never actually witnesses the scene at Marjorie's, as the story focuses on the woman the narrator meets on the way to the building and ends in a hallway before he enters the storied space. See several references to Marjorie Eliot and her weekly parlor jam sessions in Greenland, *Jazzing*, which quotes one musician saying that "Marjorie's is like a church—or, it *is* church. It's a generous environment and spiritual, I'd say." Thomas Greenland, *Jazzing New York City's Unseen Scene* (Urbana: University of Illinois Press, 2016), 151.
34. Halfon, *Monastery*, 131. For this citation and to view a list of Monk's sayings, see Shaun Usher, *Lists of Note* (San Francisco: Chronicle Books, 2015), 150. In Halfon's *Signor Hoffman*, full of wordplay and nameplay around variations of Halfon and Hoffman, E. T. A. Hoffman appears, not just as the writer and musician whose works inspired Tchaikovsky's masterpiece ballet suite *The Nutcracker* (1892), but as someone who arbitrarily assigned names to Jews in Poland, connecting the theme of famous musicians and writers to the equally important theme of names. For more on this history, see Norman Davies, *Europe: a History* (Oxford, UK: Oxford University Press, 1996), 731. There is a reference to Halfon's use of the detail in Aurelio Auseré Abarca, Luis Miguel Estrada Orozco, and Eduardo Halfon, "Eduardo Halfon: Identity Under Construction: A Conversation with Aurelio Auseré Abarca and Luis Miguel Estrada Orozco." *Latin American Literature Today*, May 2018, https://latinamericanliteraturetoday.org/es/2018/04/eduardo-halfon-identity-under-construction-conversation-aurelio-ausere-abarca-and-luis.
35. Marilyn Miller, interview with the author, Guatemala City, July 22, 2022. Some years earlier, Halfon had explained, "For me, language and literature are about music, so my writing style is very lyrical. When you're translated, there is a problem because it could be a very good, very exact translation but still be missing the music. So the deal was that the five English translators could translate, but I would be the sixth translator. Their words were all fine, but it was an issue about breathing. There has to be a certain rhythm to the way a sentence is written, and the usage of commas is really important. I very rarely say this, but my musical style comes from wanting to be a pianist when I was younger, and not being allowed. I've always been very drawn to music. What I write is based on that. Language as music." See "Characters Who Are Looking for their Roots."
36. "A Conversation with Eduardo Halfon on *The Polish Boxer*," Bellevue Literary Press, accessed May 14, 2024, https://blpress.org/author-qas/a-conversation-with-eduardo-halfon.
37. Joshua Barnes, "No Borders: An Interview with Eduardo Halfon," *Sampsonia Way*, Dec. 10, 2012, http://archive.sampsoniaway.org/literary-voices/2012/12/10/no-borders-an-interview-with-eduardo-halfon.
38. "A Conversation with Eduardo Halfon on *The Polish Boxer*."
39. Halfon, *Polish Boxer*, 93–94.
40. Halfon, *Polish Boxer*, 92. Bajramović's "Pelno me sam" can be heard here: "Saban Bajramovic—Pelno Me Sam," YouTube, posted by World Tour with Music, Jan. 28, 2019, https://www.youtube.com/watch?v=fe2upQwkpHg.
41. Garth Cartwright, *Princes Amongst Men: Journeys with Gypsy Musicians* (London: Serpent's Tail, 2007), 58–59.
42. Halfon, *Polish Boxer*, 93.
43. Halfon, *Polish Boxer*, 99.
44. Halfon, *Polish Boxer*, 98. "By early January 1942, the Gypsies were being taken to the village of Chelmno (Kulmhof) about thirty-five miles northwest of Litzmannstadt, where a killing center for Jews using gas vans had started to operate on December 8, 1941. The

practice was to kill a certain number of Jews whenever the ghetto of Litzmannstadt became overcrowded, and this same facility was now used to 'solve' the problem of the typhus epidemic among the Gypsies." Guenter Lewy, *The Nazi Persecution of the Gypsies* (Oxford: Oxford University Press, 2000), 115.
45. Halfon, *Polish Boxer*, 101–2.
46. The film in question is no doubt the 1996 *Lizst's Rhapsody*.
47. Halfon, *Polish Boxer*, 103.
48. Halfon, *Polish Boxer*, 104.
49. *The Rough Guide to Budapest* (London: Rough Guides, 2015), 216.
50. Halfon, *Polish Boxer*, 108.
51. Halfon, *Polish Boxer*, 110–11.
52. Halfon, *Polish Boxer*, 113.
53. Eduardo Halfon, *La pirueta* (Valencia: Pretextos, 2010).
54. Halfon, *Polish Boxer*, 94.
55. "Galardonada con el XIV Premio de Novela Corta José María de Pereda, esta obra es la historia insondable y prohibida de un pianista serbio, contada por alguien llamado Eduardo Halfon. Pero también es la historia de una odisea balcánica, de la obsesión por un jazzista, de una persecución misteriosa y erótica, de cómo esa historia primero se escapa de las fronteras de cualquier amistad, luego rebasa los límites de cualquier cuento, y finalmente encuentra su camino hacia estas páginas." "La pirueta," El Argonauta, accessed May 18, 2024, https://www.elargonauta.com/libros/la-pirueta/978-84-92913-22-0.
56. "A Conversation with Eduardo Halfon on *The Polish Boxer*."
57. The José María de Pereda Prize is granted annually by the government of Cantabria, Spain, with a monetary prize of 30,000 euros.
58. Halfon, *Polish Boxer*, 135.
59. Halfon, *Polish Boxer*, 142. The use of the British-flavored *stave* instead of musical *staff* here suggests this section of *The Polish Boxer* was translated by Danny Hahn.
60. Halfon, *Polish Boxer*, 150.
61. Halfon, *Polish Boxer*, 154.
62. Halfon, *Polish Boxer*, 159.
63. Halfon, *Polish Boxer*, 168.
64. Halfon, *Polish Boxer*, 169.
65. Halfon, *Polish Boxer*, 170–71.
66. Halfon, *Polish Boxer*, 94, 95.

CHAPTER 3

Epigraph. "Taller en traducción," Blogs@baruch, posted by a.galeas, June 25, 2015, https://blogs.baruch.cuny.edu/tallerentraduccion/?p=781.
1. Eduardo Halfon, *De cabo roto* (Barcelona: Littera Books, 2003), 9.
2. Halfon's work has been critically received as an outstanding example of autoficción, defined by Julia Musitano as "un género paradójico por excelencia, que vacila entre dos mundos, el de la autobiografía y el de la novela, y que no nos permite como lectores discernir entre verdad o invención" (a supremely paradoxical genre which vacillates between two worlds, that of autobiography and that of the novel, and which does not permit us as readers to discern between truth or invention). Julia Musitano, "La autoficción: Una aproximación teórica. Entre la retórica de la memoria y la escritura de recuerdos." *Acta Literaria* 52 (2016): 103–23, 110. Obviously, "verdad" y "invención" might be exchanged in this definition for "history"

and "fiction." Alexandra Ortiz Wallner, "Una escritura más allá de las fronteras: La narrativa f(r)iccional de Eduardo Halfon," *Hispanorama*, no. 144 (2014): 34–38.
3. See "Eduardo Halfon. Story and History: Bleeding into Fiction." Institute for Ideas and Imagination, Columbia University, January 16, 2020. https://ideasimagination.columbia.edu/events/eduardo-halfon.
4. While I generally cite from the 2012 English version of *The Polish Boxer*, on occasion I reference some of the Portuguese expressions retained in the Spanish original.
5. Eduardo Halfon, *Polish Boxer*, 170.
6. Halfon, *Polish Boxer*, 187.
7. "'Uma frase muito bonita, mas que me deixa confuso', revelou Eduardo Halfon, referindo-se ao tema." See "A literatura rasga a realidade," Póvoa de varzim, Feb. 15, 2008, https://www.cm-pvarzim.pt/noticias/a-literatura-rasga-a-realidade.
8. Halfon, *Polish Boxer*, 173, 174.
9. Halfon, *Polish Boxer*, 174.
10. "Nueva América | Claudio Lomnitz and Eduardo Halfon (Dec. 10th, 2020) | Writing Lives," YouTube, posted by Columbia Institute for Ideas and Imagination, Dec. 15, 2020, https://www.youtube.com/watch?v=iLivBv8AC_s. These comments occur at 11:30 and 20:30.
11. Halfon, *Polish Boxer*, 175.
12. See Tolo, "We Become the Mask"; and "Nueva América," 12:27.
13. Halfon, *Polish Boxer*, 175–76.
14. Cited in Juan Camilo Rincón, "El grandioso universo de Eduardo Halfon." *El Tiempo*, Nov. 17, 2020, https://www.eltiempo.com/cultura/musica-y-libros/eduardo-halfon-el-autor-guatemalteco-habla-de-su-universo-literario-549379.
15. In the version of "Discurso de Póvoa" that appears in the 2019 edition of *El boxeador polaco*, Halfon provides evidence for the veracity of the grandfather's story by adding a parenthesis in which he refers to a photo in black and white that shows his grandfather in jacket and tie, riding a bicycle "on some deserted street in Berlin," after being liberated from Sachsenhausen. This is the same photo that graces the cover of this more recent edition. Eduardo Halfon, *El boxeador polaco* (Barcelona: Libros del asteroide, 2019), 189.
16. Ortiz Wallner, "Una escritura más allá de las fronteras," 35.
17. Nicolás Campisi, "The Dislocation of Cosmopolitan Identities in Eduardo Halfon's *Monasterio*," *INTI: Revista de Literatura Hispánica*, no. 87–88 (2018): 113–24, 119.
18. Stephanie Pridgeon, "Silences between Jewishness and Indigeneity in Eduardo Halfon's *Mañana nunca lo hablamos*." *Revista canadiense de estudios hispánicos* 42, no. 1 (2018): 99–121, 118n7.
19. Charlotte Gartenberg, "Haunted Stories, Haunted Selves: Ghosts in Latin American Jewish Literature" (PhD diss., City University of New York, 2018), 18–19, https://academicworks.cuny.edu/gc_etds/2767. See also Chloé Habran, *Construcción posmemorial y digresión en la obra de Eduardo Halfon* (PhD diss., Faculté de philosophie, arts et lettres, Université catholique de Louvain, 2018), http://hdl.handle.net/2078.1/thesis:16593.
20. Manuel Alberca, "¿Existe la autoficción hispanoamericana?," *Cuadernos del CILHA*, No. 7/8 (2005–2006), 115–27, 115–16, my translation: "La autoficción es un relato que se presenta como novela, es decir como ficción, o sin determinación genérica (nunca como autobiografía o memorias), se caracteriza por tener una apariencia autobiográfica, ratificada por la identidad nominal de autor, narrador y personaje. Es precisa-

mente este cruce de géneros lo que configura un espacio narrativo de perfiles contradictorios, pues transgrede o al menos contraviene por igual el principio de distanciamiento de autor y personaje que rige el pacto novelesco y el principio de veracidad del pacto autobiográfico."

21. Matías Barchino, "Los cuentos de Eduardo Halfon: hiperrelato y autoficción," *LEJANA: Revista Crítica de Narrativa Breve*, no. 6 (2013): 1–13, 6.
22. Henry Miller, *Tropic of Cancer* (New York: Grove, 1961), 5.
23. "A su primera etapa, siguiendo la moda de la época, se la calificó de 'metalenguaje.' A la segunda etapa, compuesta por sus libros más conocidos, traducidos y premiados (en el 2018 recibió el Premio Nacional de Literatura en Guatemala, una tierra no sancta para escritores, como repasa en el valioso texto 'Mejor no andar hablando demasiado,' incluído en *Biblioteca bizarra*), se la cataloga con la muletilla recurrente de la 'autoficción.'" (Following the trend at the time, they characterized his early work as "metalanguage." The second period, which included his best-known works that had been translated and won awards [in 2018 he received the National Prize for Literature in Guatemala, a no-man's land for writers, as he notes in his important text "Mejor no andar hablando demasiado" included in *Biblioteca bizarra*] has been classified with the recurrent label of "autofiction"), my translation. Damián Huergo, "Eduardo Halfon: Un escritor por accidente," Entrevista, June 7, 2020. *Página 12*, https://www.pagina12.com.ar/269646-eduardo-halfon-un-escritor-por-accidente. "Mejor no andar hablando demasiado" was published in English in the *Guardian* as "Better Not Say Too Much."
24. "Ese otro Eduardo Halfon es muy diferente a mí. . . . Lleva mi nombre y mi biografía pero no soy yo." Huergo, "Eduardo Halfon." See Marjorie Worthington, *The Story of "Me": Contemporary American Autofiction* (Lincoln: University of Nebraska Press, 2018), 11, for the broad definition of autofiction.
25. Worthington, *The Story of "Me,"* 11.
26. See Per Krogh Hansen et al., eds. *Emerging Vectors of Narratology* (Berlin: De Gruyter, 2017), 49.
27. Gérard Genette, *Fiction and Diction* (Ithaca, NY: Cornell University Press, 1993), 74–79.
28. Worthington, *The Story of "Me,"* 12.
29. On translating *El boxeador polaco* into Kaqchiquel, see Escobar's "Ch'ayonel almost means boxer, in Kaqchikel."
30. Alberca, "¿Existe la autoficción hispanoamericana?," 115–16. See also Manuel Alberca, "En las fronteras de la autobiografía," in *Escritura autobiográfica y géneros literarios*, ed. Manuela Ledesma Pedraz (Jaén: Universidad de Jaén, 1999), 58–60.
31. Halfon et al., "The Purest Form of Writing," 449.
32. Huergo, "Eduardo Halfon": "No tengo una tierra propia, una ciudad, un país, un sitio que me llame," dice Halfon luego de un largo suspiro. "Lo anhelo. Quizás por eso voy por el mundo buscándolo. Puedo hacer de cualquier ciudad la mía, o mejor dicho puedo hacerla parecer la mía. Pero nunca lo es."
33. "Taller en traducción."
34. Halfon, *Polish Boxer*, 176–77.
35. Peter Ohlin, "Bergman's Nazi Past," *Scandinavian Studies* 81, no. 4 (2009): 437–74, 455.
36. Ohlin, "Bergman's Nazi Past," 454.
37. Bergman, "Film and Creativity," *American Cinematographer* 53, no. 4 (1972): 378–79, 426–31, 434, 429.
38. Werner Herzog and Moira Weigel, "On the Absolute, the Sublime, and Ecstatic Truth," *Arion: A Journal of Humanities and the Classics* 17, no. 3 (2010): 1–12, 1.
39. Herzog and Weigel, "On the Absolute," 7.

40. Herzog and Weigel, "On the Absolute," 9.
41. "Nueva América," 12:08.
42. Herzog and Weigel, "On the Absolute," 11.

CHAPTER 4

Epigraph. Andreas Huyssen, *Twilight Memories: Marking Time in a Culture of Amnesia* (New York: Routledge, 1995), 7.

1. Eduardo Halfon, *Mañana nunca lo hablamos* (Barcelona: Editorial Pre-Textos, 2011). The volume has not been released in English, although certain sections, including the title story, are available in translation.
2. David Pérez Vega, "*Mañana nunca lo hablamos* por Eduardo Halfon." *Desde la ciudad sin cine* (blog), Sept. 9, 2018, http://desdelaciudadsincines.blogspot.com/2018/09/manana-nunca-lo-hablamos-por-eduardo.html. There is considerable debate around how Halfon's texts should be classified in terms of genre. Some critics, such as Stephanie Pridgeon, study the book as a "novel," while others prefer to focus on Halfon's penchant for "border crossings between literary genres such as the novel and the short story," See Stephanie Pridgeon, "Silences between Jewishness and Indigeneity in Eduardo Halfon's *Mañana Nunca Lo Hablamos*," *Revista Canadiense De Estudios Hispánicos* 42, no. 1 (2018), 99–121; and Ortiz Wallner, "Una escritura más allá de las fronteras," 34. Vanessa Perdu similarly describes *Mañana nunca lo hablamos* as a "hybrid work." Vanessa Perdu, "Experiencias del exilio en el cuento guatemalteco contemporáneo: 'Los exiliados' de Mario Monteforte Toldeo, 'Ningún lugar sagrado' de Rodrigo Rey Rosa y 'Mañana nunca lo hablamos' de Eduardo Halfon," *Península* 11, no. 1 (2016): 155–73, 157. Chloé Habran judges it to be a collection of ten novels: see the chapter "Diez novelas cortas componen *Mañana nunca lo hablamos*" in Chloé Habran, *Construcción posmemorial y digresión*, 38. The author himself has said in relation to *Mañana nunca lo hablamos*: "I don't remember being aware that this book was the book I wanted to write. I began to write episodes from my childhood, nothing more than episodes or perhaps tales, and little by little, without realizing it, the structure of the book started to gestate on its own, the logic of those ten episodes, or stories, or chapters, became clear to me. It imposed itself on me, we might say." ("No recuerdo haber tenido consciencia de que este libro fuera el libro que yo quería escribir. Empecé a escribir episodios de mi infancia, nada más como episodios o como relatos, y poco a poco, sin darme cuenta, la estructura del libro se fue gestando sola, el sentido de esos diez episodios, relatos, o capítulos, se me esclareció. Se me impuso, digamos.") Cited in José Roberto Leonardo, "*Mañaña nunca lo hablamos* de Eduardo Halfon." *Diario del gallo* (blog), May 9, 2011, https://diariodelgallo.wordpress.com/2011/05/09/manana-nunca-lo-hablamos-de-eduardo-halfon. Related to this question of genre, Halfon has said, "My books gradually come together, they become one single thing, almost as if they were a novel in progress. Or a series, a literary project, unified. But with each one of them written very individually." ("Mis libros se van uniendo, se van volviendo una sola cosa, casi como si fuera una novela en marcha. O una serie, un proyecto literario, todo unido. Pero escritos, cada uno, muy individualmente.") "Eduardo Halfon, mi obra es una novela en marcha." YouTube, posted by Casa de América, June 7, 2018. https://www.youtube.com/watch?v=oc4I1rMPV6w.
3. Jeff Browitt, *Contemporary Central American Fiction: Gender, Subjectivity and Affect* (Portland, OR: Sussex Academic, 2018), 76, my emphasis.
4. "Sin proponérmelo, casi sin darme cuenta, vuelvo una y otra vez a las narrativas de mi infancia. A mis historias infantiles. Como si, al escribirlas, quisiera también recuperar algo, o recordar algo, o simplemente regresar a ese espacio tan blanco del cual fui

desterrado. . . . A veces pienso que por eso escribo. Para intentar regresar a la ilusoria y frágil pureza de mi niñez, en la Guatemala de los turbulentos años setenta. Para meter el plumón en la tinta de mi memoria infantil hasta encontrar allí los momentos que fueron mis puertas de salida. Para volver sobre mis pasos de niño y caminar nuevamente en aquellos pórticos y quizás así, ahora, en un puñado de páginas, y a través del prisma nebuloso de la memoria y la ficción, recuperar destellos de un paraíso perdido." My translation. The video, with Halfon narrating in Spanish, and a hand, perhaps his own, placing family photos on the sand near the water's edge, one on top of the other, is available on YouTube. Editorial Pre-Textos, "Mañana nunca lo hablamos de Eduardo Halfon: Víde Tita Portela y Fred Fuentes para Editorial Pre-Textos," YouTube, posted by Editorial Pre-Textos, Jun 13, 2011, https://www.youtube.com/watch?v=o3Kp-ME9lJ2U. The subjects of the photos appear to include older family members, a street view with earthquake damage, a mother with two young children, a class picture of young children, two different shots of two boys arm in arm (Eduardo and his brother?), a mother, father, and their two children seated on a red carpeted staircase, a beach scene with mountains in the background (the grandparents' chalet on Lake Amatitlán?), over which the hand finally places a copy of the original edition of *Mañana nunca lo hablamos*, visually connecting the book to the pre-placed photos. The sound of the sea can be heard at the beginning and end of the video.

5. Perdu, "Experiencias del exilio," 160.
6. Perdu, "Experiencias del exilio," 160.
7. "Poco a poco, el paisaje infantil de este escritor niño empieza sutilmente a verse invadido, una esquina, un horizonte, una nebulosa. Botas militares. Metralletas. Desaparecidos. Guerrilleros. Terrorismo. Guatemala años ochenta. Y la familia puede y lo hace: huye." Javier Goñi, "Mañana nunca lo hablamos," *El Pais*, July 30, 2011, https://elpais.com/diario/2011/07/30/babelia/1311984757_850215.html.
8. Browitt translates "El baile de la marea" as "The sway of the tide." A group effort with Eduardo Halfon, Anne McLean, and others produced "The Sway of the Sea." In this story, the father insists on holding his son's hand at the water's edge, explaining that as a child he had drowned further along the beach, and was rescued and revived by a US marine. See Eduardo Halfon, "The Sway of the Sea," trans. Alba Griffin et al., Newwriting, March 2012, https://www.newwriting.net/2012/03/the-sway-of-the-sea. The last story, "Mañana nunca lo hablamos," is also included in the 2012 compilation *Ni hermosa ni maldita: Narrativa guatemalteca actual*, 51–70. The twenty-four stories included in that volume "take us by the hand through spaces where the most turbulent dynamics, the strangest forms of loneliness, and the darkest conflicts come together" Alejandro Torún et al., *Ni hermosa ni maldita: Narrativa guatemalteca actual* (Guatemala Ciudad: Alfaguara, 2012), 9, my translation.
9. Browitt, *Contemporary Central American Fiction*, 75, 77.
10. Browitt, *Contemporary Central American Fiction*, 82.
11. The meaning of "Ladino" here is unrelated to its use as a term to identify the language or culture of the Judeo-Spanish diaspora that resulted from the Alhambra Decree of 1492, in which Jews were required to convert to Catholocism or leave the dominions of the Catholic monarchs later consolidated into the nation-state of Spain. "In Guatemala, any person who does not self-identify as an indigenous person is popularly called Ladino, even if they are indigenous, and this includes black people, Asians, or any type of mestizo, *criollo*, or foreigner." Luis A. Sánchez-Midence and Victorino-Ramírez Liberio, "Guatemala: Cultura tradicional y sostenibilidad," *Agricultura, Sociedad y Desarrollo* 9, no. 3 (2012): 297–313, 300.

12. Browitt, *Contemporary Central American Fiction*, 77.
13. Jorge Ramón González Ponciano, "The SHUMO Challenge: White Class Privilege and the Post-Race, Post-Genocide Alliances of Cosmopolitanism from Below," in *War by Other Means: Aftermath in Post-Genocide Guatemala*, ed. Carlota McAllister and Diane M. Nelson, 307–29 (Durham, NC: Duke University Press: 2013), 307–8. A "small but extremely powerful minority" of Euro-Americans in Guatemala are the primary beneficiaries of the regressive agrarian and fiscal structures that still govern the country, González Ponciano argues. They in turn enforce a dichotomy that is perhaps more fundamental to Guatemalan life than the distinction between Indians and ladinos: that of *gente decente* versus "everyone else," a category including not only all indigenous people but also "common" or "plebeian" ladinos stigmatized as *shumos, mucos*, or *choleros*. "*Gente decente* is a term that biologizes class distinction, but it is not, any more than *ladino* or *shumo*, reducible to race, especially in the U.S. sense of the one-drop rule." González Ponciano, "The SHUMO Challenge," 308.
14. González Ponciano, "The SHUMO Challenge," 309.
15. Judith Kay, "Jews as Oppressed and Oppressor," in *Judaism, Race, and Ethics: Conversations and Questions*, ed. Jonathan K. Crane, 66–104 (University Park: Pennsylvania State University Press, 2020), 86.
16. *Through a Glass Darkly* is the phrase Thomas Melville chose for his volume subtitled *The U.S. Holocaust in Central America* (2005), a "chronicle of mass murder in Guatemala and El Salvador" (back cover). In the introduction, Melville describes the book as "the story of a regime change executed in Guatemala by the Republican occupant of the White House" in 1954, the installation of a puppet regime that "has proven to be an economic, political, and social disaster for the Guatemalan people, the results of which remain to this day." Thomas Melville, *Through a Glass Darkly: The U.S. Holocaust in Central America* (Philadelphia, PA: Xlibris, 2005), 11.
17. Beatriz Manz, *Paradise in Ashes: A Guatemalan Journey of Courage, Terror, and Hope* (Berkeley: University of California Press, 2004), 224. For a fascinating study of the bishop's murder at the intersection of memoir, journalism, and chronicle, see Francisco Goldman, *The Art of Political Murder: Who Killed the Bishop?* (New York: Grove Press, 2007).
18. Cited in Manz, *Paradise in Ashes*, 3–4, 224. See also Daniel Rothenberg, *Memory of Silence: The Guatemalan Truth Commission Report* (New York: Palgrave Macmillan, 2012), 179.
19. Rothenberg, *Memory of Silence*, 185–86.
20. John Broder, "Clinton Offers His Apologies to Guatemala," *New York Times*, March 11, 1999. In fact, the United States' support of the Guatemalan military was not limited to the years of the civil war. In a chapter on the history of the military's rise to power, Jennifer Schirmer explains, "The army that arose after the U.S.-financed invasion of 1954 was fiercely anticommunist and bound to the Cold War fears of both Guatemala's upper class and Big Brother to the north. U.S. officers once again directed the Escuela Politécnica as they had before 1944." Between 1963 and 1982, "the army moved from being a determinant presence within the civilian state structure to assuming control of the State itself. The military began to function as a political force." Jennifer Schirmer, *The Guatemalan Military Project: A Violence Called Democracy* (Philadelphia: University of Pennsylvania Press, 1998), 14, 17.
21. Judith Zur, *Violent Memories: Mayan War Widows in Guatemala* (Boulder, CO: Westview Press, 1998), 158.
22. Primo Levi, *The Drowned and the Saved* (New York: Summit Books, 1986), 23, cited in Manz, *Paradise in Ashes*, 230.

23. "Writers on the Fly," YouTube, posted by Iowa City UNESCO City of Literature, Dec. 6, 2010, https://www.youtube.com/watch?v=9kaKeV1a0Yc, 9:08.
24. Librería Cálamo, "Eduardo Halfon presenta 'Canción,' obra publicada por Libros del Asteroide: Conversa con el editor Luis Solano," Facebook, Feb. 2, 2021, https://www.facebook.com/libreriacalamo/videos/426510551797533, 11:48, my translation.
25. See the description at the University of Oregon Libraries' Scholars Bank website for *From Silence to Memory: Revelations of the AHPN*, https://scholarsbank.uoregon.edu/xmlui/handle/1794/12928.
26. Archivo Histórico de la Policía Nacional, *Del silencio a la memoria: Revelaciones del Archivo Histórico de la Policía Nacional* (Guatemala: Archivo Histórico de la Policía Nacional, 2011), https://repositories.lib.utexas.edu/handle/2152/13521. For the English translation of the original report, see Archivo Histórico de la Policía Nacional, *From Silence to Memory: Revelations of the Archivo Histórico de la Policía Nacional*, foreword by Carlos Aguirre (Eugene: University of Oregon Libraries, 2013). https://scholarsbank.uoregon.edu/xmlui/bitstream/handle/1794/12928/ahpn_final_20130620.pdf.
27. Steffi Hobuß, "Silence, Remembering," 95.
28. For example, the first section of *Rites*, "Initiation," details the narrator's second circumcision at age six, after the first ritual, performed by a Gentile doctor, left a small flap of surviving foreskin. Victor Perera, *Rites: A Guatemalan Boyhood* (San Diego: Harcourt Brace Jovanovich, 1986), 3.
29. Perera, *Rites*, 252; also cited in Pridgeon, "Silences," 107. Written more than a decade before the CEH report, Perera's *Rites* underestimated the death toll by about 80 percent.
30. Cited in Laura Marcus, *Virginia Woolf* (Tavistock, Devon, UK: Northcote House in association with the British Council, 2004), 112. The passage focuses on the strong presence of Woolf's mother in her childhood.
31. Teresa Prudente, *A Specially Tender Piece of Eternity: Virginia Woolf and the Experience of Time* (Lanham, MD: Lexington Books, 2009), 28.
32. Halfon, *Mañana nunca lo hablamos*, 138.
33. Manz, *Paradise in Ashes*, 4.
34. CEH (Comisión para el Esclarecimiento Histórico), *Guatemala: Memory of Silence: Report of the Commission for Historical Clarification Conclusions and Recommendations* (Guatemala City: United Nations Office for Project Services, 1999), 26, https://hrdag.org/wp-content/uploads/2013/01/CEHreport-english.pdf; Rothenberg, *Memory of Silence*, 185.
35. Rothenberg, *Memory of Silence*, 186.
36. Ignacio Sarmiento Panez, *Los espectros de la guerra: Duelo, comunidad y catástrofe en la narrativa centroamericana contemporánea* (PhD dissertation, Tulane University, 2018), 211, https://library.search.tulane.edu/discovery/delivery/01TUL_INST:Tulane/12432809630006326.
37. Eduardo Halfon, "Tomorrow We Never Did Talk About It," 7.
38. Perhaps Ms. Jenkins symbolizes the US tendency to downplay the plight of the country and its people, minimizing its own role in that conflict.
39. Halfon, "Tomorrow," 8.
40. Halfon, "Tomorrow," 9.
41. Halfon, "Tomorrow," 9–10.
42. Halfon, "Tomorrow," 11.
43. In Marie Louise Seeberg, Irene Levin, and Claudia Lenz, *The Holocaust as Active Memory: The Past in the Present* (Farnham, Surrey, UK: Ashgate, 2013), 190.

44. Pridgeon, "Silences," 112.
45. Stavans, afterword to "Tomorrow We Never Did Talk About It," *Working Title* 1.3 (Hadley, MA: Massachusetts Review, 2016).
46. Halfon, "Tomorrow," 17.
47. Halfon, "Tomorrow," 18–19.
48. AHPN, *From Silence to Memory*, xiii.
49. Halfon, "Tomorrow," 19.
50. Sarmiento Panez, *Los espectros*, 215.
51. Halfon, "Tomorrow," 34.
52. Halfon, "Tomorrow," 32.
53. The full Spanish version of the APHN was not published until 2011.
54. Sarmiento Panez, *Los espectros*, 32, 217. Sarmiento Panez begins his chapter on Halfon's "Mañana Nunca Lo Hablamos" by providing an example of just such an attempt at state-mandated silencing and what he calls "forced reconciliation": In April of 2013, during the first trial for genocide of Efraín Ríos Montt, dictator of Guatemala between 1982 and 1983, a group of twelve highly influential figures in Guatemala published a notice in *El periódico* titled "Traicionar la paz y dividir a Guatemala" (Betraying the peace and dividing Guatemala). For them, the trial against the ex-dictator, far from providing a path toward justice or reparations for the victims, presented "serious dangers for our country, including the sharpening of social and political polarization that would undermine the peace reached up to now." The notice also claimed the "accusation of genocide is a juridical fabrication that does not correspond to the desire of the mourners of the victims to honor their loved ones, to finalize the mourning, and to do justice. Nor does it correspond to the desire of the majority of the population to move on from the past to find national reconciliation." Sarmiento Panez, *Los espectros*, 202. That is, the State pardoned itself, declaring its own impunity, while denying the victims and their family members of themselves exercising the right of pardon (204–5). The condition of impunity did not deter all from seeking justice and full disclosure of the state's role in torture and genocide, however. Heather Vrana notes, "After the abrogation of the verdict that had charged former president General Efraín Ríos Montt with genocide and crimes against humanity, young people from the group Sons and Daughters of the Disappeared (Hijos por la Identidad y la Justicia contra el Olvido y el Silencio [H.I.J.O.S.]) responded with the following affirmation: 'More than a failure, this can breathe life into our ongoing fight for justice.' Published on social media sites Facebook and BlogSpot, this statement seems at first eccentric, or even incidental. How could the annulled verdict breathe life—'dar aliento'—into an ongoing fight for 'justicia'? Here, H.I.J.O.S. pursues a political logic at the fringes of the liberal ideals that usually orient us, the ones that have helped us to understand mass violence in Guatemala and worked to settle accounts of loss with reparations. In place of the logic of calculability of loss and reparations, H.I.J.O.S. has issued a call for political incalculability and a loss that remains." Heather Vrana, "'Our Ongoing Fight for Justice': The Pasts and Futures of Genocidio and Justicia in Guatemala," *Journal of Genocide Research* 18, no. 2–3 (2016): 263.
55. Melville, *Through a Glass*, 101. Though De Bry never visited the New World, images such as the one used with the writings of Las Casas served as prime examples of the "Black Legend" propaganda used to challenge the might of the Spanish empire.
56. Melville, *Through a Glass*, 414. The caption of another photo in the book showing massacre victims reads, "Suspected guerrillas, victims of army 'justice.' 'They dragged

them out and killed them. They stabbed and cut them like they were animals, laughing as they killed them.'" Melville, 534. Another photo of victims of an army incursion appears on 617.

57. Amalia Ran, "Nuestra Shoá Dictaduras, Holocausto y represión en tres novelas judeo-rioplatenses," *Spanish Language and Literature* 48 (2009): 17, https://digitalcommons.unl.edu/modlangspanish.
58. Ran, "Nuestra Shoá," 26.
59. Sarmiento Panez, *Los espectros*, 210.
60. Garsd, "A Braid of Words." Garsd's comments begin at 5:07.
61. See Marileen La Haije, "'Ningún lugar sagrado' de Rodrigo Rey Rosa: Una ficción paranoica desde la diáspora centroamericana," *Neophilologus*, no. 105 (2021): 75–89, https://doi.org/10.1007/s11061-020-09666-276.
62. Eduardo Halfon, "Better Not Say Too Much," *Guardian*, Nov. 4, 2015, https://www.theguardian.com/books/the-writing-life-around-the-world-by-electric-literature/2015/nov/04/better-not-say-too-much-eduardo-halfon-on-literature-paranoia-and-leaving-guatemala. My emphasis.
63. LaHaije, "'Ningún lugar sagrado,'" 75.
64. LaHaije, "'Ningún lugar sagrado,'" 76.
65. Perdu, "Experiencias del exilio," 158.
66. Browitt, *Contemporary Central American Fiction*, 75.
67. Halfon, "Mañana," 32–33.
68. Perdu, "Experiencias del exilio," 169–70.
69. Pridgeon, "Silences," 100.
70. "El día después de cumplir diez años me partí en dos. Era agosto del 81. Eran días de disparos. Guatemala era un caos político y social. Recuerdo tiroteos, disparos sueltos, combates en las calles y barrancos y hasta uno enfrente del colegio, con todos los alumnos recluidos. Recuerdo al nuevo guardia de seguridad que llegaba a la casa en las noches y se sentaba al lado de la puerta principal envuelto en un poncho, con una enorme escopeta sobre el regazo y un tibio termo de café en las manos. Recuerdo cuando mis papás nos anunciaron que nos iríamos del país. . . . El día después de mi décimo cumpleaños, entonces, salimos huyendo con mis papás y hermanos hacia Estados Unidos, y yo me partí en dos." Eduardo Halfon, "Dicho hacia el sur," in *Sam no es mi tío: Veintidós crónicas migrantes y un sueño americano*, ed. Aileen El Kadi and Diego Fonseca, 133–41 (Ciudad Autónoma de Buenos Aires: Aguilar, Altea, Taurus, Alfaguara, 2012), 133–34. The story is also available at Plaza Pública, Dec. 14, 2012, https://www.plazapublica.com.gt/content/dicho-hacia-el-sur.
71. Editorial Pre-Textos, "Mañana nunca lo hablamos de Eduardo Halfon."
72. Eduardo Halfon, "La memoria infantil," *Cuadernos hispanoamericanos*, no. 731 (2011): 22, http://www.cervantesvirtual.com/obra/la-memoria-infantil.
73. Halfon, "Memoria infantil," 23.
74. Halfon, "Memoria infantil," 24.
75. Eudora Welty, *One Writer's Beginnings* (New York: Scribner, 2020), 121–22.
76. Halfon, "Memoria infantil," 26–27. Halfon also included a very similar text in a May 2011 email to José Roberto Leonardo, adding, "I suppose this book is my way of returning in time, to look for it." "El día después de cumplir diez años me partí en dos. Era agosto del 81. Guatemala era un caos. Recuerdo tiroteos, disparos sueltos, combates en las calles y barrancos y hasta uno enfrente de mi colegio, con todos los alumnos recluidos dentro. Recuerdo al nuevo guardia de seguridad que llegaba a la casa en las noches y

se sentaba al lado de la puerta principal envuelto en un poncho, con una enorme escopeta sobre el regazo y un tibio termo de café en las manos. Recuerdo el sonido de las palabras de mi papá—no tanto las palabras sino el sonido que hacían—, al anunciarnos que saldríamos del país . . . El día después de mi décimo cumpleaños, entonces, salimos huyendo con mis papás y hermanos hacia Estados Unidos, y yo me partí en dos. Mi lenguaje se partió en dos. Mi memoria se partió en dos. Un pedazo de mi memoria, el primero, el más diáfano y liviano, se quedó suspendido en la Guatemala de los años setenta. Supongo que este libro es mi manera de volver en el tiempo, y buscarlo." José Roberto Leonardo, "Mañana nunca lo hablamos de Eduardo Halfon," *Diario del gallo* (blog), May 9, 2011, https://diariodelgallo.wordpress.com/2011/05/09/manana-nunca-lo-hablamos-de-eduardo-halfon.

77. In Moto Leyva, "Desde el no sé, Eduardo Halfon," *El País*, Dec. 12, 2015, https://elpais.com/cultura/2015/12/15/actualidad/1450207763_402437.html.
78. Juan Camilo Rincón, "El grandioso universo de Eduardo Halfon," *El Tiempo*, Nov. 17, 2020. https://www.eltiempo.com/cultura/musica-y-libros/eduardo-halfon-el-autor-guatemalteco-habla-de-su-universo-literario-549379.
79. Claudio Guillén, *El sol de los desterrados: Literatura y exilio* (Barcelona: Quaderns Crema, 1995), 14.
80. Ortiz Wallner, "Una escritura más allá," 34.
81. We can contrast the story, as Vanessa Perdu has done, with works by Halfon's contemporaries, such as Rodrigo Rey Rosa, whose narrator in *Ningún lugar sagrado* (1998) more directly denounces US policy and activity in Guatemala: "No se vaya a ofender, pero creo que los norteamericanos tienen una asquerosa política exterior. Han hecho, siguen y mientras puedan seguirán haciendo atrocidades. Lo sé, por Guatemala. Ellos, ustedes, han financiado, planeado, supervisado, las famosas matanzas de indios, de estudiantes, de izquierdistas en los últimos treinta años." (Don't get offended, but I believe that the North Americans have a disgusting foreign policy. They've committed, continue to commit, and will keep committing atrocities. I know, because of Guatemala. They, you all, have financed, planned, supervised the famous massacres of Indians, of students of leftists in the last thirty years.) Rodrigo Rey Rosa, *Ningún lugar sagrado* (Barcelona: Seix Barral, 1998), 72, my translation, cited in the original Spanish by Perdu, "Experiencias del exilio," 164. As Perdu points out, the groups represented by the terms "ellos" and "ustedes" link the North Americans to the more proximate Guatemalan elites who also supported the military and its tactics.
82. For Sarmiento Panez, Halfon provides "a counterdiscourse that demands justice for violence and war crimes—and in broader terms, for the repression, segregation, and historical violence that have existed in the country from its foundation—and that puts an end to the silence that prevails over the atrocities committed during the conflict." Sarmiento Panez, *Los espectros*, 237. In my reading, if the text indeed offers this "counterdiscourse," it does so only implicitly.
83. Halfon, "Tomorrow," 38–39. The valences are quite different in the Spanish original: "Salió del cuarto y apagó la luz blanca del pasillo. Todo se volvió a quedar negro, inmóvil. Pronto llegó mañana y mañana nunca lo hablamos." Halfon, *Mañana*, 138. While the term *inmóvil* has stronger physical connotations than "still," the English term "still" in McLean's translation adds an important valence of the absence of sound, that is, quietude.
84. "Sentía que poco a poco me estaba acercando no solo a escribir algo sobre la vida de mi abuelo y de su identidad libanesa, sino a escribir algo sobre la historia reciente de

mi país, sobre el conflicto armado interno." In Nuria Azangot, "Eduardo Halfon: 'La literatura es insensata, inexplicable, irrepetible, como un primer beso,'" *El Español*, Jan. 12, 2021, https://www.elespanol.com/el-cultural/20210112/eduardo-halfon-literatura-insensata-inexplicable-irrepetible-primer/550696815_0.html.

85. For Sarmiento Panez, *Mañana nunca lo hablamos* inserts itself in a national context marked by forced silence and in which different forms of the work of mourning have been instrumentalized or weaponized for its benefit. He notes that unlike elsewhere in Latin America, Guatemala has no memory sites in the traditional sense, only Casa de la memoria "Kaji Tulám," created in 2014 by a private entity dedicated to legal action in human rights cases and the recognition of indigenous cultural heritage. This posture is exemplified in a speech delivered by former president of Guatemala Álvaro Arzú in 2016, on the twentieth anniversary of the peace treaty, that Sarmiento Panez quotes at length: "It is crucial to understand that the death of a human being always leaves a teaching. The thousands and thousands of deaths that our war left . . . are the proof of blood and fire of a nation. . . . We cannot plunge into oblivion those from both sides who offered their lives for a more just Guatemala. But like Lincoln, we cannot today consecrate the memory of those Guatemalans with simple words that seek to open new wounds of the past. . . . What can we the living do to guarantee that the death of all these Guatemalans was not in vain? Consecrate ourselves to this endless task of making the values of independence, liberty, and self-determination that are at the core of our founding last. Consecrate ourselves to the task of preserving the homeland." Sarmiento Panez comments, "The words of Arzú are quite eloquent and clear. The death of more than 200,000 people, and the approximately 40,000 disappeared, should fertilize the history of the nation and support the supposed historical values that have embodied the Guatemalan republic." Sarmiento Panez, *Los espectros*, 235–36, my translation.

CHAPTER 5

Epigraph. "A Conversation with Eduardo Halfon on Monastery," Bellevue Literary Press, accessed Sept. 18, 2023, https://blpress.org/author-qas/conversation-eduardo-halfon-monastery.

1. The English translation and Spanish original (*Monasterio*) were both published in 2014. In *Monasterio*, the stories that appear in the English version as "Tel Aviv Was an Inferno," "White Smoke," "Sunsets" (though a longer version than the one in *The Polish Boxer*), and "Monastery" are titled only with the numbers "Uno," "Dos," "Tres," and "Cuatro," respectively.
2. "A Conversation with Eduardo Halfon on *The Polish Boxer*."
3. "A través de sucesivos ejercicios de memoria, cual fotografías dispersas de un álbum familiar, el lector irá de la mano del narrador-protagonista Eduardo por una cartografía afectiva, emocional y subjetiva en la que éste se irá perdiendo (¿reconociendo?) mientras se desplaza por la ciudad, a veces como un turista más, a veces como un niño desorientado, a veces como un espectro, a veces como un doble de sí mismo." Alexandra Ortiz Wallner, "Autorretrato en Jerúsalen," *Iowa Literaria*, May 8, 2014, https://pubs.lib.uiowa.edu/iowaliteraria/article/id/2634.
4. Eduardo Halfon, *Monastery*, 12–13.
5. Eduardo Halfon, *Polish Boxer*, 72; *Monastery*, 105.
6. This opening section of *Monastery* suggests the genre of *autofiction*, described by Julia Musitano as a paradoxical genre that vacillates between two worlds, that of the autobiography and that of the novel, and that does not permit us as readers to discern between truth and invention. See Julia Musitano, "La autoficción: Una aproximación teórica.

Entre la retórica de la memoria y la escritura de recuerdos," *Acta Literaria* 52 (2016): 104. There are two dimensions of Halfon's autofictions, according to Ortiz Wallner: one that revolves around the possibilities and limits of artistic creation and another that is more like a large labyrinth of identities tied to the Jewish, Arab, Polish, and Guatemalan origins of the author and of his recurring narrator-protagonist, identified as Eduardo Halfon, Halfon, or simply Eduardo. "Alongside his constellations of short forms, his is a writing project which through the years has accentuated autofictionality as a trademark, but also as a game and at the same time as a constant investigation into forms of subjectivity and contemporary sensibility." Ortiz Wallner, "Autorretrato en Jerusalén."

7. Halfon, *Monastery*, 17.
8. Halfon, *Monastery*, 19.
9. "There is usually a marriage at the end of a comedy—they are life-affirming in a positive way." "Tragedy and Comedy," American Literature I, Lumenlearning.com, accessed May 14, 2024, https://courses.lumenlearning.com/suny-jeffersoncc-americanlit1/chapter/608.
10. Halfon, *Monastery*, 22.
11. Halfon, *Monastery*, 23–24.
12. Halfon, *Monastery*, 39. On the role of ultraconservative sects in contemporary Israeli political life, see Alexander Kaye, *The Invention of Jewish Theocracy: The Struggle for Legal Authority in Modern Israel* (Oxford, UK: Oxford University Press, 2020).
13. Halfon, *Monastery*, 45.
14. Halfon, *Monastery*, 27.
15. "Frente a la actitud tradicional del viajero asombrado ante el paisaje, Halfon más bien se centra en la soledad del turista y en el hastío que provocan los recorridos obligatorios de la industria del turismo." María Paz Oliver, "Los paseos de la memoria: Representaciones de la caminata urbana en Cynthia Rimsky, Sergio Chejfec y Eduardo Halfon." *Ibero-romania* 83, (2016), 16–34, https://doi.org/10.1515/ibero-2016-0003, 28.
16. Halfon, *Monastery*, 23. On the idea of touring the religious sites of Jerusalem on foot, see Oliver, "Los paseos," 28–29. On the "Jerusalem Syndrome," see Tamar Mayer and Sulieman A. Mourad, *Jerusalem: Idea and Reality* (New York: Routledge, 2008), 113–15.
17. Halfon, *Monastery*, 30.
18. "O, dicho de otro modo, la peregrinación reinscribe lo sagrado en la intimidad de la memoria familiar. La caminata genera un vínculo afectivo con la memoria y la genealogía familiar, instalando la pregunta por el 'otro' y lo extranjero en un terreno incierto, donde la peregrinación remite específicamente a la idea de una búsqueda personal y emotiva del pasado." Oliver, "Los paseos," 29.
19. Halfon, *Monastery*, 52.
20. Halfon, *Monastery*, 54. A version of "Bamboo" on the Pen America website, translated by Achy Obejas, includes a photo of several sharks on a concrete floor. Eduardo Halfon, "Bamboo," *Pen America*, April 12, 2013, https://pen.org/bamboo.
21. Halfon, *Monastery*, 52–57.
22. Halfon, *Monastery*, 75.
23. Halfon, *Monastery*, 60, 62.
24. Halfon, *Monastery*, 86.
25. Halfon, *Monastery*, 101.
26. Halfon, *Monastery*, 102–3.
27. García Márquez used clouds of yellow butterflies in several stories to prefigure the arrival of a forbidden lover. The image became so famously associated with his work that when he died in 2014, masses of yellow paper butterflies were "released" in many

of the memorial services for the Colombian author, considered Latin America's greatest proponent of magical realism. See Joseph Silcott, "Gabriel García Márquez's Yellow Butterflies," *Joseph Scissorhands* (blog), April 27, 2014, http://josephscissorhands.blogspot.com/2014/04/gabriel-garcia-marquezs-yellow.html.

28. Halfon, *Monastery*, 105, 108.
29. "A different way of approaching historical amnesia, drawing upon the insights of Ali Behdad, relates cultural forgetfulness to ideological consolidation. According to this view, forgetfulness is 'convenient.' It 'improves' history by obliterating knowledge of the past that conflicts with messages that a country or group seeks to project about itself in the present." See Jonathan D. Sarna, "The Forgetting of Cora Wilburn: Historical Amnesia and *The Cambridge History of Jewish American Literature*," *Studies in American Jewish Literature* 37, no. 1 (2018): 41.
30. According to some scholars, separating Israeli cities and Jewish settlements from Palestinian towns and villages in the West Bank has become the largest and most costly single construction project in Israeli history, converting a border unrecognized by the international community into a physical reality. See Juliana Ochs, "Seeing, Walking, Securing: Tours of Israel's Separation Wall," in *Security and Suspicion: An Ethnography of Everyday Life in Israel*, 138–60 (Philadelphia: University of Pennsylvania Press, 2011), 139.
31. Halfon, *Monastery*, 136.
32. Images and the historical context of the piece can be seen at Wikipedia, s.v. "Flying Balloon Girl," last updated Feb. 29, 2024, https://en.wikipedia.org/wiki/Flying_Balloon_Girl.
33. Anna Ball, "Impossible Intimacies: Towards a Visual Politics of 'Touch' at the Israeli-Palestinian Border," *Journal for Cultural Research* 16, no. 2–3 (2012): 176–77.
34. Ball, "Impossible Intimacies," 177. In her 2012 essay, Ball also notes that "the Wall has become so visually iconic of Palestine's occupation that the Palestinian artist Basel Abbas considers it to be 'fetishized' by the Western media. In conversation at the New Art Exchange in Nottingham, he described the frequent requests he received from American and European journalists writing about his work for him to pose in front of the Wall for publicity purposes." Ball, 175n1.
35. Halfon, *Monastery*, 136.
36. Halfon, *Monastery*, 137.
37. Nicolás Campisi, "The Dislocation of Cosmopolitan Identities in Eduardo Halfon's Monasterio," *INTI: Revista de Literatura Hispánica*, no. 87–88 (2018): 116.
38. Halfon, *Monastery*, 145.
39. Halfon, *Monastery*, 145.
40. Aarons, "Found Objects," 231–32, 238.
41. Esther Jilovsky, *Remembering the Holocaust: Generations, Witnessing and Place* (New York: Bloomsbury Academic, 2015), 94. Also cited in Aarons, "Found Objects," 252.
42. Hepworth, "From Survivor to Fourth-Generation Memory: Literal and Discursive Sites of Memory in Post-dictatorship Germany and Spain," *Journal of Contemporary History*, 54, no. 1 (2019): 145.
43. "Origin Stories: Dwyer Murphy interviews Eduardo Halfon." *Guernica*, April 15, 2013, https://www.guernicamag.com/origin-stories.
44. Aarons, "Found Objects," 240.
45. Halfon, *Monastery*, 149.
46. Jack Porter, in a chapter titled "Holocaust Suicides" in the volume *Problems Unique to the Holocaust*, notes of Kosinski, "There is much more to say about his confused

identity, his merging of truth and illusion, but the point I am trying to make is that identity problems coupled with other factors, such as deteriorating health, may have triggered his suicide, and, furthermore, the similarities of his suicide with other Holocaustal suicides are to say the least uncanny." Jack Porter, "Holocaust Suicides," in *Problems Unique to the Holocaust*, ed. Harry J. Cargas, 51–66 (Lexington: University Press of Kentucky, 1999), 59.
47. Halfon, *Monastery*, 155–56.
48. See Aurelio Auseré Abarca, Luis Miguel Estrada Orozco, and Eduardo Halfon, "Eduardo Halfon: Identidad en construcción: Una conversación con Aurelio Auseré Abarca y Luis Miguel Estrada Orozco," *Latin American Literature Today*, May 2018, https://latinamericanliteraturetoday.org/es/2018/04/eduardo-halfon-identity-under-construction-conversation-aurelio-ausere-abarca-and-luis.
49. Francine Prose, "What Can't Be Forgotten," *New York Review of Books* 65, no. 18 (2018): 38.

CHAPTER 6

Epigraph. Janina Struk, *Photographing the Holocaust: Interpretations of the Evidence* (London: I.B. Tauris, 2004), 211.
1. Eduardo Halfon et al., "The Purest Form of Writing." Born in New Haven in 1926, Wallant is best known for his novel *The Pawnbroker*, adapted into a 1964 award-winning film directed by Sidney Lumet. Other winners of the Wallant award include Chaim Potok, Cynthia Ozick, and Francine Prose, who reviewed Halfon's work for the *New York Review of Books*. Both Wallant and Halfon received Guggenheim awards to support their writing efforts. Wallant died at thirty-six of a brain aneurism. See David D. Galloway, *Edward Lewis Wallant* (Boston: Twayne Publishers, 1979).
2. Halfon et al., "The Purest Form," 457.
3. See "Eduardo Halfon: Story and History (January 16, 2020) | Rendez-vous de l'Institut." YouTube, posted by Columbia Institute for Ideas and Imagination, Mar. 5, 2020, https://www.youtube.com/watch?v=_B7iPtW_B-s.
4. Elena Hevia, "Eduardo Halfon, el Zelig guatemalteco." El Periodico, Sept. 12, 2017, https://www.elperiodico.com/es/ocio-y-cultura/20170912/eduardo-halfon-zelig-novela-duelo-6281562.
5. Thinking of how Halfon generates his texts, one of his translators, Daniel Hahn, recalls in this exchange a curious phrase used by Gregory Rabassa—who translated such works such as Gabriel García Márquez's *One Hundred Years of Solitude*—to describe his own work in translation. Rabassa claimed his task constituted "the purest form of writing," as the translator must zero in on precise details, not plot lines or big pictures. For Hahn, Halfon's choice to write "in translation," that is, to render ideas born in English into words in Spanish, affords him this same purity of language referred to by Rabassa. Cited in Halfon et al., "The Purest Form," 460.
6. The journalist in question is likely Daniel Capó, who, upon asking which books Halfon had *not* read that influenced him most, received this response: "Yo no soy judío, y no soy guatemalteco. Al menos eso me digo a mí mismo cuando escribo, o eso les digo a los demás cuando me leen, que yo no soy lo que soy. Como judío, sé que debo leer la Torá, completa, no por encima, no sólo las secciones que me convienen, no sólo el fragmento cuya fonética en hebreo me memoricé a los trece años, cuando los demás me dijeron que ya era todo un hombre y que debía entonces subir ante ellos y recitar ante ellos ese fragmento memorizado. Y como guatemalteco, sé que debo leer el Popol Vuh, entero, no por partes, no las partes mágicas o las partes que me interesan, y no

porque yo sea maya, sino porque de ahí soy, ahí nací y crecí, en su tierra, entre sus maizales. Sé que esos dos libros—si es que puedo llamarlos libros—me han marcado más que cualquier otro, como judío, como guatemalteco, como hombre, y como escritor. Pero no quiero leerlos. Me niego a leerlos. En parte, supongo, porque sé que son las dos columnas principales de mi casa, que sobre ellos se apoya y se construye todo lo demás. Y al escribir lo primero que debemos hacer es destruir nuestra casa." (I'm not Jewish, I'm not Guatemalan. Or at least, that's what I tell myself when I write, or that's what I tell everyone else who reads me, that I am not what I am. As a Jew, I know that I should read the Torah, all the way through, not just superficially, not just the sections that are convenient to me, not just the fragment whose Hebrew phonetics I memorized at thirteen, when they told me that now I was a man and that I should go up the platform and recite before them that memorized fragment. And as a Guatemalan, I know that I should read the Popol Vuh, all of it, not just some parts, not the magical parts or the parts that interest me, and not because I am a Maya, but because I am from there, that's where I was born and raised, in their land, amongst the cornfields. I know that those two books—if you can call them books—have marked me more than any other, as a Jew, as a Guatemalan, as a man, as a writer. But I don't want to read them. I refuse to read them. In part, I guess, because I know that they are the two principal columns of my house, that on top of them everything else is built and stands. And to write, the first thing we should do is destroy our own house.) See Daniel Capó, "Los libros que no he leído | Eduardo Halfon," *Daniel Capo* (blog), April 29, 2016, https://danielcapo-blog.com/2016/04/29/libros-no-leidos-eduardo-halfon.

7. Halfon et al., "The Purest Form," 449.
8. *Oh gueto mi amor* was published in 2018 with illustrations by David de las Heras. Eduardo Halfon, *Oh gueto mi amor* (Madrid: Páginas de Espuma, 2018).
9. Halfon et al., "The Purest Form," 449. "Yo duelo" is not a standard use of Spanish to convey "I hurt"; *me duele* (something hurts me) with the use of the indirect personal pronoun, would be the more common usage.
10. Eduardo Halfon, *Mourning* (New York: Bellevue Literary Press), 2018, 25.
11. Halfon, *Mourning*, 13–16.
12. For more on the Ferramonti camp, see Geoffrey P. Megargee (ed.) et al., *The United States Holocaust Memorial Museum Encyclopedia of Camps and Ghettos, 1933–1945*, vol. 3, *Camps and Ghettos under European Regimes Aligned with Nazi Germany* (Bloomington: Indiana University Press, 2018), 424–26; and Carlo Spartaco Capogreco, *Mussolini's Camps: Civilian Internment in Fascist Italy (1940–1943)* (London: Routledge, 2019), especially 4–5, 217–19.
13. Halfon, *Mourning*, 21–22.
14. Díaz Miranda, "El boxeador polaco," 44–65, 51.
15. Halfon, *Mourning*, 22.
16. Halfon, *Mourning*, 23–24.
17. Halfon, *Mourning*, 25–26.
18. Halfon, *Mourning*, 27.
19. Phillip Seymour Hoffman died on February 2, 2014. Holocaust Remembrance Day is January 27.
20. Halfon, *Mourning*, 34.
21. Halfon, *Mourning*, 36.
22. "The conditions in the camp attest to the humanity and compassion of the Italians who did all they could to help the Jewish internees maintain Jewish family life."

See Barbara Aiello, "Ferramonti," *Rabbibarbara.com*, March 2, 2018. https://www.rabbibarbara.com/ferramonti.

23. Cited in Simon Levis Sullam et al., *The Italian Executioners: The Genocide of the Jews of Italy* (Princeton, NJ: Princeton University Press, 2018), xi. In his foreword to the volume, David Kertzer also speaks of the danger "when the uncomfortable events of the past are replaced in memory—and, even worse, in historiography—by a triumphal account of virtue. . . . If Italians are, understandably perhaps, eager to *misremember* their past support for the Fascist regime and their past Alliance with Nazi Germany, they have shown themselves even more eager to construct a wholly misleading history of their responsibility for the persecution and cold-blooded murder of their fellow Italians whose only sin was being Jewish. . . . Italy's antisemitic campaign, beginning two years before Italy entered the war, can properly be placed alongside the antisemitic campaign in these years in Germany (and elsewhere in Central Europe) as a crucial step in the process that would make the Holocaust possible." Levis Sullam, *The Italian Executioners*, vii–viii, my emphasis. Though some Italian Jews were held at Ferramonti, the camp also held foreign Jews from Eastern Europe and elsewhere as well as Greeks, Chinese, Slavs, and French prisoners from Corsica. No Italian soldier or civilian was ever condemned for deportation and internment as crimes of war. See Capogreco, *Mussolini's Camps*, 125, 217.

24. *Hotel Savoy* is a 1924 novel by the Austrian author Joseph Roth. Set in the aftermath of the First World War, Roth writes of Łódź, "Life and death hang together so visibly, and the quick with the dead. There is no end there, no break—always continuity and connection." The colorful assortment of characters includes and Henry Bloomfield, a prominent Jew who has become rich in America, whose annual visit his father's grave inspires hopes he will solve the myriad economic woes of the city and its inhabitants. Joseph Roth, *Hotel Savoy; Fallmerayer the Stationmaster; The Bust of the Emperor* (London: Chatto & Windus, 1986), 107.

25. Halfon, *Mourning*, 46–47.
26. Halfon, *Mourning*, 41–43.
27. Halfon, *Mourning*, 43.
28. Halfon, *Mourning*, 44.
29. The Polish participation in Nazi genocide remains a matter of national and international debate. In fact, in September of 2023, Pope Francis beatified a Polish family executed by the Nazis for sheltering Jews. See Monika Scislowska, "The Vatican Beatifies a Polish Family of 9 Killed by the Nazis for Sheltering Jews," Associated Press, Sept. 10, 2023, https://apnews.com/article/poland-jews-ulma-family-beatification-4396a6086664fa1ea96a433e363ebd41. Struk argues that Holocaust memory films such as *Shoah* and *Schindler's List* fail to mention that ethnic Poles also suffered under the Nazis along with many other non-Jews, and "seem to have helped inflame the relationship between the Poles and the Jews. Polish guides at Auschwitz-Birkenau are sometimes harangued by Israeli and American tour groups for what they see as Poland's collaborative role in the extermination of the Jews. This fashionable folly (there was less collaboration in Poland than any other non-communist country occupied by the Nazis) has even led to tour groups of Young Israelis being warned by their guides of the 'constant danger' of being on Polish soil." Janina Struk, *Photographing the Holocaust*, 189.

30. Sinnreich notes that swastikas came into use in Łódź graffiti as an anti-Jewish symbol in the early postwar period and are even considered anti-Polish by many. However, Henry Fishel Myłarz, a Łódź resident until the 1950s, testified that "'Łódź abounded with graf-

fiti swastikas on most building walls' and linked them to insults such as 'Hitler was right' and 'Go back to Jerusalem, Jew.'" The symbol of the Jewish star hanging on a gallows may even have its origins in WWII, when the Polish Resistance used graffiti depicting a swastika in a hangman's noose. See Helene Sinnreich, "Reading the Writing on the Wall: A Textual Analysis of Łódź Graffiti," *Religion, State and Society* 32, no. 1 (2004): 54.

31. See Mark Biederman, *Schindler's Listed: The Search for My Father's Lost Gold*, with Randi Biederman (Boston: Academic Studies Press, 2019), 49, 85–86, 123. In 2001 and 2011, Polish presidents Aleksander Kwaśniewski and Bronisław Komorowski apologized on behalf of the country's role in the pogrom, but as of 2015, "the subject has again become contentious." Andrzej Duda criticized Komorowski's apology before winning the presidential election in 2015 for the rightwing Law and Justice party. See Wikipedia, s.v. "Jedwabne Pogrom," last updated July 25, 2024, https://en.wikipedia.org/wiki/Jedwabne_pogrom. On the push to have Poles acknowledge their own role in the massacre, see Jan T. Gross, *Neighbors: The Destruction of the Jewish Community in Jedwabne, Poland* (Princeton, NJ: Princeton University Press, 2001).
32. Struk, *Photographing the Holocaust*, 4.
33. This photo is reproduced in Struk's study. See Struk, *Photographing the Holocaust*, 2–5.
34. Struk, *Photographing the Holocaust*, 63–65. The scenes of Germans surrounding an Orthodox Jew with scissors, poised to cut his sidelocks, was "reenacted with precision" along with other photographic tableaus in Steven Spielberg's *Schindler's List*, Struk notes, 183.
35. Struk, *Photographing the Holocaust*, 68. The author also comments on the Nazis' use of photographic and film propaganda to show both abject poverty and luxurious lifestyles within the Jewish ghettos, in advance of their liquidation. German soldiers "gleefully photographed the dead and the accompanying relatives" as they visited Jewish cemeteries with their girlfriends as a "place of amusement." In May of 1942, Jewish men and women were stripped and forced to perform "lewd and obscene acts" on camera, as a Nazi cracked his whip over their heads, in order to later show the Jews' depravity. Struk, 80–81.
36. Halfon, *Mourning*, 48–49.
37. Halfon, *Mourning*, 50.
38. The "four cultures" refer to Poles, Jews, Germans, and Russians.
39. See "Anatewka—Łódź," 2022, Anatewka.com, accessed May 15, 2024, https://www.anatewka.com.
40. Commenting on his experience at the Anatevka restaurant, Mark Biederman writes, "It seemed to me that someone in the Lodz Chamber of Commerce finally realized what Warsaw and Krakow businessmen realized a few years earlier: Jewish tourism can be a tremendous source of revenue. . . . Upon further evaluation, I concluded that places like this restaurant serve a purpose and are the reason why all the Jewish Heritage Tours begin in Poland and finish in Israel. Lodz and its environs are a veritable theme park of anti-Semitism. Experience Poland (especially Lodz) and then continue on to Israel to be uplifted and understand the importance of the Jewish State." Biederman, *Schindler's Listed*, 123–26.
41. Halfon, *Mourning*, 51–52.
42. Halfon, *Mourning*, 53.
43. Halfon, *Mourning*, 57.
44. Lang, *Textual Silence*, 91.
45. Halfon, *Mourning*, 66–67. "Oh Gueto mi amor" appeared in Spanish in the collection *Signor Hoffman* and in 2018 as a standalone text. Eduardo Halfon, *Signor Hoffman* (Bar-

celona: Libros del Asteroide, 2015) and Halfon, *Oh gueto mi amor*. A video from the publisher of *Oh Gueto mi amor*, Editorial Páginas de Espuma, begins with a recording of a plaintive voice singing "Gueto getunya." Halfon then reads passages from the text, as scenes alternate between a hand painting—presumably that of the illustrator David de las Heras—photos of Halfon's Polish grandfather as a young man in his only remaining family portrait, and film footage of someone—presumably Madame Maroszek and Halfon, though we never see faces—ascending a staircase that leads to the apartment in Łódź where Halfon's Polish grandfather lived before being picked up by the Nazis. See "Oh gueto mi amor, de Eduardo Halfon (Editorial Páginas de Espuma)." YouTube posted by Páginas de espuma, Sept. 3, 2018, https://www.youtube.com/watch?v=KCCiZGPTHxA.

46. Halfon, *Mourning*, 64–67.
47. Halfon, *Mourning*, 69–70.
48. In 2022, the UK's National History Museum honored Daniel Nuñez as Wildlife Photographer of the Year for his photo *The Dying Lake*. "Daniel took this photograph to raise awareness of the impact of contamination on Lake Amatitlán, which receives around 75,000 tonnes of waste from Guatemala City every year. 'It was a sunny day with perfect conditions,' Daniel observed, 'but it is a sad and shocking moment.' Cyanobacteria flourishes in the presence of pollutants, such as sewage and agricultural fertilisers, forming algal blooms that block out sunlight, killing any plants below. Not only this but they also produce toxins that can poison humans and other animals. When the algal bloom dies, it sinks to the bottom and decomposes, depleting the dissolved oxygen available for fish and other animal life. Efforts to restore the Amatitlán wetland are underway but have been hampered by a lack of funding and allegations of political corruption. Jen Guyton, photojournalist and judge said, 'What really makes this image work is the element of surprise. On first glance, the right-hand side of the image looks like a grassy field. But when you realise that it's water, you immediately understand that something is sorely wrong with this picture—it's a damaged ecosystem, and something must be done to fix it." See Daniel Núñez, *The Dying Lake*, digital photograph, "Wildlife Photographer of the Year," Natural History Museum, accessed Sept. 20, 2023, https://www.nhm.ac.uk/wpy/gallery/2022-the-dying-lake.
49. Halfon, *Mourning*, 71. "The most polluted lake in Central America, Amatitlan Lake, receives its effluents from a largely urbanized watershed that extends 381 km². With more than half of Guatemala City situated within the lake's watershed, sediments, polluted runoff, and sewage constantly get deposited into the lake, turning it into a dead, eutrophic body of water with high contamination ratings comparable to a sewage tank." María Calderón, *Green Movement against Green Water* (Undergraduate Honors Thesis, Cornell University, May 2010), https://ecommons.cornell.edu/handle/1813/17514, 6.
50. Halfon, *Mourning*, 71.
51. Halfon, *Mourning*, 78.
52. Halfon, *Mourning*, 87.
53. Halfon, *Mourning*, 112.
54. Halfon, *Mourning*, 106–7.
55. "Usted no escribirá nada sobre esto, me preguntó o me ordenó mi papá, su índice elevado, su tono a medio camino entre súplica y mandamiento. Pensé en responderle que un escritor nunca sabe de qué escribirá, que un escritor no elige sus historias sino que éstas lo eligen a él, que un escritor no es más que una hoja seca en el soplo de su propia narrativa. Pero por suerte no dije nada. Usted no escribirá nada sobre esto, repitió mi papa, su tono ahora más fuerte, casit autoritario. Sentí el peso de sus palabras.

Por supuesto que no, le dije, quizás sincero, o quizás ya sabiendo que ninguna historia es imperativa, ninguna historia necesaria, salvo aquellas que alguien nos prohíbe contar." Eduardo Halfon, *Duelo* (Barcelona: Libros Del Asteroide, 2018), back cover, my translation.

56. See Ana Mendoza, "Eduardo Halfon: 'La ansiedad de vivir es algo muy judío.'" *Zenda*, June 27, 2018, https://www.zendalibros.com/eduardo-halfon-la-ansiedad-vivir-algo-judio.
57. Curiously, the "prohibition" text included on the back cover of *Duelo* is not included in the English edition. On the details of Salomón's biography, whether factual or fictional, see *Mourning*, 146–49.
58. Halfon, *Mourning*, 69.
59. Halfon, *Mourning*, 115.
60. Halfon, *Mourning*, 81.
61. Halfon, *Mourning*, 109.
62. Halfon, *Mourning*, 88–89.
63. With Madame Maroszek's help, Eduardo discovers a document in Łódź that explains how his great-uncle Zalman had died of hunger in June 1944, just a few months before the liquidation of the ghetto.
64. Halfon, *Mourning*, 89.
65. Halfon, *Mourning*, 103–4.
66. Halfon, *Mourning*, 93–94. Halfon returns in this volume as well to the grandfather's explanation of the tattoo on his arm as a telephone number he had put there himself to remember it, a lie the protagonist had believed. He even repeats the tattoo number: 69752.
67. Dora Apel, *Memory Effects*, 147.
68. Halfon, *Mourning*, 113.
69. Halfon, *Mourning*, 113.
70. For Manlio Soto Paiz, Maximón resembles Hermes from classical mythology, as well as other trickster figures such as Papa Legba (Haiti) and Edshu, suggesting other resonances with Eleggua (Cuba), Exu (Brazil), et cetera. Soto Paíz also explores Maximón from a Jungian perspective. See Soto Paiz, *Maximón y lo insconsciente colectivo: Arquetipos y simbología Maya-Tzutuhil* (Guatemala: Editorial Universitaria, Universidad de San Carlos Guatemala, 2018), especially 97–110.
71. Halfon, *Mourning*, 141–43. See also Oswaldo Chinchilla Mazariegos, "Of Birds and Insects: The Hummingbird Myth in Ancient America." *Ancient Mesoamerica*, no. 21 (2010): 45–61.

CHAPTER 7

Epigraph. "Me interesan los secretos, las historias tabú, prohibidas, lo que no se dice." "Eduardo Halfon habló de su novela 'Canción' y su interés por los tabúes," IP Noticias, April 4, 2021. https://ipnoticias.ar/nota/2600-eduardo-halfon-hablo-de-su-novela-cancion-y-su-interes-por-los-tabues.

1. Eduardo Halfon, *Canción* (New York: Bellevue Literary Press, 2022), 11. *Canción* was released in 2021 in Spanish. Eduardo Halfon, *Canción* (Barcelona: Libros del asteroide, 2021).
2. See David Ulin, "Review: How a Guatemalan Kidnapping Inspired Eduardo Halfon's Autofictional 'Cancion,'" *Los Angeles Times*, Sept. 22, 2022, https://www.latimes.com/entertainment-arts/books/story/2022-09-22/review-how-a-guatemalan-kidnapping-inspired-eduardo-halfons-autofictional-cancion.
3. See García Escobar, "'Literature is not about answers.'"

4. Domene speaks of "ese mundo de ficción que se alimenta vorazmente de lo fáctico, lo biográfico, o lo veraz." Pedro Domene, "Ficción y realidad en la novela 'Canción', de Eduardo Halfon," ¡Zas!-Madrid, Dec. 28, 2021, https://zasmadrid.com/ficcion-y-realidad-en-la-novela-cancion-de-eduardo-halfon.
5. The anthropologist Sharon Macdonald uses the term *memorylands* to argue for a deeper and fuller understanding of our relationships to the past and its material vestiges, such as museums, heritage sites, and memorials. Though her focus is on the memory phenomenon in Europe, her examination of forms of recollection and "past presencing" is useful for considering other regions as well. See Macdonald, *Memorylands: Heritage and Identity in Europe Today* (New York: Routledge, 2013), 1–4.
6. The full citation is "Ese libro ha ido engendrando otros libros, de una manera no planificada. Cuando escribí los cuentos de *El boxeador polacolo* que se presentó fue una voz, la voz de otro **Eduardo Halfon**, una voz que no es mi voz, con un temperamento muy suyo, fuma y yo no fumo, viaja mucho, dice cosas con más facilidad que yo pero también es más timorato, duda, en cambio yo soy muy ingeniero." (That book has gone on to engender other books, in an unplanned way. When I wrote the stories in *El boxeador polaco*, what was presented was a voice, the voice of another Eduardo Halfon, a voice that is not my voice, with a temperament all his own, he smokes and I don't, he travels a lot, he says things more easily than I do but he is also more timid, doubtful, while I am very much an engineer.) See Alejandra Rodríguez Ballestar, "La guerrilla secuestró a su abuelo, y su familia debió exiliarse: La nueva novela de Eduardo Halfon," *Clarín Cultura*, May 19, 2021, https://www.clarin.com/cultura/guerrilla-guatemalteca-secuestro-abuelo-familia-debio-exiliarse-nueva-novela-eduardo-halfon_0_fNmFI2XhU.html.
7. García Escobar, "'Literature is not about answers.'"
8. Halfon, *Canción* (2022), 14; Halfon, *Canción* (2021), 11.
9. "El disfraz aparece desde la primera frase del libro: 'Llegué a Tokio disfrazado de árabe'. Pero es un disfraz que luego uno encarna. Uno se vuelve el personaje. Es el disfraz ligado a la identidad. O la identidad a través de un disfraz." Carlos Aletto, "Eduardo Halfon: '¿Es la identidad un disfraz que me puedo poner y quitar cuando me lo solicitan?'" Infobae.com, March 8, 2021, https://www.infobae.com/cultura/2021/03/09/eduardo-halfon-es-la-identidad-un-disfraz-que-me-puedo-poner-y-quitar-cuando-me-lo-solicitan. The article includes a photo of Halfon's paternal grandfather.
10. On the "push" and "pull" factors that drew Sephardic Jews to Latin America in the early twentieth century, see Margalit Bejarano and Edna Aizenberg, *Contemporary Sephardic Identity in the Americas: an Interdisciplinary Approach* (Syracuse, NY: Syracuse University Press, 2012), 13–14. A chart in this volume on the distribution of the Sephardic population in Latin America does not include Guatemala, known as having only a hundred Jewish families, or perhaps even fewer, thirty. Bejarano notes elsewhere that while the term *Sephardim* is used to designate all non-Ashkenazi sectors, the fragmented character of this already complex ethnic group was further "textured" by different sub-groups such as Middle Eastern Jews, amongst whom the Arabic speakers tend to be "the most orthodox." See Margalit Bejarano, "A Mosaic of Fragmented Identities: The *Sephardim* in Latin America," in *Identities in an Era of Globalization and Multiculturalism: Latin America in the Jewish World*, ed. Judit Bokser de Liwerant, 267–86 (Leiden: Brill, 2008), 267, 286. On the two terms *Mizrahi* and *Sephardic*, as well as the catch-all label *turcos* (Turks), used to describe Middle Eastern Jewish immigrants in certain parts of Latin America, see Silvina Schamma Gesser and Susana Brauner, "Aesthetics, Politics, and the Complexities of Arab Jewish Identities in Authoritarian Argentina," in *Contemporary Sephardic and Mizrahi Literature: A Diaspora*, ed. Dario Miccoli, 43–68 (London:

Routledge, 2017), 45–47, although Halfon has been careful to point out that the Argentine and Guatemalan cases are far from analogous. Regarding the Syrian Jewish community in particular, Zenner notes the importance of transnational family and commercial networks. Walter Zenner, *A Global Community: The Jews from Aleppo, Syria* (Detroit, MI: Wayne State University Press, 2000), 106.

11. See, for example, Halfon's interview with Aloma Rodríguez, in which he states, "Mi abuelo, legalmente, era sirio, pero siempre se llamó a sí mismo libanés" (My grandfather, legally, was Syrian, but he always called himself Lebanese). Aloma Rodríguez, "Entrevista a Eduardo Halfon: 'Nuestra identidad no es más que una colección de máscaras.'" *Letras libres*, Feb. 24, 2021, https://letraslibres.com/libros/entrevista-a-eduardo-halfon-nuestra-identidad-no-es-mas-que-una-coleccion-de-mascaras.
12. Aloma Rodríguez, "Entrevista a Eduardo Halfon."
13. "Entonces, ¿qué es ser libanés, si nada tiene que ver con un país o una nacionalidad? Y en otro plano, ¿qué significa para mí ser libanés, como nieto de un libanés que no era libanés? Una pregunta con la cual me vi enfrentado al recibir una invitación a Japón para participar en un congreso de escritores libaneses, y tuve que vestirme con mi disfraz de libanés. ¿Es la identidad, entonces, un disfraz que me puedo poner y quitar cuando me lo solicitan, cuando más lo requiero?" In Aletto, "Eduardo Halfon."
14. D. Illingworth, "*Canción*," *New York Times Book Review*, Oct. 30, 2022, 26.
15. "Halfon, Eduardo: *Canción*," *Kirkus Reviews*, June 21, 2022, https://www.kirkusreviews.com/book-reviews/eduardo-halfon/cancion.
16. In the Spanish version of *Canción*, the stories or sections are untitled.
17. Halfon, *Canción* (2022), 18–20.
18. On the history and use of the mezuzah in religious practice and as a popular amulet or talisman, see Joshua Trachtenburg's *Jewish Magic and Superstition: A Study in Folk Religion* (Philadelphia: University of Pennsylvania Press, 2004), 146–49.
19. Halfon, *Canción* (2022), 31–33.
20. García Escobar, "'Literature is not about answers.'"
21. Halfon, *Canción* (2022), 46.
22. For information on how the facility was later used as a "VIP" prison for high-profile individuals, see "Matamoros: de fuerte militar a prisión exclusiva," *Prensa libre*, May 27, 2015, https://www.prensalibre.com/hemeroteca/matamoros-de-fuerte-militar-a-prision-exclusiva.
23. Halfon, *Canción* (2022), 35.
24. The scene of soldiers swarming in the grandfather's house occurs in "The Bedouin" in *Monastery* and in "El Último café turco" in Eduardo Halfon, *Mañana nunca lo hablamos* (Barcelona: Pre-Textos, 2011).
25. Halfon, *Canción* (2022), 42–43.
26. Halfon, *Canción* (2022), 43. It is common for some Mayans and other indigenous groups in Guatemala to speak little or no Spanish, a situation that complicates their bids for legal entry to or asylum in the United States. A 2019 essay by Rachel Nolan in the *New Yorker* noted, "Guatemala has a population of fifteen million people, forty per cent of them indigenous, according to the most recent census. In the past year, two hundred and fifty thousand Guatemalan migrants have been apprehended at the U.S.-Mexico border. At least half of them are Mayans, and many speak little or no Spanish. According to the Department of Justice, Mam was the ninth most common language used in immigration courts last year, more common than French. Three Guatemalan Mayan languages made the top twenty-five: Mam, K'iche', and Q'anjob'al." See Rachel Nolan, "A Translation Crisis at the Border," *New Yorker*, Dec. 30, 2019, https://www.newyorker.com/magazine/2020/01/06/a-translation-crisis-at-the-border.

27. A duplicate version of "Beni" in English was published under the Spanish title "Bienvenidos al Infierno" in the Jewish magazine *Tablet*, December 1, 2022, https://www.tabletmag.com/sections/arts-letters/articles/bienvenidos-al-infierno.
28. Halfon, *Canción* (2022), 49.
29. See "Guatemala Human Rights Commission/USA Fact Sheet. Guatemala's Elite Special Forces Unit: The Kaibiles," Guatemala Human Rights Commission/USA, accessed May 16, 2024, https://ghrc-usa.org/Publications/factsheet_kaibiles.pdf.
30. Halfon, *Canción* (2022), 50.
31. Halfon, *Canción* (2022), 55.
32. Halfon, *Canción* (2022), 56.
33. Halfon, *Canción* (2022), 44–45. See "Guatemala: Kaibiles and the Massacre at Las Dos Erres," which states that in February 1999, the Commission for Historical Clarification (CEH), established under United Nations auspices by the 1996 Peace Accords, called attention to the brutalizing nature of the training conducted by the Kaibil Center as it "included killing animals and then eating them raw and drinking their blood in order to demonstrate courage. The extreme cruelty of these training methods, according to testimony available to the CEH, was then put into practice in a range of operations carried out by these troops, confirming one point of their decalogue: 'The Kaibil is a killing machine'" (CEH, Feb. 1999). The report also references documented examples of massacres of civilians by the Kaibiles, such as the one in December 1982 at Las Dos Erres, and notes, "The Kaibiles' bloody record led the Catholic Church's Interdiocesan Project for the Recovery of Historical Memory (Proyecto Interdiocesano de Recuperación de la Memoria Histórica, REMHI) to recommend disbandment in its April 1998 report, *Guatemala: Never Again* (*Guatemala: Nunca Más*)." United States Bureau of Citizenship and Immigration Services, "Guatemala: Kaibiles and the Massacre at Las Dos Erres," GTM00003.ZNK, UNHCR, UN Refugee Agency, Feb. 2, 2000, https://www.refworld.org/docid/3ae6a6a54.html
34. Illingworth, "Canción."
35. "Esto es muy claro en los escritores agrupados bajo la denominación de HIJOS en el Cono Sur pero válido para un autor como Halfon, también 'hijo' de uno de los períodos más violentos de la historia de su país–, quienes parecen querer alejarse de este género, dominante para la generación de sus padres. Podríamos arriesgarnos a decir que este rechazo corre paralelo con la necesidad de distanciarse del tipo de práctica política de sus progenitores y construir un relato más cercano a las propias experiencias y modos de pensar." (This is very clear in the writers grouped under the label HIJOS in the Southern Cone but valid for an author like Halfon, also a "son" of one of the most violent periods of history in his country—, who seem to want to distance themselves from this genre, dominant during the generation of their parents. We could venture to say that this refusal runs parallel to the need to distance themselves from the political practices of their forbearers and construct a type of narrative closer to their own experiences and ways of thinking.) A. Amar Sánchez, "Autoficción y política: Estrategias para pensar lo real en la narrativa del siglo XXI," *Visitas al Patio* 16 no. 1, (2022), 26.
36. See, for example, Vladimir de la Cruz, "¿Qué celebramos el 15 de setiembre en Centroamérica?," which notes that indigenous uprisings occurred in every country of the continent, serving as testimony of local resistance to foreign domination: "Sublevaciones indígenas hubo en todos los países del continente, las que se recuerdan principalmente por sus líderes, que testimonian la resistencia a la dominación extranjera, como fueron en América, y el Caribe, Caonabo, Mayobanex, Guarionex, Hatuey, Guama, Lautaro,

Caupolicán, Colo Colo, Manko Inca, Tupac Amaru, Tupac Katari, Rumañahui, Atahualpa, Hayna Capac, Pelantaru, Guaicaipuro, Pacamaconi, Mara, Manaure, Cuauhtemoc, y, en Centroamérica, Presbere, Coyohe, Diriangen, Lempira, Urraca, Tecun Uman, Kaibil Balam" (There were indigenous uprisings in all parts of the continent, which are remembered principally for their leaders, who witnessed resistance to foreign domination in Latin American and the Caribbean, such as Caonabo, Mayobanex, Guarionex, Hatuey, Guama, Lautaro, Caupolicán, Colo Colo, Manko Inca, Tupac Amaru, Tupac Katari, Rumañahui, Atahualpa, Hayna Capac, Pelantaru, Guaicalpuro, Pacamaconi, Mara, Manaure, Cuauhtemoc, and in Central America, Presbere, Coyohe, Diriangen, Lempira, Urraca, Tecun Uman, Kaibil Balam). La Revista, Sept. 15, 2022, https://www.larevista.cr/vladimir-de-la-cruz-que-celebramos-el-15-de-setiembre-en-centroamerica.

37. As Rachel Nolan notes, "In the early eighties, the Guatemalan Army believed—often wrongly—that Mayans were susceptible to guerrilla ideology. Soldiers pillaged indigenous communities, raped women and girls, and stole children who survived massacres, putting hundreds up for adoption. (Guerrilla fighters also attacked Mayans whom they believed were informing for the Army.) The Army burned houses and churches as well as cornfields—sacred sources of sustenance for Mayans. Two hundred thousand people died during the war, the Western Hemisphere's bloodiest conflict of the twentieth century; eighty-three per cent of them were indigenous." Nolan, "A Translation Crisis." Nonetheless, debate continues in Guatemala around terms such as "genocide" and "holocaust," with some critics characterizing their usage as "absurd." See, for example, Irene Hernández Velasco, "'Es absurdo hablar de genocidio en el contexto de la conquista de América': Fernando Cervantes, historiador mexicano," BBC.com, Nov. 2, 2021, https://www.bbc.com/mundo/noticias-america-latina-59037914.
38. Halfon, "Tomorrow We Never Did Talk About It," 19.
39. In Aletto, "Eduardo Halfon."
40. Halfon, *Canción* (2022), 52.
41. Halfon, *Canción* (2022), 58.
42. Halfon's predecessor Victor Perera, also a Jewish Guatemalan writer who left the country at a young age to avoid the internal conflict, considered the civil war another chapter of colonial violence in the region. He wrote, "I learned from La Violencia in Guatemala how quickly one can sink beneath the anger and outrage that is translatable into purposeful energy, the will to act. I learned also that such stock phrases as 'police state,' 'totalitarian repression,' and 'systematic genocide' can be blunted by premature or inappropriate use, so that when the real thing looms in the doorway, all their energy is spent and there are no words left. There is only exhaustion, deadness of spirt, and paralyzed acquiescence." Victor Perera, *Unfinished Conquest: The Guatemalan Tragedy* (Berkeley: University of California Press, 1993), 50–51.
43. See Browitt, *Contemporary Central American Fiction*, 76–77.
44. González Ponciano argues that in the Guatemalan context, a small but powerful minority of Euro-Americans benefit from regressive structures that still determine daily life, leading to a population divided into *gente decente*, or "decent people," and everyone else, the latter group including indigenous persons as well as *ladinos*, mixed-race, Hispanicized, or non-indigenous peoples stigmatized as common or low class with the terms *shumos*, *mucos*, or *choleros*. See Jorge Ramón González Ponciano, "The SHUMO Challenge: White Class Privilege and the Post-Race, Post-Genocide Alliances of Cosmopolitanism from Below," in *War by Other Means: Aftermath in Post-Genocide Guatemala*, 307–29 (Durham, NC: Duke University Press: 2013), 308–9.

45. "'Canción' no es un libro musical. 'El boxeador polaco' no es un libro de boxeo. 'Monasterio' es un libro muy judío a pesar de tener un título tan católico. Me gusta jugar al extravío. Desarmar, desde el título. Pero es un extravío que continúa en el relato." In Aletto, "Eduardo Halfon."
46. *Canción* was released the same week in Spanish and French.
47. Halfon, *Canción* (2022), 59–60.
48. "Acaso el grupo más amorfo, pero mejor emboscado de los rebeldes sea el de las FAR-3, en el cual participaban lumpen proletarios. Está dirigido por Percy Amilcar Jacobs Fernández, exestudiante universitario, hijo de obreros y conocedor del hampa. Desde fines de 1967, comenzó la resistencia en la capital, no solo con acciones propias, sino sustentador de comandos que forman de otras zonas." Mario Monteforte Toledo, "La violencia en Centro América," *Cuadernos Americanos* 176, no. 3 (May-June 1971): 16.
49. "En la cárcel le pusieron el apodo de Canción, que en jerga caló significa carnicero. Conoció a un militante de las guerrillas que también estaba preso quien lo reclutó para la organización.... ¡Todo lo que ha pasado desde la muerte de Percy Jacobs! Medio siglo de sangrienta historia." Jaime Barrios Carrillo, "Percy y la fuga imposible," *Narrativa y ensayo guatemaltecos*, Sept. 6, 2020, https://www.narrativayensayoguatemaltecos.com/percy-y-la-fuga-imposible.
50. Halfon, *Canción* (2022), 76–77.
51. Halfon, *Canción* (2022), 76–78.
52. Halfon, *Canción* (2022), 65.
53. Halfon, *Canción* (2022), 68–70, 82.
54. Halfon, *Canción* (2022), 84–88.
55. Treacy, "Killing the Queen: The Display and Disappearance of Rogelia Cruz," *Latin American Literary Review* 29, no. 57 (2001): 41.
56. Halfon, *Canción* (2022), 90.
57. Halfon, *Canción* (2022), 99–100.
58. Halfon, *Canción* (2022), 90–92. Documents related to PBSuccess can be accessed at Kate Doyle and Peter Kornbluh, eds. "CIA and Assassinations: The Guatemala 1954 Documents," National Security Archive Electronic Briefing Book No. 4, The National Security Archive, accessed May 18, 2024, https://nsarchive2.gwu.edu/NSAEBB/NSAEBB4.
59. "Hice mucha investigación sobre eso, como sobre el presidente del país, Jacobo Árbenz, que fue derrocado por EE.UU. en un golpe de Estado." Xavi Ayén, "Eduardo Halfon: 'A mi abuelo le secuestró miss Guatemala,'" *La Vanguardia*, Feb. 23, 2021, https://www.lavanguardia.com/cultura/20210223/6257940/halfon-secuestro-miss-novela.html. The mention of a letter his grandfather sent to the local newspaper *Prensa Libre*, published on June 8, 1954, is another detail that can easily be corroborated.
60. Halfon, *Canción* (2022), 95.
61. Halfon, *Canción* (2022), 102.
62. Halfon, *Canción* (2022), 107–8.
63. "'There are three transgressions for which Jews are punished in this world and have no share in the World to Come: idolatry, sexual immorality, and bloodshed—but lashon hará is as bad as all of them combined.' The Talmud (Arachin 15b) states that each act of lashon hará does irreparable harm to three people: the victim of the gossip, the person who listened to it, and the perpetrator him/herself." See Yaakov Komisar, "Spiritual Leprosy," *Baltimore Jewish Times* 319, no. 6 (Apr. 8, 2011): 37.
64. Halfon, *Canción* (2022), 109.
65. Halfon, *Canción* (2022), 115.

66. Halfon, *Canción* (2022), 117.
67. Halfon, *Canción* (2022), 120–26.
68. Halfon, *Canción* (2022), 132–33.
69. "In Guatemala's northern Petén department, May 14, 2011, felt a lot like December 6, 1982. In May, on the Los Cocos ranch near La Libertad, 27 campesinos were slaughtered and decapitated by henchmen of a bloodthirsty Mexican drug cartel, the Zetas—whose ranks include former Guatemalan army commandos known as Los Kaibiles. That's why, for Guatemalans, the Los Cocos massacre was all too reminiscent of another 29 years ago, when witnesses say Kaibil special forces murdered 251 people in Dos Erres, also near La Libertad." Tim Padgett, "Guatemala's Kaibiles: A Notorious Commando Unit Wrapped Up in Central America's Drug War," *Time*, July 14, 2011, https://world.time.com/2011/07/14/guatemalas-kaibil-terror-from-dictators-to-drug-cartels.
70. "The Kaibiles I Special Operations Force of Guatemalan Army." YouTube, posted by Defense Daily, June 9, 2018, https://www.youtube.com/watch?v=hJZoIxoScUQ.
71. Halfon, *Canción* (2022), 131.
72. "Canción," *Publisher's Weekly*, accessed May 16, 2024, https://www.publishersweekly.com/9781954276079; and Bhattacharyya, "Canción," *Washington Independent Review of Books*, Nov. 7, 2022, https://www.washingtonindependentreviewofbooks.com/index.php/bookreview/cancion.
73. Halfon, *Signor Hoffman*, 17–18; *Mourning*, 17–18.
74. Halfon, *Mourning*, 17–18.
75. Garcia Escobar, "'Literature is not about answers.'"
76. Halfon, *Canción* (2022), 156.
77. Halfon, *Canción* (2022), 139–40.
78. Halfon, *Canción* (2022), 146, 152–53.
79. Halfon, *Canción* (2022), 154.
80. Halfon, *Canción* (2022), 157.
81. Ayén, "Eduardo Halfon."
82. Ulin, "Review."
83. Lawrence Langer, *Holocaust Testimonies: The Ruins of Memory* (New Haven, CT: Yale University Press, 1991), xv.
84. "A Conversation with Eduardo Halfon on *The Polish Boxer*," Bellevue Literary Press, accessed May 16, 2024, https://blpress.org/author-qas/a-conversation-with-eduardo-halfon.
85. See Terrence Des Pres, *The Survivor: An Anatomy of Life in the Death Camps* (Oxford: Oxford University Press, 1980), 30.
86. Burger, *Witness*, 34.
87. "La historia es siempre una fantasía sin base científica, y cuando se pretende levantar un tinglado invulnerable y colocar sobre él una consecuencia, se corre el peligro de que un dato cambie y se venga abajo toda la armazón histórica." Baroja, *El Amor, El Dandysmo y La Intriga: Novela* (Madrid: Caro Raggio, 1923), 16, my translation.
88. Burger, *Witness*, 34.

BIBLIOGRAPHY

Aarons, Victoria. "Found Objects: The Legacy of Third-Generation Holocaust Memory." In *Translated Memories: Transgenerational Perspectives on the Holocaust*, edited by Ursula Reuter and Bettina Hofmann, 231–50. Lanham, MD: Lexington Books, 2020.

———, ed. *Third-Generation Holocaust Narratives: Memory in Memoir and Fiction*. Lanham, MD: Lexington Books, 2016.

Aarons, Victoria, and Alan L. Berger. *Third-Generation Holocaust Representation: Trauma, History, and Memory*. Evanston, IL: Northwestern University Press, 2017.

Aguilar, Eduard. "Eduardo Halfon: 'Nada les gustaría más a mis editores que una novela larga.'" Alicanteplaza.es, July 28, 2018. https://alicanteplaza.es/eduardo-halfon-nada-les-gustaria-mas-a-mis-editores-que-una-novela-larga.

Aiello, Barbara. "Ferramonti." *Rabbibarbara.com*, March 2, 2018. https://www.rabbibarbara.com/ferramonti.

Alarcón, Daniel. "A Roundtable Discussion with Daniel Alarcón + Eduardo Halfon + Santiago Vaquera-Vásquez," *Believer Magazine*, no. 69 (Feb. 1, 2010). https://www.thebeliever.net/a-roundtable-discussion-3.

Alberca, Manuel. "En las fronteras de la autobiografía." In *Escritura autobiográfica y géneros literarios*, edited by de Manuela Ledesma Pedraz, 58–60. Jaén: Universidad de Jaén, 1999.

Alberca, Manuel. "¿Existe la autoficción hispanoamericana?" *Cuadernos del CILHA*, no. 7/8 (2005–2006), 115–27.

Aletto, Carlos. "Eduardo Halfon: '¿Es la identidad un disfraz que me puedo poner y quitar cuando me lo solicitan?'" Infobae.com, March 8, 2021. https://www.infobae.com/cultura/2021/03/09/eduardo-halfon-es-la-identidad-un-disfraz-que-me-puedo-poner-y-quitar-cuando-me-lo-solicitan.

Amar Sánchez, Ana María. "Autoficción y política: Estrategias para pensar lo real en la narrativa del siglo XXI." *Visitas al Patio* 16, no. 1 (2022): 23–43.

"Anatewka – Łódź." 2022. Anatewka.com, accessed May 15, 2024. https://www.anatewka.com.

Apel, Dora. *Memory Effects: The Holocaust and the Art of Secondary Witnessing.* New Brunswick, NJ: Rutgers University Press, 2002.

Apel, Dora. "The Tattooed Jew." In *Visual Culture and the Holocaust*, edited by Barbie Zelizer, 300–320. New Brunswick, NJ: Rutgers University Press, 2001.

Apter, Jeff. *Never Enough: The Story of the Cure.* London: Omnibus Press, 2005.

Archivo Histórico de la Policía Nacional. *Del silencio a la memoria: Revelaciones del Archivo Histórico de la Policía Nacional.* Guatemala: Archivo Histórico de la Policía Nacional, 2011. https://repositories.lib.utexas.edu/handle/2152/13521.

Archivo Histórico de la Policía Nacional (AHPN). *From Silence to Memory: Revelations of the Archivo Histórico de la Policía Nacional.* Foreword by Carlos Aguirre. Eugene: University of Oregon Libraries, 2013. https://scholarsbank.uoregon.edu/xmlui/bitstream/handle/1794/12928/ahpn_final_20130620.pdf.

Arias, Arturo. "Post-identidades post-nacionales: Transformaciones en la constitución de las subjetividades globalizadas." *Revista de Crítica Literaria Latinoamericana* 35, no. 69, (2009): 135–52.

Astro, Alan. "Avatars of Third-Generation Holocaust Narrative in French and Spanish." In Aarons, *Third-Generation Holocaust Narratives*, 103–30.

Auseré Abarca, Aurelio, Luis Miguel Estrada Orozco, and Eduardo Halfon. "Eduardo Halfon: Identidad en construcción: Una conversación con Aurelio Auseré Abarca y Luis Miguel Estrada Orozco." *Latin American Literature Today*, no. 6 (May 2018). https://latinamericanliteraturetoday.org/es/2018/04/eduardo-halfon-identity-under-construction-conversation-aurelio-ausere-abarca-and-luis.

"Author Eduardo Halfon in Conversation with Daniel Medin." Center for Writers and Translators, American University in Paris, Dec. 12, 2019. https://www.aup.edu/news-events/news/2019-12-12/author-eduardo-halfon-conversation-daniel-medin.

Ayén, Xavi. "Eduardo Halfon: 'A mi abuelo le secuestró miss Guatemala.'" *La Vanguardia*, Feb. 23, 2021. https://www.lavanguardia.com/cultura/20210223/6257940/halfon-secuestro-miss-novela.html.

Azancot, Nuria. "Eduardo Halfon: 'La literatura es insensata, inexplicable, irrepetible, como un primer beso.'" *El Español*, Jan. 12, 2021. https://www.elespanol.com/el-cultural/20210112/eduardo-halfon-literatura-insensata-inexplicable-irrepetible-primer/550696815_0.html.

Azses, Hayim. *The Shoah in the Sephardic Communities: Dreams, Dilemmas and Decisions of Sephardic Leaders.* Jerusalem: Sephardic Educational Center in Jerusalem, 2005.

Baer, Alejandro, and Natan Sznaider. *Memory and Forgetting in the Post-Holocaust Era: The Ethics of Never Again.* London: Routledge, 2017.

Bakhtin, M. M., Caryl Emerson, and Michael Holquist. *The Dialogic Imagination: Four Essays.* Austin: University of Texas Press, 1981.

Ball, Anna. "Impossible Intimacies: Towards a Visual Politics of 'Touch' at the Israeli-Palestinian Border." *Journal for Cultural Research* 16, no. 2–3 (2012): 175–95.
Barchino, Matías. "Los cuentos de Eduardo Halfon: hiperrelato y autoficción." *LEJANA: Revista Crítica de Narrativa Breve*, no. 6 (2013): 1–13.
Barnes, Joshua. "No Borders: An Interview with Eduardo Halfon." *Sampsonia Way*, Dec. 10, 2012. http://archive.sampsoniaway.org/literary-voices/2012/12/10/no-borders-an-interview-with-eduardo-halfon.
Baroja, Pío. *El amor, el dandysmo y la intriga, novela*. Madrid: Caro Raggio, 1923.
Barrios Carrillo, Jaime, "Percy y la fuga imposible." Narrativa y Ensayo Guatemaltecos, Sept. 6, 2020. https://www.narrativayensayoguatemaltecos.com/percy-y-la-fuga-imposible.
Barry, Des. "Eduardo Halfon and *The Polish Boxer*: Des Barry interviews Eduardo Halfon." *3:am Magazine*, May 29, 2013. https://www.3ammagazine.com/3am/eduardo-halfon-and-the-polish-boxer.
Bejarano, Margalit. "A Mosaic of Fragmented Identities: The *Sephardim* in Latin America." In *Identities in an Era of Globalization and Multiculturalism: Latin America in the Jewish World*, edited by Judit Bokser de Liwerant, 267–86. Leiden: Brill, 2008.
Bejarano, Margalit, and Edna Aizenberg. *Contemporary Sephardic Identity in the Americas: An Interdisciplinary Approach*. Syracuse, NY: Syracuse University Press, 2012.
Bergman, Ingmar. *Skammen (Shame)*. 1968. 103 min. Svensk Filmindustri.
Bergman, Ingmar. "Film and Creativity." *American Cinematographer* 53, no. 4 (1972): 378–79, 426–31, 434.
Bhattacharyya, Anaya. "Canción." *Washington Independent Review of Books*, Nov. 7, 2022. https://www.washingtonindependentreviewofbooks.com/index.php/bookreview/cancion.
Biedenbender, David. "Melodious Thunk." David Biedenbender (website), accessed May 15, 2024. https://davidbiedenbender.com/work/melodious-thunk.
Biederman, Mark. *Schindler's Listed: The Search for My Father's Lost Gold*. With Randi Biederman. Boston: Academic Studies Press, 2019.
Bolden, Tony. *Afro-Blue: Improvisations in African American Poetry and Culture*. Urbana: University of Illinois Press, 2004.
Bolton-Fasman, Judy. "Novelist Eduardo Halfon Wins Edward Lewis Wallant Award." JewishBoston, April 9, 2019. https://www.jewishboston.com/novelist-eduardo-halfon-wins-edward-lewis-wallant-award.
Brenner, Reeve Robert. *The Faith and Doubt of Holocaust Survivors*. New Brunswick, NJ: Transaction Publishers, 2014.
Broder, John M. "Clinton Offers His Apologies to Guatemala. (Foreign Desk)." *New York Times*, March 11, 1999.
Brouwer, Daniel C., and Linda Diane Horwitz. "The Cultural Politics of Progenic Auschwitz Tattoos: 157622, A-15510, 4559,..." *Quarterly Journal of Speech* 101, no. 3 (2015): 534–58.

Browitt, Jeff. *Contemporary Central American Fiction: Gender, Subjectivity and Affect*. Portland, OR: Sussex Academic, 2018.

Bukiet, Melvin Jules. *Nothing Makes You Free: Writings by Descendants of Jewish Holocaust Survivors*. New York: Norton, 2002.

Burger, Ariel. *Witness: Lessons from Elie Wiesel's Classroom*. New York: Houghton Mifflin Harcourt, 2018.

Campisi, Nicolás. "The Dislocation of Cosmopolitan Identities in Eduardo Halfon's *Monasterio*." *INTI: Revista de Literatura Hispánica*, no. 87–88 (2018): 113–24.

"Canción." *Publisher's Weekly*, July 11, 2022. https://www.publishersweekly.com/9781954276079.

Capó, Daniel. "Los libros que no he leído: Eduardo Halfon." *Daniel Capo* (blog), April 29, 2016. https://danielcapoblog.com/2016/04/29/libros-no-leidos-eduardo-halfon.

Capogreco, Carlo Spartaco. *Mussolini's Camps: Civilian Internment in Fascist Italy (1940–1943)*. London: Routledge, 2019.

Cartwright, Garth. *Princes amongst Men: Journeys with Gypsy Musicians*. London: Serpent's Tail, 2007.

CEH (Comisión para el Esclarecimiento Histórico). *Guatemala: Memory of Silence: Report of the Commission for Historical Clarification Conclusions and Recommendations*. Guatemala City: United Nations Office for Project Services (UNOPS), 1999. https://hrdag.org/wp-content/uploads/2013/01/CEHreport-english.pdf.

"Characters Who Are Looking for Their Roots: Q&A with Eduardo Halfon." *Sampsonia Way*, March 15, 2013. http://archive.sampsoniaway.org/blog/2013/03/15/characters-who-are-looking-for-their-roots-qa-with-eduardo-halfon.

Chiaravalloti, Franco. "Eduardo Halfon: 'La incomodidad es un sentir judío.'" *Revista de letras*, June 16, 2014. https://revistadeletras.net/eduardo-halfon-la-incomodidad-es-un-sentir-eminentemente-judio.

Chinchilla Mazariegos, Oswaldo. "Of Birds and Insects: The Hummingbird Myth in Ancient America." *Ancient Mesoamerica*, no. 21 (2010): 45–61.

Chowdhry, Pritika. "What is Counter-Memory?" Pritika Chowdhry (website), July 15, 2021. https://www.pritikachowdhry.com/post/what-is-counter-memory.

"Conmemoración de 20 años de la paz: Las palabras de Álvaro Arzú y Jimmy Morales." YouTube, posted by TN23 Guatemala, Dec. 29, 2016. https://www.youtube.com/watch?v=tY6r8ozncUw.

Constales, Sofie. "Posmemoria y autoficción en *Mañana nunca lo hablamos* de Eduardo Halfon y *Dios tenía miedo* de Vanesa Núñez Handal." Thesis, Universiteit Geint, 2015.

"A Conversation between Eduardo Halfon & Marilyn Miller, moderated by Avinoam Patt, UConn." YouTube, posted by UConnJUDS, Oct. 7, 2021. https://www.youtube.com/watch?v=zePg_9PB5uM.

"A Conversation with Eduardo Halfon on *Monastery*." Bellevue Literary Press, accessed May 16, 2024. https://blpress.org/author-qas/conversation-eduardo-halfon-monastery.

"A Conversation with Eduardo Halfon on *The Polish Boxer*." Bellevue Literary Press, accessed May 16, 2024. https://blpress.org/author-qas/a-conversation-with-eduardo-halfon.

Costello, Lisa A. *American Public Memory and the Holocaust: Performing Gender, Shifting Orientations*. Lanham, MD: Lexington Books, 2020.

Czarnecki, Joseph P. *Last Traces: The Lost Art of Auschwitz*. Introduction by Chaim Potok. New York: Atheneum, 1989.

Davies, Norman. *Europe: A History*. Oxford: Oxford University Press, 1996.

de la Cruz, Vladimir. "¿Qué celebramos el 15 de setiembre en Centroamérica?" *La Revista*, Sept. 15, 2022. https://www.larevista.cr/vladimir-de-la-cruz-que-celebramos-el-15-de-setiembre-en-centroamerica.

Des Pres, Terrence. *The Survivor: An Anatomy of Life in the Death Camps*. Oxford: Oxford University Press, 1980.

Díaz Miranda, Ángel M. "'El boxeador polaco': Operaciones mnemónicas e identitarias en la obra de Eduardo Halfon." *Cincinnati Romance Review* 50 (Spring 2021): 44–65.

Dicaire, David. *Jazz Musicians, 1945 to the Present*. Jefferson, NC: McFarland, 2006.

Domene, Pedro. "Ficción y realidad en la novela 'Canción', de Eduardo Halfon." ¡Zas!-Madrid, Dec. 28, 2021. https://zasmadrid.com/ficcion-y-realidad-en-la-novela-cancion-de-eduardo-halfon.

Doyle, Kate, and Peter Kornbluh, eds. "CIA and Assassinations: The Guatemala 1954 Documents." National Security Archive Electronic Briefing Book, No. 4. The National Security Archive, accessed May 18, 2024. https://nsarchive2.gwu.edu/NSAEBB/NSAEBB4.

Dreifus, Erika. "A Special Kind of Kinship: On Being a '3G' Writer." In Aarons, *Third-Generation Holocaust Narratives*, 1–16.

Durante, Erica, and Maude Havenne. "La obra en 'matryoshka' de Eduardo Halfon: Un proyecto literario global." *Revista Iberoamericana* 87, no. 274 (2021): 265–88.

Editorial Pre-Textos. "Mañana nunca lo hablamos de Eduardo Halfon: Víde Tita Portela y Fred Fuentes para Editorial Pre-Textos." YouTube, posted by Editorial Pre-Textos, Jun 13, 2011. https://www.youtube.com/watch?v=03KpME9lJ2U.

"Eduardo Halfon habló de su novela 'Canción' y su interés por los tabúes." IP Noticias, April 4, 2021. https://ipnoticias.ar/nota/2600-eduardo-halfon-hablo-de-su-novela-cancion-y-su-interes-por-los-tabues.

"Eduardo Halfon, mi obra es una novela en marcha." YouTube, posted by Casa de América, June 7, 2018. https://www.youtube.com/watch?v=0c4I1rMPV6w.

"Eduardo Halfon. Story and History: Bleeding into Fiction." Institute for Ideas and Imagination, Columbia University, Jan. 16, 2020. https://ideasimagination.columbia.edu/events/eduardo-halfon.

Edwards, Brent Hayes. *Epistrophies: Jazz and the Literary Imagination*. Cambridge, MA: Harvard University Press, 2017.

Elias, Ruth. *Triumph of Hope: From Theresienstadt and Auschwitz to Israel*. New York: John Wiley & Sons, 1998.

"En una Guatemala herida, la Casa de la Memoria clama por justicia." Nación, Feb. 9, 2014. https://www.nacion.com/revista-dominical/en-una-guatemala-herida-la-casa-de-la-memoria-clama-por-justicia/JSAZKBH6TNB6TDCQEGGWHOBNZI/story.

Ezrahi, Sidra Dekoven. "Representing Auschwitz." *History and Memory* 7, no. 2 (1995): 121–54.

Felman, Shoshana, and Dori Laub. *Testimony: Crises of Witnessing in Literature, Psychoanalysis and History*. New York: Routledge, 1992.

Fermaglich, Kirsten. *A Rosenberg by Any Other Name: A History of Jewish Name Changing in America*. New York: New York University Press, 2018.

Fischer, Nina. *Memory Work: The Second Generation*. New York: Palgrave Macmillan, 2015.

"Flying Balloon Girl." Wikipedia, last updated Feb. 29, 2024. https://en.wikipedia.org/wiki/Flying_Balloon_Girl.

Forsyth, Mark. *The Elements of Eloquence*. New York: Berkeley Books, 2014.

"From Silence to Memory: Revelations of the AHPN. Archivo Histórico de la Policia Nacional; Aguirre, Carlos; Doyle, Kate" (Abstract). University of Oregon Libraries Scholars Bank, 2013, https://scholarsbank.uoregon.edu/xmlui/handle/1794/12928.

Galloway, David D. *Edward Lewis Wallant*. Boston: Twayne Publishers, 1979.

García Escobar, José. "'Ch'ayonel almost means boxer, in Kaqchikel': Translating Eduardo Halfon into a Mayan Language." *Asymptote*, Feb. 24, 2020. https://www.asymptotejournal.com/blog/2020/02/24/chayonel-almost-means-boxer-in-kaqchikel-translating-eduardo-halfon-into-a-mayan-language.

García Escobar, José. "'Literature is not about answers. But questions': An Interview with Eduardo Halfon, Author of *Canción*." *Asymptote*, Oct. 12, 2022. https://www.asymptotejournal.com/blog/2022/10/12/literature-is-not-about-answers-but-questions-an-interview-with-eduardo-halfon-author-of-cancion.

Garsd, Jasmine. "A Braid of Words: Guest DJ Eduardo Halfon, Author of 'The Polish Boxer.'" *Alt.Latino*, National Public Radio, May 10, 2013. https://www.npr.org/sections/altlatino/2013/05/04/181136776/a-braid-of-words-guest-dj-with-eduardo-halfon-author-of-the-polish-boxer.

Gartenberg, Charlotte, "Haunted Stories, Haunted Selves: Ghosts in Latin American Jewish Literature." PhD diss., City University of New York, 2018. https://academicworks.cuny.edu/gc_etds/2767.

Gelissen, Rena Kornreich, and Heather Dune Macadam. *Rena's Promise: A Story of Sisters in Auschwitz*. Boston: Beacon Press, 1995.

Genette, Gérard. *Fiction & Diction*. Ithaca, NY: Cornell University Press, 1993.

Gerard, Christian. *The Cure FAQ*. London: Backbeat Books, 2021.

Goldman, Francisco. *The Art of Political Murder: Who Killed the Bishop?* New York: Grove Press, 2007.
Gonzalez, David. "Angels Watch Over Memories of War." Lens (blog). *New York Times*, June 4, 2012. https://lens.blogs.nytimes.com/2012/06/04/angels-watch-over-memories-of-war.
———. "A Quest for Justice in Guatemala." Lens (blog). *New York Times*, May 14, 2013. https://lens.blogs.nytimes.com/2013/05/14/a-quest-for-justice-in-guatemala.
González Ponciano, Jorge Ramón. "The SHUMO Challenge: White Class Privilege and the Post-Race, Post-Genocide Alliances of Cosmopolitanism from Below." In *War by Other Means: Aftermath in Post-Genocide Guatemala*, edited by Carlota McAllister and Diane M. Nelson, 307–29. Durham, NC: Duke University Press: 2013.
Goñi, Javier. "Mañana nunca lo hablamos." *El Pais*, July 30, 2011. https://elpais.com/diario/2011/07/30/babelia/1311984757_850215.html.
Goodwin, James. "Henry Miller, American Autobiographer." In *Critical Essays on Henry Miller*, edited by Ronald Gottesman, 297–313. New York: G. K. Hall, 1992.
Greenland, Thomas H. *Jazzing New York City's Unseen Scene*. Urbana: University of Illinois Press, 2016.
Gross, Jan T. *Neighbors: The Destruction of the Jewish Community in Jedwabne, Poland*. Princeton, NJ: Princeton University Press, 2001.
"Guatemala Human Rights Commission/USA Fact Sheet. Guatemala's Elite Special Forces Unit: The Kaibiles." Guatemala Human Rights Commission/USA, accessed May 16, 2024. https://ghrc-usa.org/Publications/factsheet_kaibiles.pdf.
Guillén, Claudio. *El sol de los desterrados: Literatura y exilio*. Barcelona: Quaderns Crema, 1995.
Habran, Chloé. *Construcción posmemorial y digresión en la obra de Eduardo Halfon*. Phd diss. Faculté de philosophie, arts et lettres, Université catholique de Louvain, 2018. http:// hdl.handle.net/2078.1/thesis:16593.
Haft, Alan Scott. *Harry Haft: Auschwitz Survivor, Challenger of Rocky Marciano*. Syracuse, NY: Syracuse University Press, 2006.
Halfon, Eduardo. *El ángel literario*. Barcelona: Editorial Anagrama, 2004.
———. "Bamboo." Translated by Achy Obejas. Pen America, April 12, 2013. https://pen.org/bamboo.
———. "Better Not Say Too Much." *Guardian*, Nov. 4, 2015. https://www.theguardian.com/books/the-writing-life-around-the-world-by-electric-literature/2015/nov/04/better-not-say-too-much-eduardo-halfon-on-literature-paranoia-and-leaving-guatemala.
———. *Biblioteca Bizarra*. Primera edición. Zaragoza: Jekyll & Jill Editores, 2018.
———. "Bienvenidos al Infierno." *Tablet*, Dec. 1, 2022. https://www.tabletmag.com/sections/arts-letters/articles/bienvenidos-al-infierno.
———. *El boxeador polaco*. Barcelona: Libros del asteroide, 2019.

———. *Canción*. Barcelona: Libros del asteroide, 2021.
———. *Canción*. New York: Bellevue Literary Press, 2022.
———. "Canción." *New York Review of Books*, Nov. 9, 2020.
———. *Clases de chapín*. Primera edición. Logroño: Fulgencio Pimentel, 2017.
———. *Clases de dibujo*. Logroño: AMG, 2009.
———. *Clases de hebreo*. Primera edición. Logroño: AMG, 2008.
———. *De cabo roto*. Barcelona: Littera Books, 2003.
———. "Dicho hacia el sur." Plaza pública, 14 Dec. 2012. https://www.plazapublica.com.gt/content/dicho-hacia-el-sur.
———. "Dicho hacia el sur." In *Sam no es mi tío: veintidós crónicas migrantes y un sueño americano*, edited by Aileen El-Kadi and Diego Fonseca, 133–41. Ciudad Autónoma de Buenos Aires: Aguilar, Altea, Taurus, Alfaguara, 2012.
———. "Domingos en Iowa." *El malpensante*, no. 210, Aug. 2019. https://elmalpensante.com/articulo/4224/domingos-en-iowa.
———. *Duelo*. Barcelona: Libros del asteroide, 2018.
———. *Elocuencias de un tartamudo*. Valencia: Pre-Textos, 2012.
———. *Esto no es una pipa; Saturno*. Guatemala Ciudad: Alfaguara, 2003.
———. *Mañana Nunca Lo Hablamos*. Barcelona: Pre-Textos, 2011.
———. "La memoria infantil." *Cuadernos hispanoamericanos*, no. 731 (2011): 21–27. http://www.cervantesvirtual.com/obra/la-memoria-infantil.
———. *Monasterio*. Segunda edición. Barcelona: Libros del asteroide, 2015.
———. *Monastery*. New York: Bellevue Literary Press, 2014.
———. *Mourning*. New York: Bellevue Literary Press, 2018.
———. *Oh gueto mi amor*. Illustrated by David de las Heras. Madrid: Páginas de Espuma, 2018.
———. *La Pirueta*. Valencia: Pre-Textos, 2010.
———. *The Polish Boxer*. New York: Bellevue Literary, 2012.
———. *Ri aj polo'n ch'ayonel = El boxeador polaco*. Translated by Raxche' Rodríguez Guaján. Primera edición bilingüe kaqchikel-español. Guatemala, Guatemala C.A: Maya' Wuj, 2019.
———. *Signor Hoffman*. Barcelona: Libros del asteroide, 2015.
———. "The Sway of the Sea." Translated from the Spanish by Alba Griffin, Avgi Daferera, Bridget Lely, Hugh Caldin, Jim Knight, Lucila Cordone, Michael McDevitt, Ollie Brock, Sabrina Steiner, Samantha Christie, Shazea Quraishi, and Tom Bunstead with the collaboration of Eduardo Halfon and Anne McLean. Newwriting, March 2012, https://www.newwriting.net/2012/03/the-sway-of-the-sea.
———. "Tomorrow We Never Did Talk About It." Translated by Anne McLean, afterward by Ilan Stavans. Working Title 1.3. Hadley, MA: Massachusetts Review, 2016.
———. *Un hijo cualquiera*. Primera edición. Barcelona: Libros del asteroide, 2022.
Halfon, Eduardo, in conversation with his translators Lisa Dillman and Daniel Hahn, with Avinoam Patt, moderator. "The Purest Form of Writing, the Most Intimate Form of Reading." *Massachusetts Review* 60, no. 3 (2019): 448–63.

"Halfon, Eduardo: CANCION." *Kirkus Reviews*, June 21, 2022. https://www.kirkusreviews.com/book-reviews/eduardo-halfon/cancion.

Hansen, Per Krogh, John Pier, Philippe Roussin, and Wolf Schmid, eds. *Emerging Vectors of Narratology*. Berlin: De Gruyter, 2017.

Hepworth, Andrea. "From Survivor to Fourth-Generation Memory: Literal and Discursive Sites of Memory in Post-dictatorship Germany and Spain." *Journal of Contemporary History* 54 no. 1 (2019): 139–62.

Hernández Velasco, Irene. "'Es absurdo hablar de genocidio en el contexto de la conquista de América': Fernando Cervantes, historiador mexicano." BBC.com, Nov. 2, 2021. https://www.bbc.com/mundo/noticias-america-latina-59037914.

Herzog, Werner, dir. *Lectionen in Finsternis* (*Lessons of Darkness*). Munich: Werner Herzog Filmproduktion, 1992. 52 min.

Herzog, Werner, and Moira Weigel. "On the Absolute, the Sublime, and Ecstatic Truth." *Arion: A Journal of Humanities and the Classics* 17, no. 3 (2010): 1–12.

Hevia, Elena. "Eduardo Halfon, el Zelig guatemalteco." El Periodico, Sept. 12, 2017. https://www.elperiodico.com/es/ocio-y-cultura/20170912/eduardo-halfon-zelig-novela-duelo-6281562.

Hirsch, Marianne. *The Generation of Postmemory: Writing and Visual Culture after the Holocaust*. New York: Columbia University Press, 2012.

Hirsch, Marianne. "Surviving Images: Holocaust Photographs and the Work of Postmemory." In *Visual Culture and the Holocaust*, edited by Barbie Zelizer, 214–46. New Brunswick, NJ: Rutgers University Press, 2001.

Hobuß, Steffi. "Silence, Remembering, and Forgetting in Wittgenstein, Cage, and Derrida." In *Beyond Memory: Silence and the Aesthetics of Remembrance*, edited by Alexandre Dessingué and Jay Winter, 95–110. New York: Routledge, 2016.

Hoelscher, Steven. "Angels of Memory: Photography and Haunting in Guatemala City." *GeoJournal* 73, no. 3 (2008): 195–217.

Huergo, Damián. "Eduardo Halfon: Un escritor por accidente." *Página 12*, June 7, 2020. https://www.pagina12.com.ar/269646-eduardo-halfon-un-escritor-por-accidente.

Huyssen, Andreas. *Twilight Memories: Marking Time in a Culture of Amnesia*. New York: Routledge, 1995.

Illingworth, Dustin. "Canción." *New York Times Book Review*, Oct. 30, 2022, 26.

Jacobs, Janet Liebman. *The Holocaust across Generations: Trauma and Its Inheritance among Descendants of Survivors*. New York: New York University Press, 2016.

"Jedwabne Pogrom." Wikipedia, last updated July 25, 2024. https://en.wikipedia.org/wiki/Jedwabne_pogrom.

Jilovsky, Esther. *Remembering the Holocaust: Generations, Witnessing and Place*. New York: Bloomsbury Academic, 2015.

JTA (Jewish Telegraphic Agency) and Emily Burack. "Why Is Holocaust Fiction Still So Popular." *Haaretz*, April 24, 2019. https://www.haaretz.com/jewish/holocaust-remembrance-day/2019-04-29/ty-article/why-holocaust-books-continue-to-be-in-high-demand/0000017f-e732-da9b-a1ff-ef7f075f0000.

"The Kaibiles I Special Operations Force of Guatemalan Army." YouTube, posted by Defense Daily, June 9, 2018. https://www.youtube.com/watch?v=hJZoIxoScUQ.

Kaitz, Marsha, Mindy Levy, Richard Ebstein, Stephen V. Faraone, and David Mankuta. "The Intergenerational Effects of Trauma from Terror: A Real Possibility." *Infant Mental Health Journal* 30, no. 2 (2009): 158–79.

Kay, Judith W. "Jews as Oppressed and Oppressor." In *Judaism, Race, and Ethics: Conversations and Questions*. Edited by Jonathan K. Crane, 66–104. University Park: Pennsylvania State University Press, 2020.

Kaye, Alexander. *The Invention of Jewish Theocracy: The Struggle for Legal Authority in Modern Israel*. Oxford: Oxford University Press, 2020.

Keith, Joseph. *Unbecoming Americans*. New Brunswick, NJ: Rutgers University Press, 2013.

Kelley, Robin D. G. *Thelonious Monk: The Life and Times of an American Original*. New York: Free Press, 2009.

Kessel, Sim. *Hanged at Auschwitz: An Extraordinary Memoir of Survival*. Lanham, MD: Cooper Square Press, 2001.

Kleist, Reinhard. *The Boxer: The True Story of Holocaust Survivor Harry Haft*. New York: Harry N. Abrams, 2014.

Komisar, Yaakov. "Spiritual Leprosy." *Baltimore Jewish Times* 319, no. 6 (April 8, 2011): 37.

LaHaije, Marileen. "'Ningún lugar sagrado' de Rodrigo Rey Rosa: Una ficción paranoica desde la diáspora centroamericana." *Neophilologus*, no. 105 (2021): 75–89. https://doi.org/10.1007/s11061-020-09666-2.

Lahiri, Jhumpa, Eduardo Halfon, and Ilan Stavans. "Three Authors Leave, Stay, Dream, and Long for Elsewhere: Jhumpa Lahiri, Eduardo Halfon, and Ilan Stavans in Conversation." LitHub, Aug. 24, 2020. https://lithub.com/three-authors-leave-stay-dream-and-long-for-elsewhere.

Lamm, Maurice. "The History, Meaning, and Significance of Kaddish." Chabad.org, accessed Sept. 16, 2023. https://www.chabad.org/library/article_cdo/aid/281617/jewish/The-History-Significance-and-Meaning-of-Kaddish.htm.

Lang, Jessica. *Textual Silence: Unreadability and the Holocaust*. New Brunswick, NJ: Rutgers University Press, 2017.

Langbein, Hermann. *People in Auschwitz*. Chapel Hill: University of North Carolina Press in Association with the United States Holocaust Memorial Museum, 2004.

Langer, Lawrence L. *Holocaust Testimonies: The Ruins of Memory*. New Haven, CT: Yale University Press, 1991.

"The Language of the Camps." JewishGen, accessed Sept. 16, 2023. https://www.jewishgen.org/ForgottenCamps/General/LanguageEng.html.

Laorden Albendea, María Teresa. "Lidiar con el pasado familiar: Posmemoria y trauma en El boxeador polaco de Eduardo Halfon." In *Tuércele el cuello al cisne: Las expresiones de la violencia en la literatura hispánica contemporánea (Siglos XX y XXI)*. Edited by Cristóbal José Álvarez López, Juan Manuel Carmona Tierno, Ana Davis González, Sara González Ángel, María del

Rosario Martínez Navarro, and Marta Rodríguez Manzano, 589–601. Madrid: Renacimiento, 2016.

Leonardo, José Roberto. "Mañana nunca lo hablamos de Eduardo Halfon." *Diario del gallo* (blog), May 9, 2011. https://diariodelgallo.wordpress.com/2011/05/09/manana-nunca-lo-hablamos-de-eduardo-halfon.

Levi, Primo. *The Drowned and the Saved*. New York: Summit Books, 1986.

———. *If This Is a Man*. New York: Orion Press, 1959.

———. *Survival in Auschwitz: The Nazi Assault on Humanity*. Translated by Stuart Woolf. New York: Touchstone, 1996.

Levin, Irene. "The Social Phenomenon of Silence." In *The Holocaust as Active Memory: The Past in the Present*, edited by Marie Louise Seeberg, 187–97. Farnham, Surrey, England: Ashgate, 2013.

Levis Sullam, Simon, David I. Kertzer, Claudia Patane, and Oona Smyth. *The Italian Executioners: The Genocide of the Jews of Italy*. Princeton, NJ: Princeton University Press, 2018.

Lewy, Guenter. *The Nazi Persecution of the Gypsies*. Oxford: Oxford University Press, 2000.

Librería Cálamo. "Eduardo Halfon presenta 'Canción,' obra publicada por Libros del Asteroide: Conversa con el editor Luis Solano." Facebook, Feb. 2, 2021. https://www.facebook.com/libreriacalamo/videos/426510551797533.

Liszt's Rhapsody. Directed by Richard Mozer. Devine Entertainment, 1996.

"A literatura rasga a realidade." Póvoa de varzim, Feb. 15, 2008. https://www.cm-pvarzim.pt/noticias/a-literatura-rasga-a-realidade.

Lizarazu, Maria Roca. "Third-Generation Holocaust Narratives: Memory in Memoir and Fiction." *Holocaust Studies* 24, no. 1 (2018): 124.

Long, Ryan. "*Canción* by Eduardo Halfon." *World Literature Today*, summer 2021. https://www.worldliteraturetoday.org/2021/summer/cancion-eduardo-halfon.

Lumet, Sidney, dir. *The Pawnbroker*. Landau Company, 1964. Distrib., Olive Films, 2014.

Macdonald, Sharon. *Memorylands: Heritage and Identity in Europe Today*. New York: Routledge, 2013.

Mandel'shtam, Nadezhda. *Hope against Hope: A Memoir*. New York: Atheneum, 1970.

Manz, Beatriz. *Paradise in Ashes: a Guatemalan Journey of Courage, Terror, and Hope*. Berkeley: University of California Press, 2004.

Marcus, Laura. *Virginia Woolf*. Tavistock, Devon, UK: Northcote House in association with the British Council, 2004.

"Martha Argerich plays Franz Liszt—The Piano Sonata in B-Minor S.178." YouTube, posted by ArgerichHD, May 24, 2013. https://www.youtube.com/watch?v=no4GkRTC_Lo.

"Matamoros: De fuerte militar a prisión exclusiva." *Prensa libre*, May 27, 2015. https://www.prensalibre.com/hemeroteca/matamoros-de-fuerte-militar-a-prision-exclusiva/.

Mayer, Tamar, and Sulieman A. Mourad. *Jerusalem: Idea and Reality*. New York: Routledge, 2008.

Megargee, Geoffrey P. (ed.), Joseph White (ed.), Mel Hecker (ed.), United States Holocaust Memorial Museum. *The United States Holocaust Memorial Museum Encyclopedia of Camps and Ghettos, 1933–1945*. Vol. 3, *Camps and Ghettos under European Regimes Aligned with Nazi Germany*. Bloomington: Indiana University Press, 2018.

Melville, Thomas. *Through a Glass Darkly: The U.S. Holocaust in Central America*. Philadelphia, PA: Xlibris, 2005.

Mendoza, Ana. "Eduardo Halfon: 'La ansiedad de vivir es algo muy judío.'" Zenda, June 27, 2018. https://www.zendalibros.com/eduardo-halfon-la-ansiedad-vivir-algo-judio.

Miller, Henry. *Tropic of Cancer*. New York: Grove, 1961.

–––. *Trópico de Cáncer*. Translated by Carlos Manzano. Barcelona: RBA Editores, 1992.

Miller, Marilyn. Interview with Eduardo Halfon. Guatemala City, July 22, 2022.

Monk, Thelonius. *Theolonious Monk Quartet with John Coltrane at Carnegie Hall*. Produced by Michael Cuscuna. Recorded November 29, 1957. Blue Note, September 27, 2005.

Monteforte Toledo, Mario. "La violencia en Centro América." *Cuadernos Americanos* 176, no. 3 (May–June 1971): 7–41.

Moto Leyva, Gustavo. "Desde el 'no sé': Eduardo Halfon." *El País*, Dec. 12, 2015. https://elpais.com/cultura/2015/12/15/actualidad/1450207763_402437.html.

Müller, Timo. *The African American Sonnet: A Literary History*. Jackson: University Press of Mississippi, 2018.

Müller-Funk, Wolfgang. "On a Narratology of Cultural and Collective Memory." *Journal of Narrative Theory* 33, no. 2 (2003): 207–27.

Musitano, Julia. "La autoficción: Una aproximación teórica. Entre la retórica de la memoria y la escritura de recuerdos." *Acta Literaria*, no. 52 (2016): 103–23.

Nolan, Rachel. "A Translation Crisis at the Border." *New Yorker*, Dec. 30, 2019. https://www.newyorker.com/magazine/2020/01/06/a-translation-crisis-at-the-border.

National Public Radio Staff. "Questions for Eduardo Halfon, Author of 'The Polish Boxer.'" National Public Radio, May 10, 2013. https://www.npr.org/2013/05/10/182258778/questions-for-eduardo-halfon-author-of-the-polish-boxer.

"Nueva América | Claudio Lomnitz and Eduardo Halfon (Dec. 10th, 2020) | Writing Lives." YouTube, posted by Columbia Institute for Ideas and Imagination, Dec. 15, 2020. https://www.youtube.com/watch?v=iLivBv8AC_s.

Numbered. Directed by Dana Doran and Uriel Sinai. Israel, 2012.

"*Numbered*. Plot." Imdb, accessed May 13, 2024. https://www.imdb.com/title/tt1921040/plotsummary?ref_=tt_ov_pl.

Núñez, Daniel. *The Dying Lake*. Digital Photograph. "Wildlife Photographer of the Year." Natural History Museum, accessed Sept. 20, 2023. https://www.nhm.ac.uk/wpy/gallery/2022-the-dying-lake.

Ochs, Juliana. *Security and Suspicion: An Ethnography of Everyday Life in Israel.* Philadelphia: University of Pennsylvania Press, 2011.

"Oh gueto mi amor, de Eduardo Halfon." YouTube, posted by Casa de América, June 7, 2018. https://www.youtube.com/watch?v=ASOMSh2gDiQ.

"Oh gueto mi amor de Eduardo Halfon. (Editorial Páginas de Espuma)." YouTube, posted by Páginas de espuma (paginasdeespuma), Sept. 3, 2018. https://www.youtube.com/watch?v=KCCiZGPTHxA.

Ohlin, Peter. "Bergman's Nazi Past." *Scandinavian Studies* 81, no. 4 (2009): 437–74.

Oliver, María Paz. "Los paseos de la memoria: Representaciones de la caminata urbana en Cynthia Rimsky, Sergio Chejfec y Eduardo Halfon." *Ibero-romania* 83 (2016): 16–34, https://doi.org/10.1515/ibero-2016-0003.

"Origin Stories: Dwyer Murphy interviews Eduardo Halfon." *Guernica*, April 15, 2013. https://www.guernicamag.com/origin-stories.

Ortiz Wallner, Alexandra. "Autorretrato en Jerusalén." *Iowa Literaria*, May 8, 2014. https://pubs.lib.uiowa.edu/iowaliteraria/article/id/2634.

Ortiz Wallner, Alexandra. "Una escritura más allá de las fronteras: La narrativa f(r)iccional de Eduardo Halfon," *Hispanorama*, no. 144 (May 2014): 34–38, http://otrolunes.com/35/wp-content/files/2015/01/OrtizWallner_EHalfon.pdf.

Padgett, Tim. "Guatemala's Kaibiles: A Notorious Commando Unit Wrapped Up in Central America's Drug War." *Time*, July 14, 2011. https://world.time.com/2011/07/14/guatemalas-kaibil-terror-from-dictators-to-drug-cartels.

Perdu, Vanessa. "Experiencias del exilio en el cuento guatemalteco contemporáneo: 'Los exiliados' de Mario Monteforte Toldeo, 'Ningún lugar sagrado' de Rodrigo Rey Rosa y 'Mañana nunca lo hablamos' de Eduardo Halfon." *Península* 11, no. 1 (2016): 155–73.

Perera, Victor. *Rites: A Guatemalan Boyhood.* San Diego: Harcourt Brace Jovanovich, 1986.

Perera, Victor. *Unfinished Conquest: The Guatemalan Tragedy.* Berkeley: University of California Press, 1993.

Pérez Vega, David. "*Mañana nunca lo hablamos* por Eduardo Halfon." *Desde la ciudad sin cine* (blog), Sept. 9, 2018. http://desdelaciudadsincines.blogspot.com/2018/09/manana-nunca-lo-hablamos-por-eduardo.html.

Perkowska, Magdalena. "Infancia e historia: Actos de la memoria en *Dios Tenía Miedo* de Vanessa Núñez Handal y *Mañana Nunca Lo Hablamos* de Eduardo Halfon." *Revista de Estudios Hispanicos* 51 no. 3 (2017): 595–620.

"Permiso para que inventes todo: Unas breves notas sobre Eduardo Halfon." *Iletradoperocuerdo* (blog), May 26, 2015. https://iletradoperocuerdo.com/2015/05/26/permiso-para-que-inventes-todo-unas-breves-notas-sobre-eduardo-halfon.

Piglia, Ricardo. "Tesis sobre el cuento." University of Sao Paolo, E-Disciplinairies, 1986. https://edisciplinas.usp.br/pluginfile.php/2544967/mod_resource/content/1/RicardoPigliaTesissobreelcuento.pdf.

"La pirueta." El Argonauta, accessed May 18, 2024. https://www.elargonauta.com/libros/la-pirueta/978-84-92913-22-0.

"The Polish Boxer." Bellevue Literary Press, accessed May 18, 2024. https://blpress.org/books/the-polish-boxer.

"The Polish Boxer." *Publishers Weekly*, July 9, 2012. https://www.publishersweekly.com/978-1-934137-53-6.

"The Polish Boxer by Eduardo Halfon (book trailer)." Youtube, posted by Polish Boxer, Sept. 5, 2012. https://www.youtube.com/watch?v=kq1UzG_wmIs.

Porter, Jack Nusan. "Holocaust Suicides." In *Problems Unique to the Holocaust*, edited by Harry J. Cargas, 51–66. Lexington: University Press of Kentucky, 1999.

Pridgeon, Stephanie. "Silences between Jewishness and Indigeneity in Eduardo Halfon's *Mañana Nunca Lo Hablamos*." *Revista Canadiense De Estudios Hispánicos* 42, no. 1 (2018): 99–121.

"Prof. Marilyn Miller, 'Eduardo Halfon and the Itinerary of Memory' at UConn Halfon Mini-Symposium." YouTube, posted by UConn JUDS, Oct. 7, 2021. https://www.youtube.com/watch?v=zePg_9PB5uM.

Prose, Francine. "What Can't Be Forgotten." *New York Review of Books* 65, no. 18 (2018): 38. https://www-nybooks-com.libproxy.tulane.edu/articles/2018/11/22/eduardo-halfon-what-cant-be-forgotten/.

Prudente, Teresa. *A Specially Tender Piece of Eternity: Virginia Woolf and the Experience of Time*. Lanham, MD: Lexington Books, 2009.

Ran, Amalia, "Nuestra Shoá: Dictaduras, Holocausto y represión en tres novelas judeorioplatenses" *Spanish Language and Literature*, no. 48 (2009). https://digitalcommons.unl.edu/modlangspanish/48.

Rebiger, Bill, ed. *Yearbook of the Maimonides Centre for Advanced Studies 2018*. Boston: De Gruyter, 2018.

Reiter, Dan. "Remembering as Deconstruction: Eduardo Halfon's *Mourning*." *The Rumpus*, Sept. 25, 2019. https://therumpus.net/2019/09/mourning-by-eduardo-halfon.

"Relato y cuento corto: Diferencias." Las letras del alba, accessed May 18, 2024. https://www.lasletrasdealba.es/diferencias-entre-relato-y-cuento-corto.

Rey Rosa, Rodrigo. *Ningún lugar sagrado*. Barcelona: Seix Barral, 1998.

Rincón, Juan Camilo. "El grandioso universo de Eduardo Halfon." *El Tiempo*, Nov. 17, 2020. https://www.eltiempo.com/cultura/musica-y-libros/eduardo-halfon-el-autor-guatemalteco-habla-de-su-universo-literario-549379.

Rodríguez, Aloma. "Entrevista a Eduardo Halfon: 'Nuestra identidad no es más que una colección de máscaras.'" Letras Libres, Feb. 24, 2021. https://www.letraslibres.com/espana-mexico/libros/entrevista-eduardo-halfon-nuestra-identidad-no-es-mas-que-una-coleccion-mascaras.

Rodríguez Ballestar, Alejandra. "La guerrilla secuestró a su abuelo y su familia debió exiliarse: La nueva novela de Eduardo Halfon." *Clarín Cultura*, May 19, 2021. https://www.clarin.com/cultura/guerrilla-guatemalteca-secuestro-abuelo-familia-debio-exiliarse-nueva-novela-eduardo-halfon_0_fNmFI2XhU.html.

The Rough Guide to Budapest. London: Rough Guides, 2015.
Roth, Joseph. *Hotel Savoy; Fallmerayer the Stationmaster; The Bust of the Emperor*. London: Chatto & Windus, 1986.
Rothenberg, Daniel. *Memory of Silence: The Guatemalan Truth Commission Report*. New York: Palgrave Macmillan, 2012.
"Saban Bajramovic—Pelno Me Sam." YouTube, posted by World Tour with Music, Jan. 28, 2019. https://www.youtube.com/watch?v=fe2upQwkpHg.
Sánchez-Midence, Luis A., and Victorino-Ramírez Liberio. "Guatemala: Cultura tradicional y sostenibilidad." *Agricultura, Sociedad y Desarrollo* 9, no. 3 (2012): 297–313. https://www.redalyc.org/articulo.oa?id=360533092004.
Sankovitch, Nina. *Tolstoy and the Purple Chair: My Year of Magical Reading*. New York: Harper, 2011.
Sarmiento Panez, Ignacio. *Los espectros de la guerra: Duelo, comunidad y catástrofe en la narrativa centroamericana contemporánea*. Phd diss., Tulane University, 2018. https://library.search.tulane.edu/discovery/delivery/01TUL_INST:Tulane/12432809630006326.
Sarna, Jonathan D. "The Forgetting of Cora Wilburn: Historical Amnesia and *The Cambridge History of Jewish American Literature*." *Studies in American Jewish Literature* 37, no. 1 (2018): 73–87.
Schamma Gesser, Silvina, and Susana Brauner. "Aesthetics, Politics, and the Complexities of Arab Jewish Identities in Authoritarian Argentina." In *Contemporary Sephardic and Mizrahi Literature: A Diaspora*, edited by Dario Miccoli, 43–68. New York: Routledge, Taylor & Francis Group, 2017.
Schirmer, Jennifer G. *The Guatemalan Military Project: A Violence Called Democracy*. Philadelphia: University of Pennsylvania Press, 1998.
Schult, Tanja. "From Stigma to Medal of Honor and Agent of Remembrance." In *Entangled Memories: Remembering the Holocaust in a Global Age*, edited by Marius Henderson and Julia Lange, 257–91. Heidelberg: Universitätsverlag, 2017.
Schwab, Gabriele. *Haunting Legacies: Violent Histories and Transgenerational Trauma*. New York: Columbia University Press, 2010.
Schwarz, Daniel R. *Imagining the Holocaust*. New York: St. Martin's Press, 1999.
Seeberg, Marie Louise, Irene Levin, and Claudia Lenz. *The Holocaust as Active Memory: The Past in the Present*. Farnham, Surrey, England: Ashgate, 2013.
Sharenow, Robert. *The Berlin Boxing Club*. New York: Balzer + Bray, 2012.
Silcott, Joseph. "Gabriel García Márquez's Yellow Butterflies." *Joseph Scissorhands* (blog), April 27, 2014. http://josephscissorhands.blogspot.com/2014/04/gabriel-garcia-marquezs-yellow.html.
Sinnreich, Helene J. "Reading the Writing on the Wall: A Textual Analysis of Łódź Graffiti." *Religion, State and Society* 32, no. 1 (2004): 53–58.
Soto Paíz, Manlio. *Maximón y lo inconsciente colectivo: Arquetipos y simbología Maya-Tzutuhil*. Guatemala: Editorial Universitaria, Universidad de San Carlos Guatemala, 2018.
Spiegelman, Art. *Maus II: A Survivor's Tale: And Here My Troubles Began*. New York: Pantheon Books, 1992.

Stavans, Ilan. Afterword to "Tomorrow We Never Did Talk About It." *Working Title* 1.3. Hadley, MA: Massachusetts Review, 2016.

Stein, Arlene. "'As Far as They Knew I Came from France': Stigma, Passing, and Not Speaking about the Holocaust." *Symbolic Interaction* 32, no. 1 (2009): 44–60.

Stoppelman, Gabriela. "Tizas blancas sobre humo negro." El Anartista, Sept. 29, 2020. https://www.elanartista.com.ar/2020/09/29/tizas-blancas-sobre-humo-negro.

Straus, Nina Pelikan. "Sebald, Wittgenstein, and the Ethics of Memory." *Comparative Literature* 61, no. 1 (2009): 43–53.

Struk, Janina. *Photographing the Holocaust: Interpretations of the Evidence*. London: I.B. Tauris, 2004.

"Taller en traducción." Blogs@baruch. Posted by a.galeas, June 25, 2015. https://blogs.baruch.cuny.edu/tallerentraduccion/?p=781.

"Tattoo Jew Documentary Trailer." YouTube, posted by Andy Abrams, Dec. 13, 2011. https://www.youtube.com/watch?v=nLszeZgvU5s.

Templin, E. "Pio Baroja: Three Pivotal Concepts." *Hispanic Review* 12, no. 4 (1944): 306–29.

"Their Name: 'Roma'? 'Sinto'? 'Gypsy'?" USC Shoah Foundation, accessed May 14, 2024. https://sfi.usc.edu/education/roma-sinti/en/conosciamo-i-roma-e-i-sinti/chi-sono/da-dove-vengono-il-nome/il-nome-rom-sinto-zingaro.php.

Tolo, Julia Johanne. "We Become the Mask That We Wear: An Interview with Eduardo Halfon." Electric Literature, Nov. 10, 2015. https://electricliterature.com/we-become-the-mask-that-we-wear-an-interview-with-eduardo-halfon.

Torún, Alejandro, Juan Pensamiento, Eduardo Halfon, Julio Calvo, Rafael Romero, Mildred Hernandez, Eduardo Juarez, et al. *Ni hermosa ni maldita: Narrativa guatemalteca actual*. Guatemala Ciudad: Alfaguara, 2012.

Trachtenberg, Joshua. *Jewish Magic and Superstition: A Study in Folk Religion*. Philadelphia: University of Pennsylvania Press, 2004.

"Tragedy and Comedy." American Literature I, Lumenlearning.com, accessed May 14, 2024. https://courses.lumenlearning.com/suny-jeffersoncc-americanlit1/chapter/608.

Travers, Peter. "Triumph of the Spirit." *Rolling Stone*, Dec. 8, 1989. https://www.rollingstone.com/movies/movie-reviews/triumph-of-the-spirit-252966.

Treacy, Mary Jane. "Killing the Queen: The Display and Disappearance of Rogelia Cruz." *Latin American Literary Review* 29, no. 57 (2001): 40–51.

"Tumbalalaika." Wikipedia, last updated June 4, 2024. https://en.wikipedia.org/wiki/Tumbalalaika.

Tyler, Imogen. *Stigma: The Machinery of Inequality*. London: Zed Books, 2020.

"UFM.edu—Libro El Boxeador Polaco por Eduardo Halfon: Entrevista con Luis Figueroa." YouTube, posted by Newmedia UFM, Feb. 27, 2009. https://www.youtube.com/watch?v=AYfqh6CbmG4.

Ulin, David L. "Review: How a Guatemalan Kidnapping Inspired Eduardo Halfon's Autofictional 'Cancion.'" *Los Angeles Times*, Sept. 22, 2022. https://

www.latimes.com/entertainment-arts/books/story/2022-09-22/review-how-a-guatemalan-kidnapping-inspired-eduardo-halfons-autofictional-cancion.

United States Bureau of Citizenship and Immigration Services. "Guatemala: Kaibiles and the Massacre at Las Dos Erres," GTM00003.ZNK. UNHCR, UN Refugee Agency, Feb. 2, 2000. https://www.refworld.org/docid/3ae6a6a54.html.

Usher, Shaun. *Lists of Note.* San Francisco: Chronicle Books, 2015.

Van der Bliek, Rob. *The Thelonious Monk Reader.* Oxford: Oxford University Press, 2001.

Van Hecke, A. "Memoria, ficción y multilingüismo en 'El Boxeador polaco': Un cuento de Eduardo Halfon." *Connotas: Revista de crítica y teoría literarias*, no. 21 (Jan. 2021): 9–31. https://connotas.unison.mx/index.php/critlit/article/view/335.

Vargas Llosa, Mario. *Tiempos recios.* Barcelona: Alfaguara, 2019.

Scislowska, Monika. "The Vatican Beatifies a Polish Family of 9 Killed by the Nazis for Sheltering Jews." Associated Press, Sept. 10, 2023. https://apnews.com/article/poland-jews-ulma-family-beatification-4396a6086664fa1ea96a433e363ebd41.

"Versos de cabo roto." *Lenguarelio* (blog), Feb. 27, 2011. http://lenguaurelio.blogspot.com/2011/02/versos-de-cabo-roto.html.

Vrana, Heather A. "'Our Ongoing Fight for Justice': The Pasts and Futures of Genocidio and Justicia in Guatemala." *Journal of Genocide Research* 18, no. 2–3 (2016): 245–63. https://doi.org/10.1080/14623528.2016.1186949.

Welty, Eudora. *One Writer's Beginnings.* New York: Scribner, 2020.

Worthington, Marjorie. *The Story of "Me": Contemporary American Autofiction.* Lincoln: University of Nebraska Press, 2018.

"Writers on the Fly: Eduardo Halfon." YouTube, posted by Iowa City UNESCO City of Literature, Dec. 6, 2010. https://www.youtube.com/watch?v=9kaKeV1a0Yc.

Zenner, Walter P. *A Global Community: The Jews from Aleppo, Syria.* Detroit, MI: Wayne State University Press, 2000.

Zur, Judith N. *Violent Memories: Mayan War Widows in Guatemala.* Boulder, CO: Westview Press, 1998.

INDEX

Aarons, Victoria, 104, 105
Aguilar, Eduard, 7
Alarcón, Daniel, 8–9
Alberca, Manuel, 64, 66
Amar Sánchez, Ana María, 136
Antigua, 41–42, 46, 49–53, 95, 101–2
Apel, Dora, 127, 156n17, 158n45
Arab identity, 96–97
Arbenz, Jacobo, 141–42
archival activism, 76–77, 82
Archivo Histórico de la Policía Nacional (AHPN), 76, 81, 92
Argentina, 84
Arouch, Salamo, 158n58
Arzú, Álvaro, 174n85
Astro, Alan, 152n19
Auschwitz
    boxers at, 28–30, 158n58, 159n60
    Czarnecki's *Last Traces*, 28–29
    diary entries from, 120
    grandfather's two stories of, 61–63
    number tattoos in *The Polish Boxer*, 21–28, 35, 39–40
    in "Oh Ghetto My Love," 114, 118
    protagonist's travel to, 39, 104–5
    See also Łódź
autobiography, questions of, 11–12, 32

autofiction (*autoficción*), 11–12, 64–66, 84, 164n2, 174n6
Ayén, Xavi, 141–42

"Baile de la marea, El" (Halfon), 71, 168n8
Bajramović, Šaban, 48, 51–52
Ball, Anna, 102–3, 176n34
"Balloon Debate" (Banksy), 102–3
"Bamboo" (Halfon), 98–99
Banksy, 102–3
Barchino, Matías, 64
Baroja, Pío, 150
Barrios Carrillo, Jaime, 139
Barry, Des, 9, 10–11
Basquiat, Jean-Michel, 28
Batz Chocoj, Roberto, 81
"Bedouin, The" (Halfon), 132–33
Bejarano, Margalit, 183n10
Belgrade, 54–56
"Beni" (Halfon), 133–38
Bergman, Ingmar, 61, 66–68
"Better Not Say Too Much" (Halfon), 85–86, 138
Biederman, Mark, 116, 180n40
"Birds Are Back, The" (Halfon), 99
Bolden, Tony, 44
Borges, Jorge Luis, 16, 65

Boxeador polaco, El (Halfon), 16–17, 40, 60–61, 64–65, 118, 165n15
Brouwer, Daniel, 27
Browitt, Jeffrey, 70–72, 86–87, 138
Bukiet, Jules, 36
Burack, Emily, 7

Campisi, Nicolás, 64, 103
Canción (Halfon)
  "The Bedouin," 132–33
  "Beni," 133–38
  "Canción," 138–46
  "The Conference," 129–31
  kidnapping of grandfather, 129, 131–33, 138–45, 148–49
  "Kimono on the Skin," 146–49
  Mourning and, 146
  narrator identity/positioning and disguises, 1–3
  The Polish Boxer and, 130, 139
  publication of, 153n32
  relato form and, 11
  Signor Hoffman and, 139, 146
  "Tomorrow We Never"/*Mañana nunca lo hablamos* and, 132, 133, 137, 138, 142
"Canción" (Halfon), 138–46
Capó, Daniel, 177n6
Carroll, Lewis, 89
Cartwright, Garth, 52
Castellanos Moya, Horacio, 85
CEH (Comisión para el Esclarecimiento Histórico), 73–74, 78, 185n33
Central Intelligence Agency (CIA), 74, 133, 141
Cervantes, Miguel de, 19, 65
Chelmno (Kulmhof), 52–53, 163n44
Chopin, Fréderic, 48
cinema verité, 69
civil war, Guatemalan
  AHPN documents and *From Silence to Memory* report, 76, 81, 92
  archival activism and, 76–77, 82–83

  "Dicho hacia el sur" and, 88
  as holocaust, 83–85
  Kaibiles, 134–38, 145, 185n33, 188n69
  Mayan genocide, 77–85, 134–37, 184n26, 186n37
  "La memoria infantil" and, 89–91
  Memory of Silence (CEH report), 73–74, 76, 78
  race, class, and, 71–73
  Ríos Montt trial, 171n54
  silence, silencing, and, 74–83, 85–86
  United States and, 74, 135, 169n20
  the untold and, 74–75, 77–78
  See also *Canción*; "Tomorrow We Never Did Talk About It"
class positioning, 71–73, 133
Clinton, Bill, 74
Comisión para el Esclarecimiento Histórico (CEH), 73–74, 78, 185n33
concentration camps
  Chelmno (Kulmhof), 52–53, 163n44
  Ferramonti di Tarsia, 110–13
  Neuengamme, 35
  Niš, 52
  Sachsenhausen, 34–35, 114, 118, 126–27, 165n15
  See also Auschwitz
"Conference, The" (Halfon), 129–31
Contreras, Felix, 84
Cortázar, Julio, 50
Costello, Lisa, 26
Cruz Martinez, Rogelia, 141–42
cryptonomy, 160n90
Cuenca, João Paolo, 60–61
Czarnecki, Joseph, 28–29

Dead Sea, 93–94, 96, 104
De cabo roto (Halfon), 59
Derrida, Jacques, 160n90
Díaz Miranda, Ángel, 29–30, 110–11
Dicaire, David, 43–44

"Dicho hacia el sur" (Halfon), 5, 88, 90
Dillman, Lisa, 107–8
"Discurso de Póvoa," 60–61, 63, 65, 165n15
"Distant" (Halfon), 18–19, 85
"Domingos en Iowa," 162n30
Dreifus, Erika, 7, 38
Duelo (Halfon), 108–9, 123
Durante, Erica, 13, 16

Edwards, Brent Hayes, 44
Elias, Ruth, 25
"Epistrophy" (Halfon), 41–48, 55, 57
"Epistrophy" (Monk), 43–44, 47
eroticism and sexuality, 45–46, 90, 104, 106, 112
Estrada, Manuel, 99
exile, 86–88, 91
Ezrahi, Sidra, 37

Fermaglich, Kirsten, 159n68
Ferramonti di Tarsia, 110–13
fiction and history as adjacent domains, 59–60
Figueroa, Luis, 19
Fischer, Nina, 25, 33
"Flying Balloon Girl" (Banksy), 102–3
food and memory, 32–33
Forsyth, Mark, 40–41
Foucault, Michel, 80
From Silence to Memory (AHPN), 76, 81, 92

García Escobar, José, 133, 146
García Márquez, Gabriel, 9, 101, 175n27
Garsd, Jasmine, 84
Gartenberg, Charlotte, 64
Genette, Gerard, 65
Gerard, Christian, 49, 162n31
Gerardi, Juan, 73
"Ghosts" (Halfon), 55
Goñi, Javier, 71
González Ponciano, Jorge Ramón, 72, 169n13, 186n44

Goodwin, James, 159n72
graffiti, antisemitic, 115–16
grandfather, maternal. *See* Tenenbaum, Leon
grandfather, paternal. *See* Halfon, Eduardo (paternal grandfather character)
Gras, Eric, 8
Guatemalan civil war. *See* civil war, Guatemalan
Guatemalan Human Rights Commission (GHRC), 135
Guatemalan identity
   in *Canción*, 133–34
   in *Monastery*, 98–102
   Mourning and, 109, 122
   Popul Vuh and, 108, 128, 178n6
Guatemala Nunca Más! (REMHI), 73
Guillén, Claudio, 91
Guyton, Jen, 181n48
Gypsies (Roma)
   correct term for, 161n1, 162n28
   Holocaust and, 52–53, 163n44
   Jewishness, parallels with, 54–57
   music and, 41, 48, 51–55
   nomadism and, 48, 52
   race and, 53–54

Hahn, Daniel, 107–8, 177n5
Halfon, Eduardo (author)
   at Correntes D'Escritas festival, 60–61, 63
   identity, placement, and position of, 1–8
   as Jewish writer, 6–8
   languages, publics, and audiences of, 8–10
   Latino identity, Latino literature, and, 4–6
   as Lebanese writer, 3
   publications and awards, 10, 107–8
   relationships between texts and *matryoshka* diagram, 12–14, 18
   thresholds and genres of, 10–12
   See also specific works

Halfon, Eduardo (paternal grandfather character)
  about, 97
  kidnapping of, 70, 75, 80, 129, 131–33, 138–45, 148–49
  Lebanese identity and, 2, 130
  surname of, 4
Halfon, Eduardo (protagonist/narrator character)
  family-member directives resisted by, 2
  identity, placement, and disguises of, 1–4
  name of, 11
  narrative voice, 12
  See also specific works
Havenne, Maude, 13, 16
Hepworth, Andrea, 105
Herskowitz, Yankele, 120
Herzog, Werner, 62, 68–69
Hijo cualquiera, Un (Halfon), 133
Hijos por la Identidad y la Justicia contra el Olvido y el Silencio (H.I.J.O.S.), 171n54
Hirsch, Marianne, 26
Hobuß, Steffi, 30, 77
Hoffman, E. T. A., 119–20
Hoffman, Phillip Seymour, 111–12, 178n19
Holocaust (Shoah)
  artifacts of memory and, 104
  Italy and, 112–13, 179n23
  Mayan genocide as holocaust, 83–85
  number tattoos, 21–28, 35, 39–40
  photography and, 113–18
  Poland and, 115, 179n29
  survival in and of, 34
  third frame for, 127–28
  tourism and, 110–13, 126–27
  See also Auschwitz; concentration camps; *Polish Boxer, The*
Holocaust Fiction genre, 7. See also *Polish Boxer, The*

Holocaust memory. *See* memory
Holocaust Remembrance Day, 110, 112
Holocaust testimony
  hearers of, 20
  in *Mourning*, 120–21
  The Polish Boxer and, 19–21, 63
  post-testimony, 38, 120
  testimonial literature, 37–38, 156n17
  third generation (3G) as inheritors of, 36–37
Horwitz, Linda Dian, 27
Hotel Savoy (Roth), 179n24
Huehuetenango, 99
Huergo, Damián, 66
hypernarrative, 64

identity
  Arab, 96–97
  author and narrator identity and positioning, 1–6
  Guatemalan, 98–102, 108, 109, 122, 128, 133–34, 178n6
  Latino, 4–6
  Lebanese, 1–3, 92, 124, 130–31
  See also Jewishness
Illingworth, Dustin, 136
Indigenous Guatemalans
  in "Distant," 18–19
  Mayan genocide, 77–85, 134–37, 184n26, 186n37
International Latino Book Award, 107
Israel, 49, 93–99, 102–4, 152n20, 176n30, 180n40. See also *Kotel*
Italy, 112–13, 179n23. See also *Mourning*

Jacob, Janet, 21, 31
Jacobs Fernández, Percy Amilcar, 139
Jewishness
  in *Canción*, 133–34, 148
  exile and, 87
  Halfon as Jewish writer, 6–8

Mañana nunca lo hablamos and, 83
in *Monastery*, 93–98, 101, 105–6
in *Mourning*, 109
in *The Polish Boxer*, 39
Torah reading and, 108, 178n6

Kaddish (prayer of the dead), 23–24, 33
Kaibiles, 134–38, 145, 185n33, 188n69
Kalian, Moshe, 98
kapo, 29
Kay, Judith, 73
Kertzer, David, 179n23
"Kimono on the Skin" (Halfon), 146–49
Kolbe, Maximilian, 29
Kornreich, Rena, 40
Kosinski, Jerzy, 106, 176n46
Kotel (Wailing Wall)
  in *Monastery*, 94
  "Wailing Wall" (The Cure), 49, 97, 162n31

ladinos, 72, 143, 168n11, 169n13, 186n44
lager literature, 7
LaHaije, Marileen, 86
Lajkó, Félix, 54–55
Lake Amatitlán, 121–22, 181nn48–49
Lang, Jessica, 36, 37, 120
Langbein, Hermann, 158n58
Langer, Lawrence, 149
language, 178n6
  Halfon and English vs. Spanish, 5–6, 8–10
  Hebrew, 4, 26, 39, 57, 95, 101, 108, 112, 120, 157n42
  other languages, in *The Polish Boxer*, 33–34
  as weapon, in *The Polish Boxer*, 30
  Yiddish, 31, 33, 39, 120
Las Casas, Bartolomé de, 83
lashon hara (evil speech), 143, 187n63

Last Traces (Czarnecki), 28–29
Latin American fiction, 9
Latino literature genre, 5–6
Laub, Dori, 20
Lebanese identity, 1–3, 92, 124, 130–31
Lech l'cha, 39, 161n97
Lessons of Darkness (film; Herzog), 68–69
Levi, Primo, 24, 25–26, 30, 40, 74
Levin, Irene, 80
Liszt, Franz, 45–48, 53–57, 162n16
literature
  autofiction (*autoficción*), 11–12, 64–66, 84, 164n2, 174n6
  as biographical, 65
  blurred with reality, 59–60
  filling empty spaces of memory, 90
  healing power of, 36
  lager, 7
  Latin American, 8–9
  Latino, 5–6
  music and, 163n35
  as prayer, 93
  the questions and, 129
  "tearing at reality," 60–63, 67–69
Litzmannstadt, 163n44
Łódź, 104–5, 113–21, 179n24, 179n30, 180n40
Los Cocos massacre, 188n69

Macdonald, Sharon, 183n5
Mãe, Valter Hugo, 60
magical realism, 9
Mañana nunca lo hablamos. See "Tomorrow We Never Did Talk About It"
"Mañana nunca lo hablamos" (Halfon), 168n8
Mandel'shtam, Nadezhda, 156n17
Manz, Beatriz, 74
Massacre at Las Dos Erres, 136–37, 142, 188n69
Mayan genocide, 77–85, 134–37, 184n26, 186n37

McLean, Anne, 77
Mein, John Gordon, 140, 145
Melchor de Mencos, 100
Melville, Thomas, 83, 169n16, 171n56
"Memoria infantil, La" (Halfon), 89–91
memory
    absent witnesses and, 38–39
    artifacts of, 104
    Auschwitz tattoos and, 25–28, 31, 37
    communicative and cultural, 105
    as creative or restorative, 32
    cultural forgetfulness, 102, 176n29
    episodic forms and, 11
    fallibility of, 74, 124
    family history, complexity of, 123–24
    family treasures and, 100–101
    fiction portraying truth and, 34, 37–38
    filling empty spaces of, 90
    food and, 32–33
    forgetting and ecstatic truth, 66–69
    Holocaust Remembrance Day, 110, 112
    intertextual, 17–18
    itinerary of, 129–30
    jazz and, 44–45
    memorylands, 129–30, 183n5
    music, creative quest, and, 48–51
    pendular, 32
    photographic, 113–18
    postmemory, 26, 37–38
    silence, silencing, and, 74–83, 85–86
    trauma and, 71, 123
    triggers of, 31–34
    whiskey and, 19, 21, 33, 57, 62
    See also specific works
Memory of Silence (CEH), 73–74, 76
Mendoza, Ana, 36–37
mezuzah, 132
migrants, Mayan, 184n26
Miller, Henry, 32, 64, 159n72
Monasterio (Halfon), 174n1

Monastery (Halfon)
    autofiction and, 174n6
    "Bamboo," 98–99
    "The Birds Are Back," 99
    Canción and, 144
    grandfather's Polish address, 7–8, 104, 144
    Jewish memory as theme, 7–8
    legacy of betrayal in, 2
    "Monastery," 93–94, 102–6, 109
    Mourning compared to, 99
    Peter (Yosef), 3
    "Surviving Sundays," 50
    "Tel Aviv was an Inferno," 7, 49, 93–98
    "White Sand, Black Stone," 100–101
    "White Smoke," 12, 28, 49–50, 101–2
"Monastery" (Halfon), 93–94, 102–6, 109
Monk, Thelonious, 39, 41, 43–44, 47, 50, 56–57
Monteforte Toledo, Mario, 139
Mota Leyva, Gustavo, 91
Mourning (Halfon)
    awards, 107–8
    Canción and, 146
    Duelo, 108–9, 123
    English title of, 109–10
    Monastery compared to, 99
    "Mourning," 5, 34–35, 121–28
    "Oh Ghetto My Love," 113–21, 153n33
    "Signor Hoffman," 4, 110–13, 117, 146
    Tanakh epigraph, 108–9
"Mourning" (Halfon), 5, 34–35, 121–28
Müller, Timo, 44
Murphy, Dwyer, 20–21, 40, 105
music
    classical, 41–42, 44–48, 162n30
    Gypsy, 41, 48, 51–55
    improvisation, 41, 43, 47, 53–54

jazz, 39, 41–45, 50, 52–55
memory, creative quest, and, 48–51
as refuge, 50
rock, 49
translation and, 163n35
Musitano, Julia, 164n2, 174n6

narrative voice, 12
Neuengamme, 35
Neves, Pedro Teixeira, 60
New Orleans, 42. *See also* Storyville
"Ningún Lugar Sagrado" (Rey Rosa), 86
Niš, 52
Nolan, Rachel, 184n26, 186n37
nomadism, 4, 14, 48, 52, 131
novela en marcha form, 13–14
Numbered (documentary), 25–26
numbers
    69752 as almost character, 21–23
    as artifacts of memory, 104
    erasure of names and identity, 25–26, 31, 109
    faith based on, 23
    for prisoner identification, 127
    profusion of, in grandfather's Holocaust story, 35
    in video trailer for *The Polish Boxer*, 22–23
    in *yizkor* (prayer to honor the dead) in "Mourning," 126
number tattoos
    body as living Holocaust memorial and, 158n45
    covering of, 25, 40
    legibility across space, language and time, 24–25
    meaning and significance of, 24–28, 39–40
    "phone number" story and the untold, 20–21, 28, 34, 37, 123, 182n66
    in *The Polish Boxer*, 21–28, 35, 39–40
    progenic, 26–27, 31
    ritual of being tattooed, 24
Nuñez, Daniel, 181n48

"Oh Ghetto My Love" (Halfon), 113–21, 153n33
Oh gueto mi amor (Halfon), 109
Ohlin, Peter, 67
Ortiz Wallner, Alexandra, 3, 64, 91, 175n6

Parker, Charlie, 39, 42
Pascal, Blaise, 68–69
Patt, Avinoam, 108
Paz Oliver, María, 97
Perdu, Vanessa, 71, 86–87, 167n2, 173n81
Perera, Victor, 77, 186n42
Perez, Jung, 159n58
Pérez Vega, David, 70
photography and Holocaust memory, 113–18
Pietrzykowski, Tadeusz "Teddy," 29, 158n58, 159n60
Piglia, Ricardo, 18, 155n9
"Pirouette, The" (Halfon), 41, 55–58
Poland
    antisemitism and, 115–16, 118
    Łódź, 104–5, 113–21, 179n24, 179n30, 180n40
    warning against visiting, 2, 39, 114–15, 118
    See also Auschwitz
Polish Boxer, The (Halfon)
    the Auschwitz number tattoo, 21–28, 35, 39–40
    bilingual publication of, 10, 15
    El boxeador polaco, 16–17, 40, 60–61, 64–65, 118, 165n15
    the boxer character, 28–31
    Canción and, 130, 139
    "Distant," 18–19, 85
    "Epistrophy," 41–48, 55, 57
    flow charts, 45–48

Polish Boxer, The (Halfon) *(continued)*
   as foundation volume, 15–16
   gestation and global project, 19–21
   "Ghosts," 55
   Holocaust Fiction and, 7
   honors, 16
   intertextual memory and, 17–18
   jazz obsession and memory as renewable resource, 42–45
   memory triggers, 31–34
   Monastery and, 93
   "Mourning" and, 34–35
   "The Pirouette," 41, 55–58
   "The Polish Boxer," 21–24, 28–38, 109
   "Postcards," 41, 51–55
   publicity video, 22–23
   "A Speech at Póvoa," 38, 60–69
   "Sunsets," 38–40
   third generation writers and postmemory, 35–40
   translations and reconfigurations, 16–17
   "Twaining," 19, 38
   "White Smoke," 12, 27–28, 38, 49–50
"Polish Boxer, The" (Halfon), 21–24, 28–38, 109
Popul Vuh, 108, 128
Porter, Jack, 176n46
"Postcards" (Halfon), 41, 51–55
Potok, Chaim, 29
Premio de Las Librerías de Navarra, 107
Pridgeon, Stephanie, 64, 80, 87, 88, 167n2
Prix du meilleur livre étranger, 107
progenic tattoos, 26–27
Prose, Francine, 106
"Purest Form of Writing, The" (Halfon), 108

Rabassa, Gregory, 177n5
race
   in *Canción*, 133
   Mañana nunca lo hablamos, civil war, and, 71–73
   whiteness and white privilege, 73, 138

Rachmaninoff, Sergei, 47–48
Ran, Amalia, 84
Razon, Jacques, 158n58
readability, 36–37
Rebel Armed Forces (FAR), 138–45
Recuperación de la Memoria Histórica (REMHI), 73
Reinhardt, Django, 53
Reiter, Dan, 6
relato form, 11, 17
Rey Rosa, Rodrigo, 86, 173n81
Rincón, Juan Camilo, 3
Ríos Montt, Efraín, 84, 171n54
Rites (Perera), 77
Rodriguez, Raxche', 10
Roth, Joseph, 179n24

Sachsenhausen, 34–35, 114, 118, 126–27, 165n15
Salomón, Uncle, 121–28, 132–34
Sam no es mi tío (Halfon). See "Dicho hacia el sur"
Sankovitch, Nina, 34
Sarmiento Panez, Ignacio, 82–83, 84, 171n54, 173n82, 174n85
Sarna, Jonathan, 102, 176n29
Schirmer, Jennifer, 169n20
Schult, Tanja, 26, 31, 158n45
Schwab, Gabriele, 160n81
Sebald, W. G., 162n20
Sephardim, 96, 183n10
sexuality and eroticism, 45–46, 90, 104, 106, 112
Shoah. *See* Holocaust
Signor Hoffman (Halfon), 4, 109, 139, 146, 163n34
"Signor Hoffman" (Halfon), 4, 110–13, 117, 146
silence and silencing
   civil war, *Mañana nunca lo hablamos*, and, 74–83, 85–86
   Foucault, Levin, Pridgeon, and Stavans on, 80
   as survival tactic, 85

Sinnreich, Helen, 115, 179n30
Skammen (*Shame*) (film; Bergman), 66–68
"Speech at Póvoa, A" (Halfon), 38, 60–69
Spiegelman, Art, 26
Spreti, Karl von, 145
Stavans, Ilan, 80
Stein, Arlene, 156n17
Stoppelman, Gabriela, 4
Storyville, 42, 44, 57
Stravinsky, Igor, 42
Struk, Janina, 116–17, 179n29
Sullam, Simon Levis, 112
"Sunsets" (Halfon), 38–40
"Surviving Sundays" (Halfon), 50
swastikas, 115–16, 179n30
Sway of the Sea, The. *See* "Baile de la marea, El"

Tanakh (Hebrew Bible), 108–9
tattooed numbers. *See* number tattoos
"Tel Aviv was an Inferno" (Halfon), 7, 49, 93–98
Tenenbaum, Leon (Leib), 35, 38, 118, 123, 144. See also *Mourning*; *Polish Boxer, The*
third generation (3G) authors, 35–40, 120
Through a Glass Darkly (Melville), 83, 171n56
Tokyo, 129–30, 146–49
"Tomorrow We Never Did Talk About It" and *Mañana nunca lo hablamos*
  about, 9, 70–72
  autofictional form and, 84–85
  "El baile de la marea" (The Sway of the Sea), 71, 168n8
  Canción and, 132, 133, 137, 138, 142
  CEH report, AHPN documents, archival activism, and, 73–74, 75–76, 78, 81–82, 92
  child's perspective, 70–72, 91–92
  "Dicho hacia el sur" and, 88

  "exile" and, 86–88, 91
  genre, question of, 167n2
  "Mañana nunca lo hablamos," 168n8
  Mayan genocide and, 77–85
  "La memoria infantil" and, 89–91
  music in, 48
  narrator protagonist and class/race positioning, 71–73
  publicity video, 71, 89
  REMHI report, 73
  Spanish edition and, 12
  "El último café turco," 132
  the untold and, 74–75, 77–78
Torah, 27, 108, 132, 178n6
tourism, 110–13, 126–27
Treacy, Mary Jane, 141
Triumph of the Spirit (film), 158n58
Tropic of Cancer (Miller), 32, 64, 159n72
Twain, Mark, 19
"Twaining" (Halfon), 19, 38
Tyler, Imogen, 25

Ubico, Jorge, 140
Ulin, David, 149
"Último café turco, El" (Halfon), 132
untold, the, 74–75, 77–78

Vainshtein, Marina, 158n45
Valle, Ignacio del, 60
Vaquera-Vasquez, Santiago, 8–9
Vargas Llosa, Mario, 142
Vista Hermosa, Guatemala City, 79–83
Vrana, Heather, 171n54

Wailing Wall. *See Kotel*
"Wailing Wall" (The Cure), 49, 97, 162n31
Wallant, Edward Lewis, 107
Wallant Award, 107–8, 177n1
Welty, Eudora, 90
whiteness, 73, 138
"White Sand, Black Stone" (Halfon), 100–101

"White Smoke" (*Monastery*) (Halfon), 12, 28, 49–50, 101–2
"White Smoke" (*Polish Boxer*) (Halfon), 12, 27–28, 38, 49–50
Wittgenstein, Ludwig, 46, 50, 162n20
Witztum, Eliezer, 98

Woolf, Virginia, 77
Worthington, Marjorie, 65

yizkor prayer, 126

Zur, Judith, 74

www.ingramcontent.com/pod-product-compliance
Lightning Source LLC
Chambersburg PA
CBHW030650230426
43665CB00011B/1031